THE INVISIBLE ART: A CENTURY OF MUSIC IN IRELAND 1916–2016

THE INVISIBLE ART

A Century of Music in Ireland 1916–2016

EDITED BY MICHAEL DERVAN

BORD NA MÓNA
Naturally Driven

NEW ISLAND

RTÉ

The Invisible Art: A Century of Music in Ireland 1916–2016
First published in 2016 by

New Island
16 Priory Hall Office Park
Stillorgan
Co. Dublin
www.newisland.ie

Print ISBN: 978-1-84840-574-5
EPUB ISBN: 978-1-84840-575-2
MOBI ISBN: 978-1-84840-576-9

Executive Editor: Clíodhna Ní Anluain
Design: Fidelma Slattery
Illustrations Researcher: Caitríona Ní Dhunáin
Printed in Poland by Przedsiebiorstwo Uslugowo-Produkcyjne Introkar

This book is typeset in Cycles.

A CIP catalogue record for this book is available from the British Library.

5 4 3 2 1

Contents

•

Foreword

How we choose to mark key moments tells us a lot about ourselves. The idea behind *Composing the Island* was originally conceived as part of *RTÉ 1916*, and later developed in conjunction with the National Concert Hall to become a festival made possible through the financial support of Bord na Móna and Ireland 2016. The intention was to view the centenary through a specifically artistic lens, creating an opportunity for us to reflect on the journey we have travelled this past century through the story told by some of the music that was written by Irish composers. The music both speaks for itself, directly reflecting the personal vision and creative imaginations of so many Irish composers and, as is exemplified by this fascinating new book, also invites commentary, reflection and critical debate.

RTÉ itself played a unique role in how this story unfolded, a role that dates back to 1926 and the very earliest days of broadcasting. In particular, the formation of the orchestras in 1948—followed later by the string quartet and choirs—and their commitment to commissioning and otherwise providing both live and broadcast access to the work of Irish composers had a fundamental and catalytic impact. The burgeoning of original creative output across the century will be heard over the course of *Composing the Island* in live performances, broadcast across RTÉ lyric fm and online, and through subsequent recordings.

Just as the festival enables us to view ourselves through the prism of some of the music that has emerged thus far, it will offer a provocation—and perhaps also some inspiration—as to how we commit now to ensuring a bright and confident future.

The Invisible Art: A Century of Music in Ireland 1916–2016 will form part of a significant legacy from the project and RTÉ is proud to collaborate with Bord na Móna in facilitating this important publication.

Moya Doherty, Chair, RTÉ Board

Foreword

Composing the Island is a major retrospective festival focused on music composed in Ireland in the century 1916–2016.

The members of the Board of Bord na Móna are delighted to sponsor, in association with RTÉ and the NCH, this festival, the largest festival of Irish music that's ever been undertaken.

For many, music is a universal language. It gives voice to ideas and feelings that simply can't be expressed in any other way. Over the course of the three weeks of the festival we will hear the voices and experience emotions that are unique to the many different concepts of Irishness. The question of whose music qualified for inclusion appears to have been resolved in line with Dr Conor Cruise O'Brien's dual definition. 'Irishness is not primarily a question of birth or blood or language; it is the condition of being involved in the Irish situation, and usually being mauled by it.' All the composers meet the first criterion, too many, alas, met the second.

The concerts and recitals of *Composing the Island* will give renewed voice to over eighty-five composers in performances by our greatest musicians. Our hope is that these concerts will not only win thousands of new friends for Irish music, but that by celebrating the composers of the past and present they will also inspire the composers of the future.

Now is a good time to be fêting Irish music. Our composers are flourishing at home and abroad as never before. The range and vitality of music by the multitude of composers currently active is truly impressive.

This volume, commissioned by Bord na Móna to accompany the festival, documents the development of the art of music in Ireland over the last hundred years. The story is told through the voices of expert commentators, the words of composers themselves, and insights provided by some of the performers who have succeeded brilliantly in bringing new music vibrantly to life. It is intended to be a tangible reminder of the music making during September 2016.

John Horgan, Chairman, Bord na Móna

Photographer Lee Miller visited Dublin in 1946 on an assignment from *Vogue* for illustrations to accompany Constantine Curran's article, 'When James Joyce Lived in Dublin' . In Duke Street near the location of the pub Davy Byrnes, which Joyce frequented and which Leopold Bloom visits in *Ulysses*, she photographed American Vogue models Aleene Tallmey, left, and Rosamund Riley, right, with an unidentified street musician.

Player's Please
LENNON'S
13
3504

TIVOLI
TIVOLI
TIVOLI
WAIT HER
FOR EARLY
6D PIT
ENTRANC
TIVOLI
STALL
Entranc
TIVOLI
7 TWICE NIGHTLY 9
CHOOSING
A HUSBAND
HUGH WARD
TOM FRANKS
3 KELLINOS 3

Introduction

MICHAEL DERVAN

The Tivoli Theatre on Burgh Quay, one of Dublin's lost venues, was built in 1843 as the Conciliation Hall, a meeting place for Daniel O'Connell's Loyal National Repeal Association. It was converted to a concert hall in 1897 as the Grand Lyric Hall, and became the Tivoli in 1901. It closed in 1928 and was later adapted as the headquarters of the Irish Press newspaper group. Detail from Robert French photograph in the National Library of Ireland

Ireland stands unique among the nations of the world in having a musical instrument, the harp, as its national emblem. Irish musicians of all hues are widely celebrated. *Riverdance* has been an international phenomenon for two decades. Flautist James Galway and the rock band U2 are known all over the world. Singer Sinéad O'Connor is famous enough for her behaviour on US chat shows to create international headlines. And traditional music is even more widely dispersed than the phenomenon of the Irish pub.

Other Irish musical figures have been making waves, too. When Gerald Barry dared to turn Oscar Wilde's *The Importance of Being Earnest* into an opera, the 2011 concert premiere by the Los Angeles Philharmonic Orchestra prompted Mark Swed of the *Los Angeles Times* to call the work 'maybe the most inventive Oscar Wilde opera since Richard Strauss's *Salome* more than a century ago.' Kasper Holten, director of opera at the Royal Opera House in London, called it simply 'the first great comic opera of the twenty-first century.' *Earnest* won the composer the RPS Music Award for Large-Scale Composition, and its CD recording was nominated for a Grammy. It has now been seen or heard in London, Birmingham, Nancy, Dublin, Cork, Belfast, Derry and New York.

Barry is not alone. Donnacha Dennehy's opera *The Last Hotel*, with a libretto by playwright Enda Walsh, premiered at the Edinburgh Festival in 2015, and the Wide Open Opera/Landmark production was later seen in London, Dublin and New York. Early in 2016 Dennehy was taken on by the American publisher Schirmer, joining Barry, Ian Wilson and David Fennessy in having been signed by an international publishing house.

Composing the Island, the September 2016 festival of twenty-seven concerts over nineteen days, was a pretty hefty event by any measure. And it was not even designed to celebrate the full history of composition in Ireland, just the works of the last hundred years. There has been nothing quite like it before. Anywhere. Ever. Yet the tradition of music it salutes has long had in

Ireland a Cinderella-like position, an invisibility that can sometimes seem like the airbrushing or photoshopping into non-existence of a major art form.

Composers have felt the slight acutely. 'I'm a Composer'—'You're a What?' was the title Frank Corcoran gave an essay he contributed to *The Crane Bag* back in 1982. It was his way of explaining that Irish people simply didn't see being a composer as a serious or full-time occupation. In 1995 Raymond Deane wrote an essay on classical composers in Irish society for the third volume of *Irish Musical Studies*. Its self-explanatory title, 'The Honour of Non-Existence', has taken on a life of its own in reflecting the rather nebulous position of composers in Irish cultural life.

Over forty years earlier, in 1952, Frederick May wrote about the plight of composers in the symposium *Music in Ireland*, edited by Aloys Fleischmann. May painted a less than pretty picture. He bemoaned the lack of an adequate concert hall (a deficiency which would take nearly thirty years to rectify), as well as the absence of a national academy of music and a fully functioning music publisher in Ireland. In the area of commissioning, he pointed to the fact that copyists were being paid more for copying scores than composers were for composing them.

The composer's lot, it is true, is rarely easy. But the invisibility of composers in Irish life goes a lot further than you might imagine. The thousand-plus pages of the *Encyclopedia of Irish History and Culture*, published by Thomson Gale under its Macmillan Reference USA imprint in 2004, include articles on Early Modern Music and Modern Music as well as Popular Music. Just two Irish composers are mentioned, Seán Ó Riada and Mícheál Ó Súilleabháin, both included for their genre-crossing involvement with both classical and traditional music. Apart from that, the only reference is to the eighteenth century:

> At the end of the early modern era, Dublin's predilection for Western art music, which reached an epitome in 1742 with the premiere of Handel's *Messiah*, would decline with the drift of colonial society to London after the Act of Union.

The Cambridge Companion to Modern Irish Culture, published in 2005, shows a similar bias. Charles Villiers Stanford, Ó Riada and Ó Súilleabháin get mentioned in connection with traditional music. Wexford Festival Opera is included as an aside in connection with the traditional music organisation Comhaltas Ceoltóirí Éireann, because they were both founded in the same year, 1951. The book lists a trio of Englishmen, Peter Warlock, Arnold Bax and Ralph Vaughan Williams, who 'produced works that revealed some engagement with Irish culture'. There is one sentence which refers to 'the gifted but stricken progressive Frederick May and the prolific nativist Éamonn Ó Gallchobhair.' Apart from that composers are ignored as completely as if they had never existed.

I've often wondered why music written in Ireland—by natives and visitors, from the eighteenth century to the present—should feature only peripherally in such surveys. Perhaps it's because so much of it has featured only peripherally in our musical lives. The simplest way for me to understand and explain the situation has been to think back and remember how I began to accumulate my own knowledge of Irish music, probably in a way not much different from many of the composers covered in this book.

I grew up in what you would call a musical family, traditional music on one side, classical on the other. My first instrument was the accordion, when I joined a band at school at around the age of ten. I showed eagerness by working out how to read the bass clef in order to teach myself piano pieces, and I was sent to a Miss Humboldt in Phibsborough for piano lessons.

At that age Irish music meant for me, first and foremost, traditional Irish music, and also the music that was played by Irish pop groups and showbands. The first actual Irish composer I became aware of was John Field, through learning his Nocturne No. 5 in B flat.

I was very surprised that a celebrated composer, famous enough to be dubbed 'the inventor of the nocturne', should be an Irishman. But he seemed unique, isolated, like a single tree on an otherwise barren plain. I had no idea who might have come before him or after him. He seemed like a special case, an aberration, an anomaly, a one of a kind phenomenon for whom no explanation was offered or expected.

It was years later before I came across a second Irish composer. 'Ruffle the Old Hag in the Corner', one of Havelock Nelson's *Three Irish Diversions*, was a set work for one of my grade exams. It was the first piece I studied in which I got to play a glissando.

Away from the piano, I knew of two other Irish composers. A. J. Potter appeared as a judge on a national talent contest that featured on Telefís Éireann's *Joe Linnane Show*. I remember Potter as being what schoolchildren called a hard marker. The scores he gave were very low, and he offered technical comments in a way that no other judge did. Brian Boydell's almost hypnotically plummy voice was familiar from the radio programmes he presented. But the two men's status as composers was somehow abstract. It may have been what explained their presence on television and radio. But I knew them as composers without being aware of ever having heard a note of their music.

My teachers were highly conservative. My music teacher at secondary school used to cite Michael Tippett as a kind of bogeyman epitomising everything he believed to be wrong with contemporary composition. I hadn't heard a note of his work, either. I was promised an LP of my choice as a reward if I scored above a particular mark in my music exams in Fifth Year. I don't think my teacher ever got over the fact that I asked for an album of the jazz pianist Fats Waller.

Looking back at some stage, I began to realise that my ignorance was anything but accidental. I was in the privileged position of learning a number of instruments—I also played euphonium in the school band—but I had never been called upon to know much about Irish music apart from the Irish melodies I had to study, analyse and be able to write out from memory for the Leaving Certificate exam. And when I went on to study music at Trinity College Dublin there was nothing on the course to ensure that I would end up with any familiarity with the history of music in my own country.

My parents' interests had never extended to concert-going. It was only after I went to university that I began attending concerts. And I did it with a vengeance. H. H. Stuckenschmidt's book *Twentieth Century Music* presented a vast range of unfamiliar music in a way that made me hungry to get to know it. Fortunately, this was in the days when many of RTÉ's orchestral, choral and chamber concerts were free, and the repertoire planners had little fear of the new or rare. I opened myself to everything.

Schoenberg's Second String Quartet with soprano Minnie Clancy and the RTÉ Quartet at the National Gallery was a landmark experience. I soaked it up as readily as I did much more recent works by John Kinsella and Gerard

These highly distinctive New Irish Recording Company LP covers were designed by Bill Bolger. The illustrations are, left, of Kildare House (now Leinster House) from a 1756 map of Dublin by John Roque; and right, part of a print of the Rotunda Hospital and Concert Rooms by J. Owen after W. H. Bartlett from *Ireland Illustrated, from original drawings*, London, 1831.

Victory. I went to the Dublin Festivals of 20th Century Music and argued with friends about the merits of various works and composers. I joined record libraries and I saved up so that I could scour shops for music that would expand my horizons. Virtually everything from the twentieth century was new to me.

It wasn't actually that difficult in the early 1970s to get a picture of what contemporary Irish composers were writing. It was the pre-contemporary music that remained obscure.

There was, of course, Irish music that was inescapable—traditional arrangements, Thomas Moore, Herbert Hughes. I had experienced a surge of national pride when I discovered that Handel's *Messiah* had been first performed in Dublin. And my passion for chamber music led me to read Francesco Geminiani's *The Art of Playing on the Violin* of 1751. Geminiani had spent a lot of time in Dublin, and actually died there in 1762. There was of course John Field, although the gap in my knowledge between Field and the present felt uncomfortably hazy.

Stanford came to my attention when I borrowed the complete music criticism of George Bernard Shaw from the public library. I may still be tinged with Shaw's negativity towards the composer. I became aware that some of the most successful operas in English in the nineteenth century were written by Irishmen, Michael William Balfe and William Vincent Wallace, whose *Bohemian Girl* and *Maritana* still get bundled together with German composer Julius Benedict's *The Lily of Killarney* as the *Irish Ring*—never mind the fact that the original sobriquet seems to have been the 'English Ring' as a derisory comparison with Wagner. I saw a portrait of Robert Prescott Stewart (1825–94) in TCD, but didn't hear any of his music.

Hamilton Harty first came to my attention as a conductor of note rather than a composer. The Ulster Orchestra's pioneering recordings of his music conducted by Bryden Thomson were still in the future. And it was through Nicolas Slonimsky's mammoth *Music Since 1900* that I first came to know of O'Brien Butler's opera *Muirgheis*, produced in Dublin in 1903, and Robert O'Dwyer's *Eithne*, first heard in 1909. But a listing is no substitute for listening.

In the 1970s the Claddagh label, and the short-lived New Irish Recording Company, filled in a range of gaps. Claddagh took the laurels with recordings of Frederick May's String Quartet from the mid 1930s and Seán Ó Riada's *Hercules Dux Ferrariae* from the mid 1950s. These works had a vitality that made their neglect hard to fathom. Something had to be wrong if this music was not making its way into concert programmes.

And there was a huge information gap. When a slender booklet on *Four Centuries of Music in Ireland*, edited by Brian Boydell, appeared in 1979, the publisher was the BBC, and the text was based on the scripts of a radio series Boydell had edited to commemorate the fiftieth anniversary of broadcasting in Northern Ireland.

It seemed crazy for it to fall to the British Broadcasting Corporation to issue a volume surveying the history of music in Ireland. But it was still simply not possible to get a broad picture of Irish composers' endeavours in the twentieth century. The coverage on LP was patchy, to say the least, and there was no study laying out the information and putting it into some sort of perspective.

What was becoming clear to me was that Ireland had a musical heritage that was rather richer than most Irish music lovers seemed to suspect. But it was neglected and largely inaccessible to the general public.

It took until 1996 for a survey of the twentieth century to make it into print, when Axel Klein filled a major gap, with *Die Musik Irlands im 20.*

Jahrhundert (*Irish Music in the Twentieth Century*), still the broadest study of its kind. And the book was obviously closed to anyone who didn't read German.

The flow of information has not exactly become a flood since then. RTÉ Radio 1's Thomas Davis Lectures of 1998 surveyed *Music in Ireland 1848–1998* in connection with the 150th anniversary of the Royal Irish Academy of Music, and the series' commissioning editor, Richard Pine, has also co-edited, with Charles Acton, a book on the RIAM itself, and written a history of music in Irish broadcasting.

Books by and about composers are more often making it into print now. When Patrick's Zuk's book *Raymond Deane* was published as one of a series on Irish composers by Field Day in 2006, the flyleaf was able to proclaim proudly that it was 'the first comprehensive study of an Irish composer to appear in print in his lifetime'. Another landmark was the publication in 2013 of the two-volume, 1,200-page *Encyclopaedia of Music in Ireland*, edited by Harry White and Barra Boydell.

The issuing of CDs also got into gear in the 1990s, with Irish composers' series from Marco Polo and Black Box, followed in the new millennium by the RTÉ lyric fm and Ergodos labels.

Compositional activity grew apace. The increase in composer numbers is documented on the website of the Contemporary Music Centre, from eighteen born in the 1930s to a peak of fifty-three born in the 1970s, from a very low female base to over twenty-seven per cent of those born in the 1980s. Edgar Deale's 1973 *Catalogue of Contemporary Irish Composers* listed two dozen living composers. A collection of brochures published by the Arts Council in 1980 covered twenty-nine, and a more compact catalogue published by the Irish Transport & General Workers Union (with which the Association of Irish Composers was affiliated) in 1983 featured twenty-eight AIC members. Fast forward to 2016, and the CMC website lists over 190 living composers, and the Irish Composers' Collective has over 60.

How did all this come about? It doesn't seem to me that the 1969 introduction of an income tax exemption on artists' earnings from their creative work had any real impact. Composers were not earning enough from their compositions for the exemption to make much of a difference. The leading composers of the 1970s continued to make their living through normally-taxed, full-time jobs in academia or broadcasting.

If you wanted to point to a key change through the emergence of a new composer, the moment would probably be the appearance of Raymond Deane playing his own music at the young composers' concert of the first Dublin Festival of 20th Century Music in 1969. Deane was the first of a new breed to make a splash.

If you wanted to link it to the more solid evidence of composers establishing careers, the change would lie in the 1980s, when Deane, Gerald Barry, John Buckley and Roger Doyle all established formidable presences as composers. What set these thirty-somethings apart was the way in which they endeavoured to make a living purely from composing.

It was the creation in 1981 of Aosdána, the Arts Council-funded affiliation of artists, that made their ambition plausible. Aosdána offers members a tax-free annual stipend or Cnuas that's currently valued at €17,180. This support enabled the generation of Barry and Deane to be the first in which key individuals would succeed in concentrating their available energy on their creative work. The Cnuas is still an essential buffer, with 18 of the 31 current music members of Aosdána in receipt of one.

Aosdána was created in 1981 as the result of the Arts Council's concern regarding the working conditions of artists, and was intended to address questions of honour, support and pensions. The formal description has always been 'affiliation', though the Arts Council director who oversaw its introduction, Colm Ó Briain, preferred to call it a collective, as in this 1983 interview published in the music magazine *Soundpost*, at the time Aosdána became a self-electing entity.

The opening of the National Concert Hall in 1981 gave classical music an official home and an identity. It was and is anything but state-of-the-art. But as a national cultural institution devoted to music, it served to normalise the activities of performers and composers.

The Ennis Composition Summer School—composers organising tuition for composers—was established in 1983, and the Contemporary Music Centre was founded in 1985. A later fillip was the appointment in 1996 of Donnacha Dennehy as lecturer in music and media technology at TCD. Dennehy seems to have had a gift for encouraging his students to try their hand at composition, and the intake for the course included musicians from rock and other backgrounds who were initially attracted by the technology aspect of the course. Dennehy was also one of the founders of the Crash Ensemble, which in 1997 joined Jane O'Leary's Concorde, established in 1976, as specialist performers of new music.

SOUND POST

RIAM Summer School
Gruppen in London,
Stimmung in Belfast,
and Stockhausen's latest record
Earl 'Fatha' Hines
The possibilities of improvisation
Reviews of Sonorities,
Victoria de los Angeles,
Hermann Prey, Smetana Quartet,
Electric Phoenix

June/July 1983
95p (including VAT in the Republic of Ireland)
75p in UK

AOSDÁNA: THE CREATIVE COLLECTIVE

Arts Council Director Colm O'Briain talks to Michael Dervan

There's no doubt that Ireland's membership of the European Economic Community from 1973 opened up not just new educational opportunities for students from Ireland, but also new artistic vistas. Britain didn't seem quite as interesting when other European countries no longer seemed so far out of reach.

Britain, of course, has functioned like a distorting lens when it comes to the consideration of Irish music. That distortion has operated far beyond these islands. Composers like Harty and Stanford, and Balfe and Wallace before them, are routinely treated as British, sometimes even as English. British law, after all, regarded everyone born on the island of Ireland as British citizens until 1 January 1949, after which it effectively disowned those born in the Republic. And British taste still embraces many of these composers with an enthusiasm that's not quite matched in the country of their birth.

I don't want to rehearse arguments here regarding the Irishness or Britishness of long-dead composers. I just wonder why, since Irish history is so shy when it comes to composers, we just don't accept them as ours the way we're happy to cheer footballers whose ancestry allows them play for the Irish team, or highlight our connection with American presidents whose roots we can trace back to Irish soil.

The rejection of the likes of the staunchly Unionist Stanford seems to have a lot to do with political nationalism. Stanford spent his life as a hugely important mover and shaker in England, and he may still be tainted by the kind of thinking that rejected as un-Irish the Irish men and women who fought in the British Army during two world wars. The rehabilitation of such people has been accelerated by the 1916 centenary celebrations, and the process could valuably also be applied to composers and musicians.

It's hardly surprising then that it was not an Irish record company, but an English one, Chandos, which first recorded the orchestral works of Hamilton Harty in the 1980s (with the Ulster Orchestra) and followed up with the symphonies and Irish rhapsodies of Stanford.

'Resurrecting a Pillar of British Music' ran the headline for a 1990 *New York Times* review of some of Chandos's Stanford recordings, though admittedly the article itself did characterise the composer as 'an Anglo-Irish Dvořák'. In Ireland he still seems to be treated as more Anglo than Irish.

The creation of the Army School of Music was set in train in 1922 during the Civil War, one of Ireland's most difficult periods. The composer John F. Larchet advised the Commander-in-Chief of the Irish Army, General Mulcahy, that 'The original Bandmaster must come from without and the future Bandmasters can be developed from within.' His advice was taken and the German conductor, military bandmaster and composer Fritz Brase (right) was chosen for the task.

It's not just long-dead composers that Britain is happy to claim. Gerald Barry, Donnacha Dennehy and others are featured on the NMC Label, which was originally set up specifically to promote British music. There's an undoubted career advantage for any Irish composer in having a level of advocacy on record in Britain that they can't always have at home. Benefits can cut both ways.

The priorities of the young Irish state are revealing. The band of An Garda Síochána, the Irish Free State's police force, was established within months of the force itself. The German conductor and bandmaster, Fritz Brase (1875–1940), was invited to Ireland as early as 1923 to establish the Army School of Music. The establishing of a professional symphony orchestra took a further quarter of a century, and it was arranged at arm's length from the government by the national broadcaster.

The support of a professional orchestra has never been directly undertaken by either the state or any arm of local government, and all attempts to establish a full-time opera company have also come to nought. One of the stranger consequences of the state's priorities has been the fact that until the 1990s, the army was the biggest employer of full-time professional musicians in the country. When RTÉ overtook it in that regard, that was a matter of reductions in the army rather than increases in RTÉ.

If Ireland had the same interest in the ancestry of composers and musicians as in footballers and American presidents, then we would be able to claim composers like Henry Cowell (1897–1965) and Terry Riley (b. 1935). Riley is widely regarded as the father of minimalism, and Cowell was one of the twentieth century's leading avant-gardists. His explorations included tone-clusters—playing the piano with his arms—and pieces which call on performers to use their hands directly on the strings of the piano. That's how the eerie sounds of his *The Banshee* (1925) are created.

Working on this book brought into focus individuals and works which don't actually feature in its pages. There's the Clonmel-born violinist Maud MacCarthy (1884–1967), who appeared as soloist with the symphony orchestras of Boston and Chicago. Neuritis ended her concert career, and she travelled to India with Annie Besant and studied Indian music and mysticism. She wrote the text for English composer John Foulds's *World Requiem*, which was performed on Armistice Nights at the Royal Albert Hall in London in the 1920s, and later published poetry under the name Tandra Devi.

Kathleen Schlesinger (1862–1953), from Holywood in Co. Down, was a music archaeologist and curator of musical instruments at the British Museum. Her work on Greek music influenced microtonal composers on two continents, Harry Partch (1901–74) in the U.S., and Elsie Hamilton (1880–1965) in Australia.

Partch designed and made his own instruments in order to play music using scales of his own invention, and he visited Yeats in Dublin in 1934 to discuss setting the poet's modern version of Sophocles's *Oedipus Rex*. He later asked, 'Is it not remarkable that a man of literature with an eager and anxious temperament should one day explode over the much-marvelled artifices in the modern degeneration of words in music, or, the art of song.'

There's another interesting connection with Yeats. The American composer George Antheil (1900–59), self-proclaimed 'bad boy of music', whose fans included the poet Ezra Pound, also impressed Yeats, who asked him to write the music for the play *Fighting the Waves* at the Abbey Theatre in 1929.

Through the digital archive of *The Irish Times* I came across Digby La Touche (ca 1880–1957), whose operetta *Thémidor* was a success in Munich in 1911. Max Reinhardt directed and Alexander Zemlinsky conducted. The paper gave a lengthy description of the composer's ancestry. It began with the information that he was 'the youngest son of the late Lieutenant General William Paget La Touche, by his marriage with Frances, second daughter of General Sir Anthony Stranshaw, GCB, [and] is a great-grandson of the well-known David La Touche (the younger), of St Catherine's, Leixlip, Co. Dublin.'

And how many people know that the Irish-American composer Swan Hennessy (1866–1929) dedicated his Second String Quartet of 1920 'à la Mémoire de Terence McSwiney, Lord Mayor de Cork'—the use of French is explained by the fact that Hennessy spent much of his life in Paris, where the work was published. Plans are underway for a performance of the work in Cork, and also for a revival of Robert O'Dwyer's opera *Eithne*, first staged at the Oireachtas festival in 1909.

The period that's documented in this book includes its fair share of artistic hardship, resilience and fighting against the odds. The Irish state does not come well out of international comparisons when it comes to support of the arts. Aosdána is a valuable institution, but it can't magic away the fact that Ireland is close to the bottom of the EU table when it comes to expenditure on culture and the arts. And, within that limited spend, music is less kindly treated than in other countries.

The musical world cannot overturn these facts by an act of will. But the mere fact that a nineteen-day, twenty-seven-concert festival could be put on is a statement about the amount of music that is there to be celebrated. A similarly sized festival with an entirely different selection of works would not be that difficult to devise. After all, the Contemporary Music Centre, focusing primarily on the work of living composers, holds over 9,600 Irish scores.

The longer-term importance of the festival will be gauged by the way it impacts the concert programmes of the future, ideally stimulating new ideas and explorations that will continue to breathe the life of performance into a larger proportion of our musical heritage. The essays of this book provide historical information and context, suggest leads for further exploration, and offer thought-provoking perspectives on how we got to where we are today. And, in spite of all the difficulties and obstructions, there are more composers, and more successful composers, active in Ireland today than ever before.

1916–1922

1916

Dublin-born Victor Herbert writes one of the first orchestral feature film scores, for Thomas Dixon Jr's *The Fall of a Nation*, the sequel to D. W. Griffith's *The Birth of a Nation*.

1917

Finn Varra Maa, an 'Irish fairy pantomime' with music by Geoffrey Molyneux Palmer, is performed at the Theatre Royal in Dublin.

1918

The first use of the term céilí band is credited to Frank Lee for a St Patrick's night céilí in London.

1919

Ina Boyle composes her orchestral work *The Magic Harp*, which becomes the only work by a woman ever selected for publication by the Carnegie Trust.

1920

Hillsborough-born Hamilton Harty is appointed permanent conductor of the Hallé Orchestra in Manchester.

1921

The Antient Concert Rooms concert hall on Dublin's Great Brunswick Street (modern-day Pearse Street) is transformed into the Palace Cinema.

1922

Irish violinist and composer Mary Dickenson-Auner gives the world premiere of Bartók's First Violin Sonata with pianist Eduard Steuermann at the Konzerthaus in Vienna on 8 February.

Before the beginning

JOSEPH RYAN

Ireland entered the twentieth century as a quiet musical backwater, unaffected by any of the major movements in European music.

On Tuesday 25 April 1916 *The Irish Times* reported upon what was described as 'The Outbreak'. It noted that 'this newspaper has never been published in stranger circumstances than those which obtain today.' The paper, which adopted a conservative and indeed Unionist perspective, had insufficient information at that stage to report on other parts of the country, and noted of Dublin that 'an attempt has been made to overthrow the constitutional government of Ireland.' Understandably, neither the significance nor the consequences of the armed insurrection that would become known as the Easter Rising were at that time apparent. 'At this critical moment,' the paper cautioned, 'our language must be moderate, unsensational, and free from any tendency to alarm. As soon as peace and order have been restored the responsibility for this intended revolution will be fixed in the right quarter.'

The column immediately following provided insight into an opposing quarter at play and revealed a similar estimation of the events unfolding. 'We are glad to learn that, in spite of the present troubles in Dublin, The Royal Dublin Society's Spring Show will be opened today.' The article proceeded to record that the society had a run of bad luck with the show in recent years, including the prevalence of foot-and-mouth disease, but concluded with the hope 'that the show arrangements will not be very much upset by the effects of yesterday's disturbance.'

The proclamation of martial law issued that day by Baron Wimborne, Lord-Lieutenant General and General Governor of Ireland, told another story. The regulations required that all persons within the city and county of Dublin remain within their houses between 19.30 and 05.30. This impacted all social life and entertainment at the very time of year when the lengthening evenings were inviting a convivial people abroad. Ever helpful, *The Irish Times* suggested that the citizenry might put the time to good use: putting the garden into a state of decency, painting about the house, or even acquiring, or reacquiring, the art of reading.

It was music performance, a staple of urban social life, that suffered. Not until the week of Monday 8 May did the various venues begin to reopen. The Royal Irish Academy of Music announced that it was resuming operations on that day, as did such diverse places of entertainment as the Theatre Royal Winter Gardens on Hawkins Street and the year-old Carlton Cinema on Sackville Street, today's O'Connell Street. That the period had occasioned hardship was indicated in correspondence in *The Irish Times* on 15 May, which referred to a proposed concert to be given by Mr John McCormack in New York in aid of those who had suffered as a result of the recent rebellion, and made the proposal that special consideration should be reserved for Dublin musicians, of whom it stated some 100 were now out of work.

From being the second city of the British Empire in the eighteenth century, Dublin had regressed following the Act of Union in 1800, and cultural life had suffered accordingly. Urban centres, and notably Dublin, maintained a level of musical activity, but this was modest compared to other European capitals. Music had, to some degree, also become politicised: it was sufficiently low in the scheme of things to be of no significant moment, but it was in evidence nonetheless. In Ireland, European art music had associations of an establishment, of the old order, of foreignness. It contrasted with an indigenous expression which was lauded as simple, pure and unadulterated. Traditional Irish music, or the notion of such a tradition, had the benefit of constituting a badge of distinctiveness, further evidence of a distinguishing and honourable culture.

But there remained some appetite for the repertoire that one would encounter in a city such as London. On that fateful Easter Monday in 1916 the D'Oyly Carte Repertoire Opera Company was scheduled to open a fortnight's season in the Gaiety Theatre. Specialising in the performance of Gilbert and Sullivan's Savoy Operas, the season was due to open with *The Gondoliers* and was to include performances of *Iolanthe*, *The Mikado*, *The Pirates of Penzance*, *Trial by Jury*, *Patience* and *The Yeomen of the Guard*. The arrangements for the season were inevitably to collapse due to the restrictions of martial law which followed from the Rising. This occasioned considerable loss to the Gaiety Theatre, which enjoyed full houses during the regular D'Oyly Carte seasons. While the theatre suffered financially, the fabric of the building escaped damage as it was not close to the centre of the conflict. The same could not be said of the more modern and capacious Coliseum Theatre off Henry Street and Prince's Street, which had opened the previous Easter, and suffered devastating damage from the bombardment and the resultant fire.

It was a loss that magnified the city's dearth of performance venues. This was highlighted in correspondence to *The Irish Times* published on 30 May, which notes that following the lease of the Antient Concert Rooms on Great Brunswick Street—today's Pearse Street—to a business following enforced relocation due to the recent troubles, and the redesignation of the Rotunda as a temporary General Post Office, there was no longer a single hall in the capital capable of hosting a public concert. It was to prove a recurrent cry; the competitions and concerts of that year's Feis Ceoil had to rely on the generosity of the Commissioners of National Education, who lent their schools on Marlborough Street for the competitions of 1916. The call for a concert hall in Dublin was to continue for decades, but the absence of such a facility speaks to the low priority that was afforded to music during these perfervid political times.

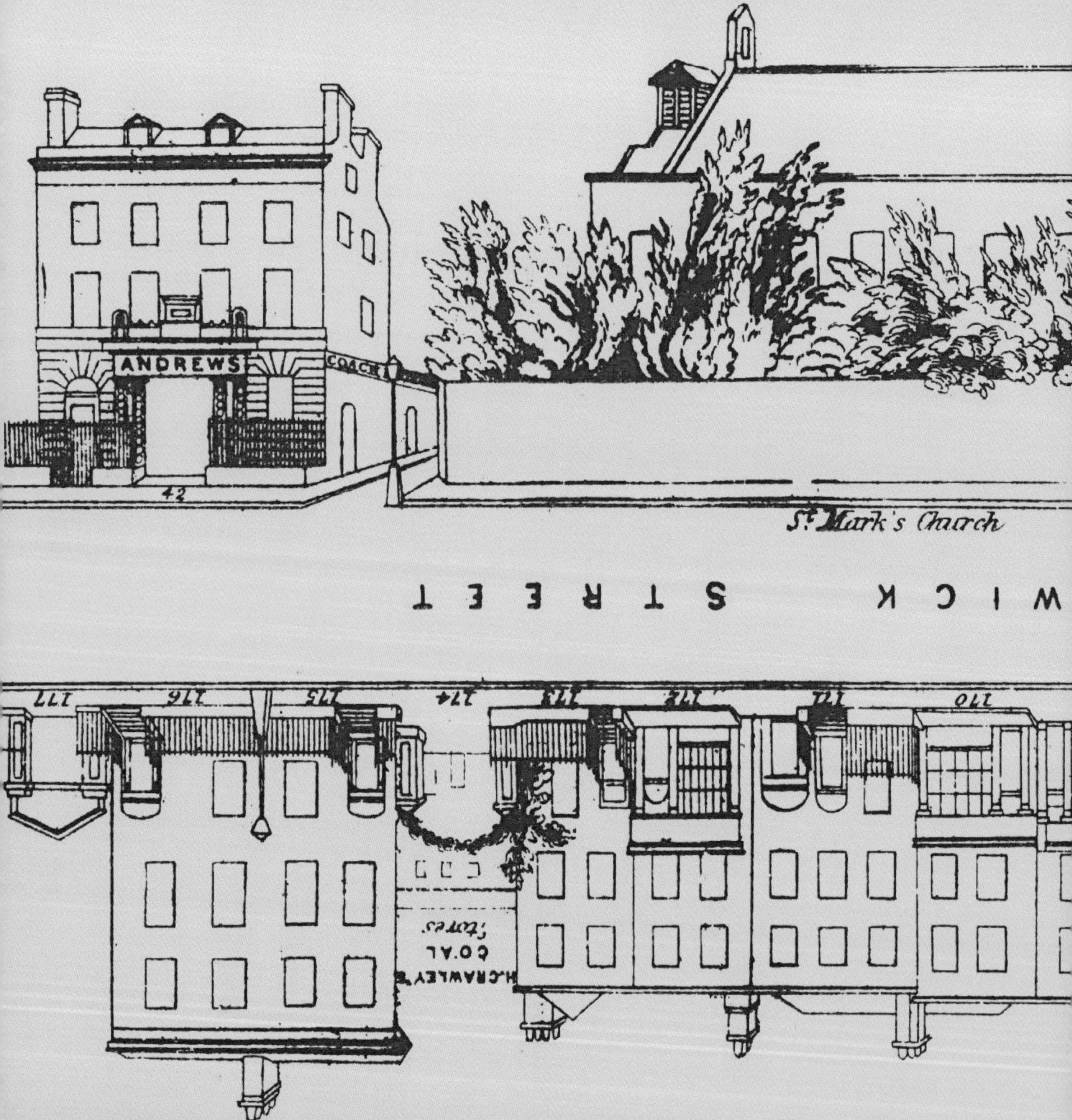

ANDREWS
COACH
42
St. Mark's Church
WICK STREET
177
176
175
174
173
172
171
170
H.CRAWLEY'S
COAL
Stores

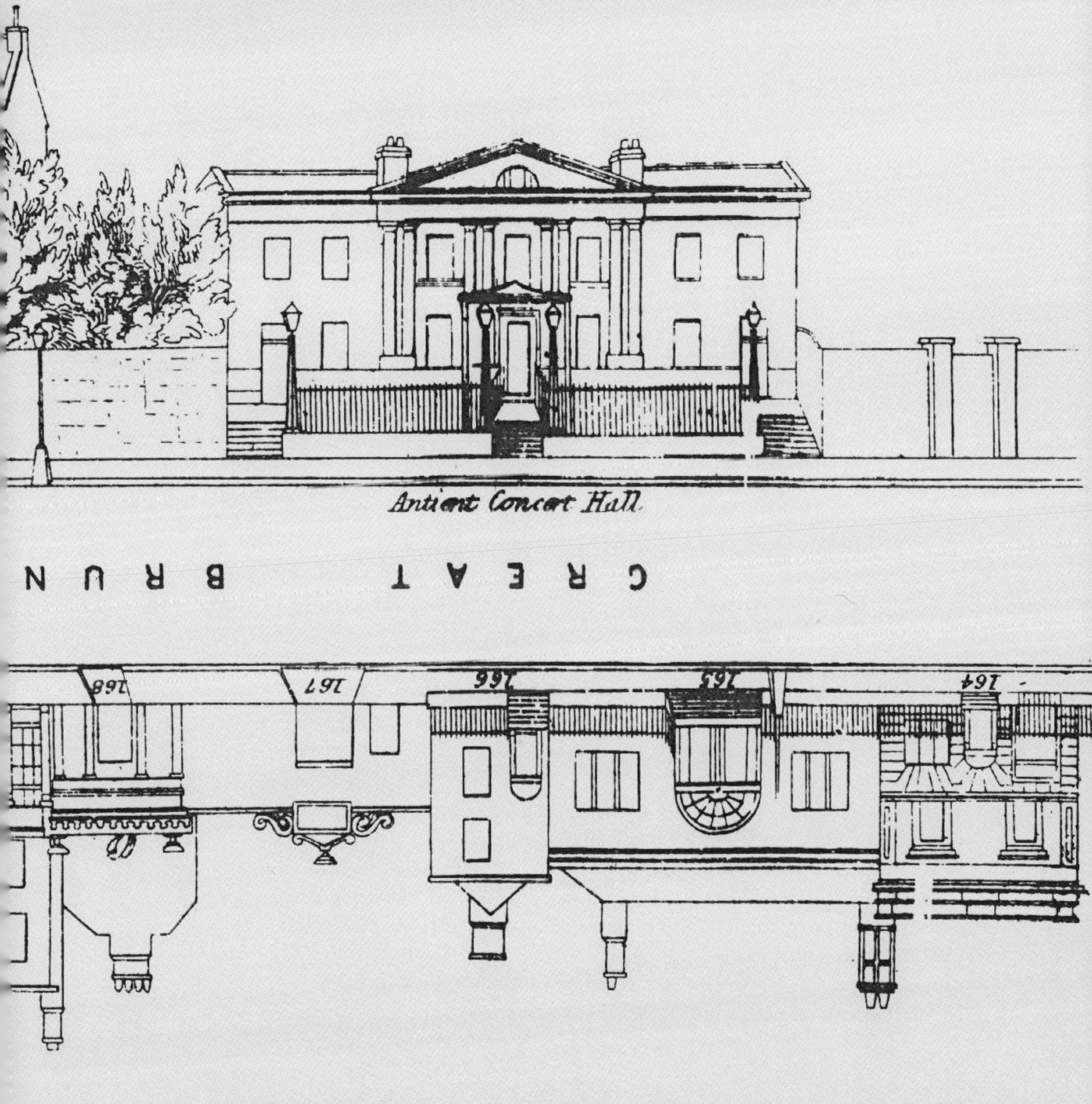
Antient Concert Hall
GREAT BRUN
164
165
166
167
168

Traditional music had passed through a period of collection, codification and celebration, but this was not synonymous with preservation within a living context. While Carl Hardebeck (1869–1945), one of the strongest campaigners for a distinctly Irish music, was willing to support and compete within the Feis Ceoil in its initial years, a more extreme and controversial opinion was proposed by fellow advocate, the Rev Dr Richard Henebry (1863–1916), who made some of the earliest surviving field recordings of traditional Irish music. 'The present pervading ignorance concerning Irish music,' he wrote in his 1903 booklet, *Irish Music*, 'is entirely on the outside, and arose from the habit of regarding it from the standpoint of the vulgar music.'

Henebry was being characteristically adversarial and provocative. His view that traditional music represented a system of music wholly at odds with what he described as the 'vulgar' tradition helped to seed the sense of difference and opposition that was to inform the following decades. He criticised the 'modern style' that he saw as being promoted through Irish cultural feiseanna and attacked what he viewed as the false ideals of nationality that were now being foisted upon the population.

The truth is that music in Ireland at the beginning of the twentieth century was in a debilitated condition. Politicisation resulted in a fractured expression: Gaelic Ireland sponsored its own practice, predominantly monophonic and imbued with melodies of surpassing beauty; the more cosmopolitan or European aesthetic was predominantly celebrated in urban centres and was supported by the educated and travelled classes.

But the two traditions were not mutually exclusive, and increasingly there were attempts at fusion. Some of these emanated in unpredictable ways. The future Master of the King's Music, Arnold Bax (1883–1953), had travelled to Ireland as a young man, adopted a *nom de guerre*, Dermot O'Byrne, and become enthralled with the Irish spirit and friendly with Padraig Pearse and that circle which espoused an independent Ireland. Following the execution of Pearse, Bax penned his tribute *In Memoriam (1916)*, scored for cor anglais, harp and string quartet. He also wrote an orchestral *In Memoriam* with the dedication '*I gcuimhne ar Padraig mac Piarais*' ['In memory of Padraig Pearse'], which would not become well known until the 1990s after the original full score resurfaced and the piece was performed and recorded. He had

Previous pages: The Antient Concerts Society founded by Joseph Robinson bought the Dublin Oil Gas Light Company's building at 52 Great Brunswick Street (today's Pearse Street) in 1843, and transformed it into a concert hall, the Antient Concert Rooms. American composer Daron Hagen's one-act opera, *The Antient Concert*, with a libretto by Paul Muldoon, is premised on the fact that both John McCormack and James Joyce competed there at the Feis Ceoil of 1904, though in fact they didn't. McCormack's success was in 1903.

Right: The cover of the booklet *Irish Music* by the multi-talented Catholic priest and musical polemicist, Fr Richard Henebry. He also made early field recordings of traditional Irish music, which can be sampled on the Irish Traditional Music Archive's website, www.itma.ie.

Irish Music

Rev. R. Henebry

Ph. D

already invested significantly in the notion, as he described it, of writing 'Irishly' through tone poems such as *Cathaleen-ni-Hoolihan* (1905), *Into the Twilight* (1908), *In the Faery Hills* (1909) and *Roscatha* (1910).

Another who viewed Ireland as an exotic musical location was Ernest John Moeran (1894–1950), who had first come to Ireland in 1917 as a commissioned officer in the British Army to counter republican unrest following the Rising of the previous year. Moeran was enchanted by the indigenous tradition and spent much of his time collecting folk songs, which were to inform his original pastoral style. In later life he was to return to Co. Kerry, which was to prove a source of solace and creative inspiration; his last completed work was the set of *Songs from County Kerry* shortly before his untimely death—he fell from the pier during a storm in Kenmare in December 1950, and the inquest established that he died from natural causes before his fall. Ever the miniaturist, his passion for Ireland was presaged in the sensitive short piano work from 1926, the *Irish Love Song*.

The history of music in other European countries suggests that opera offers itself as an ideal proselytising vehicle; the central place of opera in the rise of nationalism in nineteenth-century Italy provides a prime example. Despite Ireland's consistent record in fostering creative literary talent, there is no parallel record of endeavour in the genre of music drama. Opera lent itself to the portrayal and celebration of the regional accent. One might reasonably have anticipated that the Ireland of the nineteenth century, with its burgeoning interest in antiquarian studies and identification of distinctively national characteristics, might have turned to opera for one manifestation of this individuality. The artistically inclusive nature of the form along with its dramatic power and spectacle would naturally appeal to any progressive cultural and political movement. But while one can find sporadic forays into the world of opera throughout the nineteenth century, composers largely eschewed any exercises in what might have been described as the development of a national operatic expression.

Performances of opera did take place, and there was clearly an audience for such performances. Smock Alley (1662–1787), the Theatre Royal (1821–80 and, as a new building, 1897–1934) and previously the Musick Hall in Crow Street (1731–57, and, operating as a theatre, 1758–1820) had provided

The 2,011-seat, Frank Matcham-designed Theatre Royal (1897–1934) was the second Theatre Royal built on Hawkins Street in Dublin. The theatre's last concert, with the Orchestra of the Dublin Philharmonic Society under Fritz Brase, featured Hungarian violinist Adila Fachiri in Beethoven's Violin Concerto plus works by Wagner and Elgar. Its successor, a third and larger Theatre Royal, closed in 1962 and was demolished to make way for one of the city's least-loved buildings, Hawkins House, itself now scheduled for demolition.

venues in Dublin. The Ulster Hall, which was opened in 1862 with a capacity that could reach 2,000 with a large portion of the audience standing, had taken over as the principal venue in Belfast from the Music Hall of 1840, which had been built by subscriptions from members of The Anacreontic Society. The Theatre Royal in Cork, which itself existed on a number of sites, provided the focus for larger-scale performances in the southern city. Opera, provided by touring companies such as the English Carl Rosa Opera Company and the Moody Manners Company, and variety performances provided the staple diet. Italian opera and performances of Mozart operas also featured with some regularity, although in November 1916 *The Irish Times* drew attention to a performance of *Die Zauberflöte* in Dublin's Gaiety Theatre with the note that, 'It has been so seldom heard in Dublin during recent years that very few persons last evening seemed to be familiar with it.'

Shamus O'Brien by Charles Villiers Stanford (1852–1924) is a romantic comic opera in two acts set to a libretto by George H. Jessop and is based on a poem by Joseph Sheridan Le Fanu. Following its successful premiere at the Opera Comique Theatre in London on 2 March 1896, it moved to the

William Orpen's 1920 portrait of Charles Villiers Stanford, the greatest composer to come out of Ireland in the late nineteenth century. He held professorships at the Royal College of Music in London (composition) and at Cambridge University (music), and trained a generation of British composers.

Broadway Theatre in New York, where it was received with acclaim. The critics of the day declared that it was one of the finest comic operas that had been seen in years. The work features spoken dialogue, and the music is invested with the distinct flavour of native song and dance. The tale is set in the mountains of Cork in the aftermath of the rebellion of 1798, and the eponymous hero is an outlaw who is on the run from the British Army. The libretto was an uncanny pre-echo of the coming times. Stanford's characteristic mastery of orchestration is evident from the lively opening of the overture, which features one of the few original Irish tunes employed in the opera *Father O'Flynn*, a fruit of an earlier cooperation with the poet and folklorist Alfred Perceval Graves.

Stanford's success with *Shamus O'Brien* encouraged additional exploration of musical drama as a vehicle for exploring the prospect of cultivating a distinctively Irish opera. It led to what was described as the first Irish grand opera ever produced on any stage, which was initially presented on 7 December 1903 in Dublin's Theatre Royal. This was *Muirgheis* by Thomas O'Brien Butler (1861–1915). This composer's birth name was Thomas Butler, which he later changed to Whitwell Butler before finally settling on O'Brien Butler as a consequence of engaging with the Irish literary revival. *Muirgheis* featured an exclusively Irish company including dancers from the Keating Branch of the Irish League. What ultimately made this work most notable was the fact that it was championed by the *Freeman's Journal* as 'the first Irish Grand Opera'. The premiere clashed with a performance by the Brodsky Quartet in the Royal Dublin Society on the same evening, but it still managed to attract a reasonably sized audience. *The Irish Times* review praised the intent, but noted a number of telling reservations:

> Visitors who went to hear the work for the first time laboured under a double disadvantage. In the first place, no copy of the libretto was available; in the second, the singers being amateurs, and knowing little of the art of pronunciation, it was almost impossible to follow the story of the work, and absolutely impossible to form any notion of the character of the libretto. One would fain encourage Irish art, but it must be confessed that *Muirgheis* does not possess the elements of popularity.

The unnamed critic concluded that the opera was no more characteristically Irish than *Shamus O'Brien* and that it compared poorly to the earlier work. The libretto was an adaptation of *The Sea Swan* by Nora Hopper Chesson (1871–1906), an archetypal Celtic Twilight poet. Her early *Ballads in Prose* (1894) were much admired by W. B. Yeats, who described the publication as 'the most distinguished volume we had had out of Ireland this decade.' The English libretto used in the first performance was later translated into Irish by Tadhg Ó Donnchadha (1874–1949), who was to become professor of Irish at University College Cork in 1916. In preparing the plot for *Muirgheis*, Chesson was assisted by fellow Irish writer George Moore. *Muirgheis* betrays the composer's technical limitations, but it does consciously set out to be Irish in flavour and, having sought letters of introduction from fellow Kerryman The O'Rahilly, O'Brien Butler had travelled to the United States in 1914 to promote his work. Along with the opera, this included a setting of *Marching Song of the Irish Volunteers* by Thomas MacDonagh. There is some poignancy in the fact that the trumpeting of an opera which is set by the sea was ultimately to lead to the composer's demise whilst returning from that promotional visit on the RMS *Lusitania* in 1915. Some 1,200 passengers and crew perished when the *Lusitania* was sunk by a German U-boat off the Old Head of Kinsale on 15 May as it travelled from New York to Liverpool.

A determinedly Irish opera of a different flavour was created by the Neapolitan musician Michele Esposito (1855–1929). He had arrived in Dublin from Paris in 1882 and had contributed significantly to the musical life of the city as professor of piano at the Royal Irish Academy of Music. His name became known throughout the country as a chamber musician and frequent piano recitalist. Esposito's regular appearances at the annual recital series under the auspices of the Royal Dublin Society and his support for a series of Sunday afternoon concerts in the city's Antient Concert Rooms were significant contributions to the musical calendar, as was his inauguration of the Dublin Philharmonic Society through public subscription in 1899. *The Postbag* was an operetta he composed to a libretto by A. P. Graves. It was first staged in London in January 1902 and was given its Irish premiere in the Gaiety Theatre, Dublin, on 14 March of the same year. The music

Sarah Cecilia Harrison's 1926 portrait of Neapolitan pianist Michele Esposito, who joined the staff of the Royal Irish Academy of Music in 1882, and was an influential figure in Irish musical life as a performer, educator, conductor, composer and publisher until his departure in 1928. He is commemorated through a piano competition which carries his name in Dublin's Feis Ceoil.

SONATE
1926

features settings of traditional airs and original elements based on the traditional idiom. The work is set in the kitchen of the heroine's home. In a comic *ménage à trois*, Kitty is joined by two other characters, a postman and a smith, and the plot makes play of the heroine's inability to understand a letter written to her in Irish by her absent lover, Brian.

The Postbag was essentially a fruit of the Irish Literary Society and signified one example of the artistic contribution to the re-emergence of a national sensibility. Esposito had earlier collaborated with T. W. Rolleston on a dramatic cantata, *Deirdre,* which was a successful entrant in the very first Feis Ceoil in 1897. A second opera, *The Tinker and the Fairy* (1904), enjoyed a libretto from one of the guiding founders of the literary revival, Douglas Hyde, later to be the first President of Ireland. It too features three characters, but the concision of the libretto and Esposito's harmonic mastery make this a work of substance. The inaugural performance of this opera as part of the spring season by the Dublin Amateur Operatic Society in March 1910 was notable for a different reason: the performances attracted small, if enthusiastic, audiences. However, on the last night, Esposito, who had conducted the performances, left the Gaiety Theatre before the final curtain calls, clearly despondent at what he perceived as the apathy of the public towards the ambitious efforts of the society. It was to be a tale oft repeated in Irish musical life.

Robert Dwyer (1862–1949) was a Bristol-born composer who took the patronymic 'O' when he returned to Ireland. O'Dwyer, as he preferred to be known, had commenced his career in 1891, first conducting the Carl Rosa Opera Company and later touring with the Rousbey Opera Company until 1896. He settled in Dublin in 1897, where he held various posts as organist, conductor, composer and teacher. His most famous work was the opera *Eithne,* written for the annual Oireachtas festival in 1909; the Oireachtas was intended as an annual and determinedly Gaelic cultural festival based on the Welsh Eisteddfod. The Rev Thomas O'Kelly's libretto was later translated into Irish, gaining the work particular attention as another opera to employ an Irish text. The same librettist, a Sligo native who was more commonly known under the Irish form, Fr Tomás Ó Ceallaigh, had earlier supplied the first translation of Yeats's *Cathleen ni Houlihan.*

The Gaelic League and Aonach Tailteann (Tailteann games), a purposeful initiative named after the ancient figure of Queen Tailté and focused on building unity around culture and sport and locating this within a decidedly Gaelic tradition, provided the occasion for further essays in drama through music, notably from Harold R. White (1872–1943), who also wrote under the name Dermot Macmurrough. White's contribution as an arranger, occasional composer and music critic speaks to the importance of the Churches in the formation of musicians and in the broader musical life of the major urban centres in Ireland. Edward Martyn's initiative in founding the Palestrina Choir under Vincent O'Brien in Dublin's Pro-Cathedral in 1903 and the major contributions made by the Robinson family to Christ Church Cathedral and within neighbouring St Patrick's, the dedication of Sir Robert Prescott Stewart, teacher of Stanford, along with the work of Charles George Marchant and George Hewson would be difficult to overstate. The same can be said of the work of Captain Charles Brennan, organist of Elmwood Presbyterian Church, University Road, Belfast from 1901 and of St Anne's Cathedral in Belfast from 1904 until his retirement an astonishing sixty years later. The organist of St Fin Barre's Cathedral, Cork, was J. C. Marks, who also served in St Bartholomew's Church, Dublin in 1883, where he was succeeded by another long-serving organist, William Henry Vipond Barry. The cross-generational work of George A. Osborne, organist at St John's Cathedral until his departure from Limerick in 1825, and his father, George W. Osborne, who was the organist at Limerick Cathedral, is also notable. The want of a musical literacy and of any proper system of training for church musicians forced the Catholic Church to look abroad, which led to the appointment of a number of Belgian and German musicians from such as the Lemmens Institute in Malines. Franz Born and Karl Seeldrayers in Carlow, Ernest de Regge in Ennis, Staf Gebruers in Cork, Louis Evers in Galway and Michael Van Dessel in Dundalk all played a significant part in the broader musical life of their areas, and it points to the consistent dependence on foreign-born musicians. The history of the Fleischmann family in Cork offers a leading and lasting example.

Returning to the secular world, if Arthur Sullivan had been somewhat discomfited by the association with operetta, his contemporary Victor

August Herbert (1859–1924) had no such qualms. Herbert was born in Dublin in February 1859 of Irish Protestant stock. The early death of his father led to a nomadic few years where he lived for a period in London with his grandfather, the celebrated Irish novelist, poet and composer Samuel Lover, before a further period in Stuttgart, when his mother remarried. He met and married the soprano Therese Förster there and they sailed to the United States in 1886, where Therese had been engaged by the Metropolitan Opera to sing the title role in the American premiere of Verdi's *Aida*. Herbert, himself an instrumentalist of note, was appointed principal cellist in the orchestra, and the couple settled in New York.

He was to immerse himself in the musical life of the east coast, and by 1893 he had also become director of the 22nd Regiment Band, founded by

Aloys Fleischmann's parents. Aloys Snr was photographed in 1916 in the internment camp in Oldcastle, Co. Meath, where he was held as an enemy alien before his transfer to the Isle of Man and post-war deportation to Germany. Cork-born pianist Tilly Fleischmann, née Swertz, the daughter of the organist of the city's North Cathedral, is pictured at the family home in Dachau in 1903.

fellow Irishman Patrick Sarsfield Gilmore. He had a successful career as a conductor, and maybe even more tellingly as an advocate for the legal rights of composers. His campaigning strongly influenced the American copyright law of 1909, which secured composers' royalties on the sales of sound recordings. He had met with and advised O'Brien Butler during the latter's promotional foray in the United States. As a composer himself, Herbert was active in many genres but the stage remained his principal focus. His origins were evident in the abiding desire to compose an Irish operetta, which he finally realised with the production of *Eileen* in 1917. Originally entitled *Hearts of Erin*, the work demonstrates a strong score with clear influence of the wind band tradition, and the libretto is based on the Irish rebellion of 1798. That spirit informed a band setting he made under the title of *Soldiers of Erin* in 1916 of the popular Irish Volunteers' marching song *The Soldiers' Song*, which a decade later was to be adopted as the national anthem.

Political independence brought with it calls for more focused and consistent support for the building and shaping of an artistic infrastructure. This was initially realised through the work of Vincent O'Brien (1871–1948) in gradually building a station orchestra from the inception of 2RN, the precursor of Radio Éireann, in 1926, and Colonel Fritz Brase (1875–1940), the first director of the fledgling Army School of Music. Brase worked with John Turner Huggard (1893–1944) to position the Dublin Philharmonic Society as a principal contributor to the musical life of the capital for a decade.

Belfast provided a strong template for Dublin in this regard. On 9 April 1925, the Belfast Philharmonic Society celebrated its jubilee with a performance of Elgar's *The Dream of Gerontius* conducted by Sir Henry Wood, founder of the Promenade Concerts in London. Exactly fifty years previously, the society had performed Handel's *Judas Maccabeus* to close its inaugural season. The society was an amalgamation of the Classical Harmonists' Society and the older Belfast Musical Society. The Belfast Philharmonic Society had prospered under the direction of Francis Koeller, from 1887 to 1912, and Edward Godfrey Brown, from 1912 to 1950. Like its younger Dublin counterpart, the society gave a small number of concerts annually and attracted visiting musicians of high calibre; it also provided a focus for the development of local musicians such as the composer and critic Edward Norman Hay (1889–1943).

Like many other contemporary aspiring creative musicians, Hay had won competition prizes at the Feis Ceoil. Another more famous musician from the North followed a similar fostering path. Within the pantheon of Irish music, Herbert Hamilton Harty (1879–1941) stands as the direct successor to Sir Charles Villiers Stanford. Harty's family had moved north to Co. Down the year before his birth in 1879, when his father had assumed the post of organist and choirmaster in Hillsborough. Unlike Stanford, he was one of a large family. Also in contrast to the older man, he was, like Edward Elgar, largely self-taught, although he benefited hugely from the influence of his father, who he described as having 'unerringly good taste in music'. Harty proved a precocious talent and moved to take up a position in Christ Church, Bray, in Co. Wicklow, when he was still shy of his seventeenth birthday. It was a fortuitous move as it brought him into contact with Esposito, who was to be his mentor. It was under the influence of the latter that Harty wrote his first major orchestral work, the *Irish Symphony*, for the Feis Ceoil festival of 1904, where it won the prize for an orchestral work based on traditional airs. More at home as a creator in shorter forms, Harty would nonetheless rework this symphony, first in 1915 and then definitively in 1924 for performances with Manchester's Hallé Orchestra which, while its principal conductor, from 1920 to 1933, he had restored to its former

Hillsborough-born composer and pianist Hamilton Harty was also the most successful Irish conductor of the first half of the twentieth century. He was a passionate advocate of Berlioz, conducted the world premiere of William Walton's First Symphony and the British premieres of Shostakovich's First Symphony and Mahler's Ninth. In 1951 it was decided to use royalties from his music to create the Hamilton Harty Chair of Music at Queen's University Belfast, where there is also a recital room named in his honour.

glory. The work is best remembered today for the refulgent orchestration of the second movement, 'The Fair Day', based on 'The Girl I left behind me', or under its Irish title, '*Spailpín Fánach*'.

This determination to write an 'Irish' symphony had survived decades and rhymed with the prevalent focus on the creation of a distinct Irish identity. Sir Arthur Sullivan (1842–1900), the son of an Irish bandmaster, harboured the ambition to be regarded seriously as an original voice, and while he much appreciated the fame derived from his fecund collaboration on the Savoy Operas with W. S. Gilbert, he maintained the hope that his reputation could move beyond the realm of operetta. An early symphony was performed at the Crystal Palace on 10 March 1866 and was later dubbed the 'Irish' Symphony. Stanford's contribution in this regard, his Symphony No. 3, *Irish*, in F minor, was first performed in London on 27 June 1887. Esposito himself had given Harty a lead with an *Irish* Symphony in 1902. This too was written for the Feis Ceoil, which had elected at a meeting of the festival committee in 1901 to offer a prize for a suite or symphony based on traditional airs. It was an interesting departure as it was likely to attract extended arrangements of original airs rather than foster any distinctive 'Irish' voice. It was predictable that such a liberal encouragement would result also in the accommodation of traditional expression within the predominant framework of European art music; it was also precisely the approach that had fuelled the antagonism of such as Henebry.

A later *Irish* Symphony was penned in 1941 by the Dublin-born violinist, composer and music teacher Mary Dickenson-Auner (1880–1965). From a privileged background, Dickenson-Auner had a distinguished career as a violin soloist in Prague, Transylvania, the Netherlands and finally Vienna before political events conspired somewhat later in her career to turn her attention to composition. The *Irish* Symphony is one of six essays in the genre and is distinctively Irish in flavour with the final movement being a series of variations on an adapted traditional theme, 'The Banks of Moorlough Shore'. Dickenson-Auner's progress points to a truism about Irish creative musicians in the decades before and after independence: if one wished to pursue a high-level career as a professional musician, it was necessary to travel abroad. Indeed the Irish public had an expectation that musicians would be travelled, foreign, or least have an exotic name. Gabriel, the hero of the 'The Dead', the final, culminating story in Joyce's *Dubliners*, states:

> Mr Browne could go back farther still, to the old Italian companies that used to come to Dublin—Tietjens, Ilma de Murzka, Campanini, the great Trebelli, Giuglini, Ravelli, Aramburo. Those were the days, he said, when there was something like singing to be heard in Dublin.

Similarly, that the composer Augusta Holmès (1847–1903) of Irish parentage published her earliest songs under the pseudonym Hermann Zenta tells something of the challenges faced by female creative artists at the close of the nineteenth century. While her life was centred on France, her works include the symphonic wind poem, *Irlande,* which was performed at the opening season of the Feis Ceoil in 1897. Within Ireland, Dr Annie Patterson (1868–1934), who succeeded Hardebeck as lecturer in Irish music at UCC in 1924, was a consistent advocate for women in music and had been a formative influence in the initiation of the Feis Ceoil in 1897. Another female composer who benefited from the platform of the Feis Ceoil was Alicia Adélaïde Needham (1863–1945), who had been born in Co. Meath and wrote over 600 songs. Such pioneers encouraged later generations that included the good friends Ina Boyle (1889–1967) and Elizabeth Maconchy (1907–94).

Charlotte Milligan-Fox (1864–1916) from Omagh, Co. Tyrone, made a highly significant contribution through her work as a collector and champion of traditional music and as a founder-member of the Irish Folk Song Society in London in 1904 and then editor, along with Herbert Hughes, of its journal. It was her arrangement and publication of the traditional air, 'The Banks of Moorlough Shore', in her *Songs of the Irish Harpers* (1910), that helped popularise the 'The Foggy Dew', which had earlier been published by A. P. Graves in *Father O'Flynn and other Irish Lyrics* in 1889 and was separately arranged by Stanford.

It has been suggested that the traditional love song 'The Banks of Moorlough Shore', employed by Dickenson-Auner, had been collected near Holy Hill close to Strabane in Co. Tyrone. This was the home area of George Sigerson (1836–1935), a true renaissance man, who was president from 1893 of the Irish National Literary Society and also served as early acting chairman of the Feis Ceoil executive committee in its formative days. This annual festival has made an immeasurable contribution to the musical life of Ireland. It was designed as a resolutely Irish musical festival with an original focus on both ancient and modern Irish music; the twinned inaugural concerts in Dublin and Belfast in May 1897 were consciously so fashioned. The notion of an all-Ireland festival was further endorsed with the unanimous support for the proposal delivered by Koeller that the Feis of 1898 be held in Belfast on the basis that it 'was to be an Irish and not merely a Dublin festival.'

The rotation, which was meant to be 'the means of cementing the hearts of the people of the South and the North,' did not survive. But the endurance of the Feis Ceoil in Dublin is testimony to the vision of its founders and to a musical spirit that has proved to be enduring.

From the vantage point of an independent and confident Irish state and the hindsight of a century, one can marvel at the opening decades of the twentieth century as a defining episode in Ireland's modern history. Musical creativity, however, was never to the fore, and there was a failure to foster the infrastructure necessary for a vibrant musical expression. Some four decades after his initial introduction to Ireland, Sir Arnold Bax was to record that in his Dublin days, 'there was no talk of music whatever.' In spite of this, the resilience and dedication of a few key individuals and organisations helped to lay a foundation that would enable others to construct a more active musical landscape in the decades that followed.

The power of persistence

ITA BEAUSANG

When Ina Boyle was born in Enniskerry, Co. Wicklow, in 1889, Ireland was part of the United Kingdom. By the time she was thirty-three years old the twenty-six-county Irish Free State had been established, with an Irish government and administration, independent of the Houses of Parliament at Westminster. As a member of the Protestant Ascendancy she could be categorised as a typical representative of the Anglo-Irish social class. Her Crampton maternal lineage included powerful members of the medical, military, legal and diplomatic professions; her father, Rev William Foster Boyle, was a graduate of Trinity College Dublin.

A young Ina Boyle playing her John Betts cello at Bushey Park, Enniskerry, holding the instrument side-saddle, as was dictated by Victorian decorum. Her first complete work was a Romance for cello and piano which she wrote in 1913 and later orchestrated, changing the title to *Elegy*. The *Elegy* won first prize in the composers' competition at the 1913 Sligo Feis Ceoil and her song 'The Last Invocation' won second prize.

Overleaf: An extract from Ina Boyle's 1928 diary detailing a difficult moment in a lesson in London with Ralph Vaughan Williams. She is believed to have made this copy of her 1928 entries in the 1950s.

What were the musical influences that gave her the impetus and ambition to compose continuously from childhood to old age? She grew up in the then remote village of Enniskerry and from the age of eleven had private theory and harmony lessons with Samuel Myerscough. She enjoyed music-making with her sister and her father, who made violins as a hobby. Her cousin Charlotte was married to the Armagh-born composer Charles Wood, and from 1904 she took correspondence lessons from him.

The series of concerts in 1913 and 1914 by the London Symphony Orchestra under Hamilton Harty at Woodbrook, near Bray, residence of the music patron Sir Stanley Cochrane, were probably her first opportunity to hear an orchestra in live performance. Soon afterwards she launched into serious composition and studied privately with two English musicians who had settled in Dublin, Percy Buck and C. H. Kitson. It is surprising that she never attended classes at the Royal Irish Academy of Music or at Trinity College Dublin, where women had been admitted as students since 1904.

The years from 1914 to 1918 reveal conflicting aspects of her life. The music that she composed reflects the impact of WWI, in which two members of her family lost their lives and ten members of the parish of St Patrick's Church, Enniskerry, were killed. On the other hand there is no echo in her music or mention in her papers of the Easter Rising, or later of the War of Independence.

After the war she entered five works, including her orchestral rhapsody, *The Magic Harp,* for composers' competitions in London. In 1920 she had the greatest success of her career when the rhapsody was selected for publication by the Carnegie United Kingdom Trust. She was the only woman composer ever to be chosen by the trustees. The press paid attention, and a headline in London's *Evening Standard* recorded 'Sudden fame for Irish woman composer' (22 May 1920).

After Buck and Kitson returned to London she decided to find a new composition teacher. She approached Ralph Vaughan Williams requesting composition lessons. By February 1923 a date

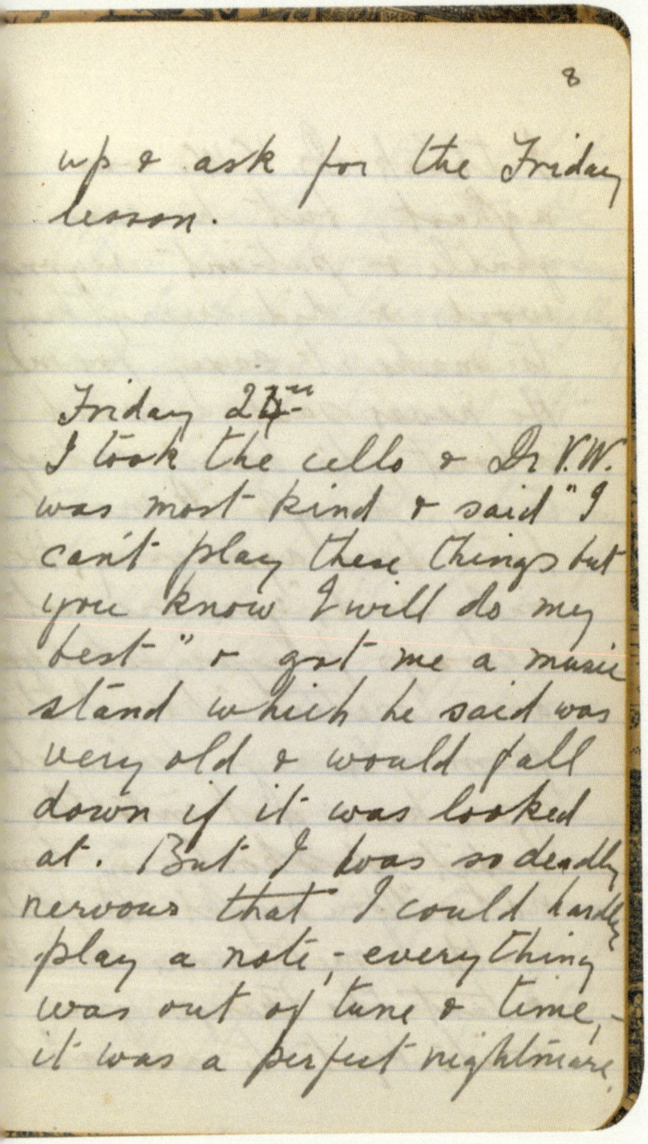

8

up & ask for the Friday lesson.

Friday 27th
I took the cello & Dr V.W. was most kind & said "I can't play these things but you know I will do my best" & got me a music stand which he said was very old & would fall down if it was looked at. But I was so deadly nervous that I could hardly play a note – everything was out of tune & time – it was a perfect nightmare.

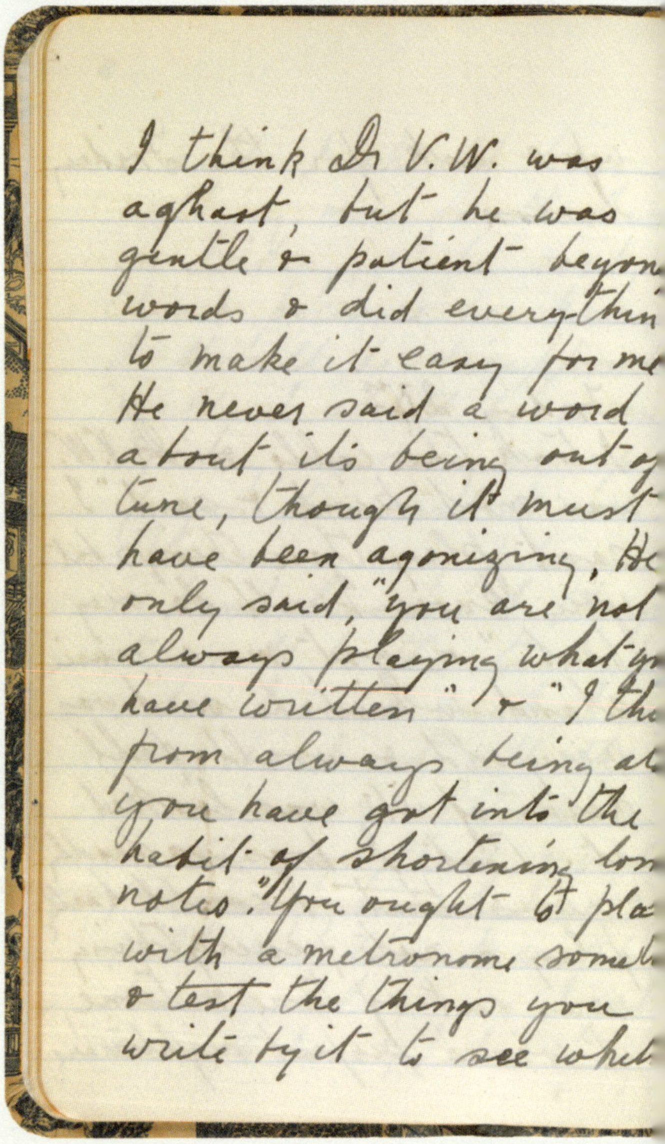

I think Dr V.W. was aghast, but he was gentle & patient beyon words & did everythin to make it easy for me He never said a word about its being out o tune, though it must have been agonizing. He only said, "you are not always playing what yo have written" & "I thi from always being at you have got into the habit of shortening lon notes." You ought to pla with a metronome somet & test the things you write by it to see whet

was arranged and the lessons, which required her to travel to London and continued until the outbreak of war in 1939, began in his home at the rate of £1 per hour; this was equivalent at the time to almost one-third of the average weekly wage.

The establishment of the Irish Free State's first broadcasting station, 2RN (later Radio Éireann) in 1926 proved to be the most important development for Irish composers in the twentieth century. Between 1936 and 1955 music by Ina Boyle was broadcast

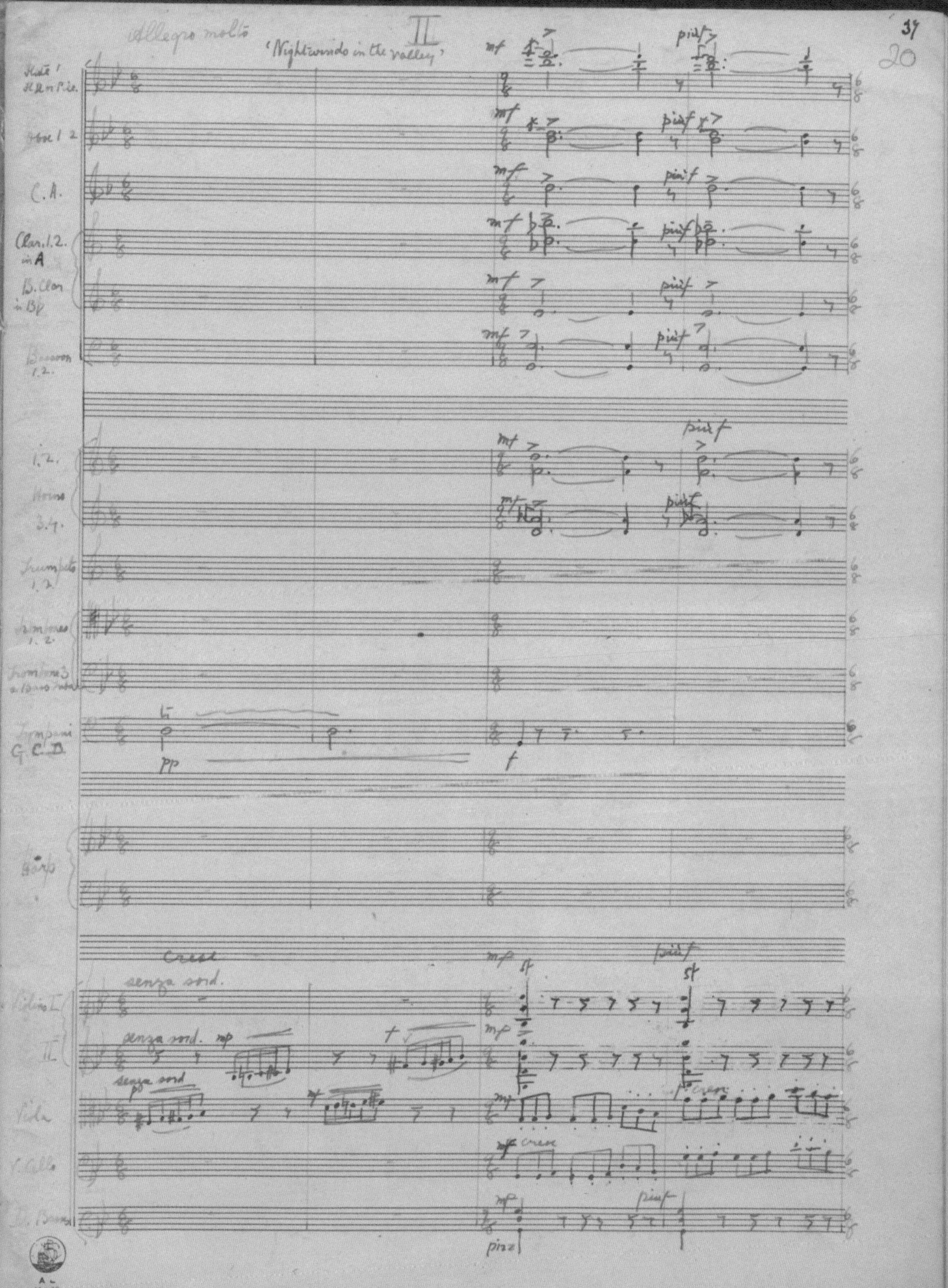
Allegro molto
II
'Nightwinds in the valley'
Flute I
Oboe 1 2
C. A.
Clar. 1.2. in A
B. Clar in B♭
Bassoon 1.2.
1.2.
Horns
3.4.
Trumpets 1.2
Trombones 1.2.
Trombone 3 & Bass tuba
Timpani G C D
Harp
Violins I
II
Viola
V. Cello
D. Bass
mf
più f
pp
f
cresc
senza sord.
mp
pizz

from Radio Éireann on twenty-one occasions.

Conductors of the orchestral works included Arthur Duff, Edmond Appia, Jean Martinon, Milan Horvat and Éimear Ó Broin. It was somewhat out of character for her when in her late fifties she attended Jean Martinon's composition classes in 1947 and 1948 at the Department of Education Summer School. She was working on her Third Symphony, *From the Darkness*, and used the opportunity to bring several orchestral scores to Martinon for his advice. In 1948 when she joined the newly founded Music Association of Ireland she did not attend meetings, although she contributed to its policies. She was an outsider who wanted to make her mark on a world that she could not quite bring herself to inhabit.

Ten years after her death, Charles Acton, music critic of *The Irish Times,* asked why Boyle's distinguished music was so little heard during her lifetime. She is not the only Irish woman composer of the twentieth century whose work has been neglected, but she was certainly one of the most prolific.

Over sixty years she produced a steady stream of orchestral, choral and vocal compositions, three symphonies, a violin concerto, an opera and ballet music. She set texts by many Irish poets including Padraig Pearse, W. B. Yeats, Eva Gore-Booth and James Stephens.

Her musical style changed little over her lifetime and is firmly rooted in the harmonic language of the early twentieth-century English School. This is often combined with rhapsodic string melodies enhanced by judicious use of harp and woodwind. She drew inspiration from Celtic mythology for her most successful composition, *The Magic Harp*, which, from the moment of its magical opening, captures an other-worldly atmosphere. The *Glencree* Symphony depicts the changing moods of the picturesque Wicklow landscape. Her voice-friendly choral music and songs are notable for her skilful technique and understanding of the text, in particular her masterly settings of two John Donne poems—'Thinke Then My Soul' and 'Hymne to God, my God, in my Sicknesse'—for tenor solo and string quartet.

Previous page: The opening page of the second movement from the full score of Ina Boyle's Symphony No. 1, *Glencree* (*In the Wicklow Hills*). The work started out as a suite in 1924, and the first movement was rehearsed and performed by Adrian Boult with the London Symphony Orchestra at the Royal College of Music in London in 1925. Vaughan Williams thought it 'sounded well but needed pulling together'. The first movement was added last, in 1927, to make the work a symphony.

Opposite: The cast list and the composer's costume drawings from the manuscript score of Ina Boyle's still unperformed 1966 chamber opera *Maudlin of Paplewick*.

Robin Hood, the Chief Woodman, Master of the Feast		Baritone
Friar Tuck, his Chaplain and Steward		Bass
Little John, Bow-bearer.		Baritone
Scathlock, Huntsman.		Bass
George-a-Green, Huisher of the Bower.		Baritone
Much, Bailiff or Acater.		Baritone
The Guests invited		
AEglamour, the Sad	Shepherds	Tenor
Lionel, the Courteous	Shepherds	Baritone
Alken, the Sage	Shepherds	Bass
Karolin, the Kind	Shepherds	Tenor
Lorel, the Rude, the Witch's son		Bass
Puck-Hairy or Robin Goodfellow, their Hind		Tenor
Marian, Robin Hood's Lady		Contralto
Earine, the Beautiful, (sister to Karolin)	Shepherdesses	Soprano
Mellifleur, the Sweet	Shepherdesses	Mezzo
Amie, the Gentle, (sister to Lionel)	Shepherdesses	Soprano
Maudlin, the Envious, the Witch of Paplewick		Contralto
Douce, the Proud, (her daughter)		Mezzo
2 Young Woodsmen.		
3 Musicians, Foresters, etc		

Scene, Sherwood.

By birth, gender, social background, religion and education, Ina Boyle was dislocated in the new Irish Free State. Like many other members of the Protestant Anglo-Irish class who had to adapt to living in the new nationalist Ireland, she gradually adjusted to the changes and became integrated in the environment. She continued to compose until the end of her life as she lived in seclusion in the family home. In 1963, four years before her death, she wrote in a letter to her friend Sheila Wingfield (18 August 1963):

> I love this dear house so much that I never mind about lack of musical success, though of course it would have been very welcome, and as long as I can stay here I am well content.

She went on, without any prospect of a performance, to complete a chamber opera, *Maudlin of Paplewick,* to a libretto she had written after Ben Johnson. Her indomitable spirit, which had spurred her on as a composer all her life, endured to the end.

Right person, right time

DAVID BYERS

'What's the use of going on with [my music]? … It never comes to anything. What's the use of writing music that is never published and never played?' The composer William Brown Reynolds (1874–1925) from Coleraine was complaining to his friend, the novelist Forrest Reid, ca 1915.

In earlier times, industrial Victorian Belfast had its music societies and concert venues, but home-grown composers were few and far between. Then as now, the lack of performance opportunities, appreciative audiences and patronage was a major draw-back for creative souls.

A Hay family outing around 1930, with, from left, Elizabeth Haughey (Hay's sister-in-law), Norman Hay, his wife, Hessie (née Haughey) and their two sons, Norman and, partly hidden, Michael.

An *Inaugural Ode* to mark the installation of the Ulster Hall organ in 1862 was commissioned from its new organist, Edmund Chipp (1823–1886) from London. Belfast-born organist and pianist Benjamin Hobson Carroll (1835–1921) wrote an instrumental ode in 1871 for the opening of the Belfast Working Men's Institute. Armagh-born Charles Wood (1866–1926) left to study at London's Royal College of Music (RCM) with Stanford, Parry and others when he was seventeen. He didn't return.

Hamilton Harty (1879–1941), from Hillsborough, was taught by his organist father. During his couple of years as an organist in Belfast, he surely gained valuable experience as an occasional viola player in the orchestra of the Belfast Philharmonic Society under Francis Koeller (1858–1926) from Aix-la-Chapelle. Harty moved to Dublin towards the end of 1896, studied with Esposito, and settled in London in 1901.

Choral and orchestral standards improved with Koeller's appointment to the Philharmonic in 1887. Norman Hay, who was born in 1889, inherited the autograph score of Koeller's large-scale Wagnerian cantata *Reullera* (1896), performed at the second Feis Ceoil in 1898, held in Belfast. *Reullera* earned Koeller his Oxford D.Mus in 1899, and probably led to his commission for the Ode to mark the opening of Belfast's City Hall in 1906.

Chronologically, W. B. Reynolds comes between Wood and Harty. He and Herbert Hughes (1882–1937) were Gaelic Revivalists and involved in the founding of the Antrim Glens Feis (*Feis na nGleann*) in 1904. A year later, Reynolds was writing of his concerns that young Hughes and Arthur Monnier Harper (1886–1916) might leave Ulster for the bright lights and ignore the heritage of Irish folk music in their own compositions.

Well, he got that half right. Hughes studied with Stanford and Wood at the RCM in London, where he settled as the music critic for the *Daily Telegraph*, helped found the Irish Folk Song Society, and made wonderful arrangements of traditional Irish songs. Harper died in the Netherlands, remembered for

A relaxing time being had by, from left, Herbert Hughes, Aloys Fleischmann Snr, Suzanne McKernan (Hughes's second wife) and Arnold Bax. This 1936 photograph was taken by Tilly Fleischmann in west Cork, where the Hughes family was living,

his early flying exploits rather than his music-making.

Theatre provided another platform for composers. Reynolds was an active supporter of the Ulster Literary Theatre, and in 1909 he provided the opening music for Harry Morrow's burlesque *Suzanne and the Sovereigns*. His *Overture 1690* was a parody of the *Tannhäuser* overture, based on Orange tunes including 'The Boyne Water' and 'The Boys of Wexford'.

He was also one of the first composers to set poems from Joyce's *Chamber Music*, followed closely by Hughes. Joyce spent a convivial evening with Reynolds on his trip to Belfast in November 1909. Alas, Reynolds' songs are lost, as is the music for his unfinished opera, *The Lovers of Shulam*, to a libretto by Forrest Reid. The overture and orchestral music from the first scene were performed in the Ulster Hall before World War I.

For twenty years, Reynolds was music critic of the *Belfast Telegraph*, writing under the pen name of 'Rathcol', the name derived from the Irish for Coleraine—*Cúil Raithin*. When he died in 1925, he was succeeded, also using the name 'Rathcol', by the now well-established composer Edward Norman Hay.

The family was from Coleraine, but Hay was born in Faversham, Kent, where his father, an Inland Revenue official, had been posted. He wasn't two-years-old when his mother died and he was hospitalised with polio. He was shipped home to be brought up by his aunts and was unable to walk until he was twelve, ever afterwards having a permanent limp.

'Hay, who I know well, is a difficult and pugnacious person, but honest', wrote the BBC's Director-General in London in 1938. That character, so stereotypically Ulster, was probably moulded in those difficult childhood years.

Eventually there were regular visits to Belfast, where Koeller was one of his teachers. Studies with Dr Eaglefield Hull, a champion of Scriabin and Cyril Scott, were most likely mainly by correspondence. He also played in the Philharmonic's orchestra—'second violin, cello, sometimes the triangle, and on one fearsome occasion second oboe'.

'I learnt much from my mentors,' he wrote. 'But, remember, I had few chances of hearing music. No wireless or gramophone then. ...' However, there were Feis Ceoil successes (like Harty before him), a Cobbett prize for a *Phantasy String Quartet on Irish Folk Tunes*, and an Oxford D.Mus earned with a large-scale cantata, *The Gilly of Christ*, setting words by Ulster poet Joseph Campbell.

When Hay's father died in 1918, Norman wrote a richly argued string quartet in his memory. Awarded a Carnegie Trust Award and published by Stainer & Bell in 1920, it's an important work in the early history of the string quartet in Ireland.

In 1912, Godfrey Brown (1874–1955) succeeded Koeller as the conductor of the Philharmonic. He became a crucial advocate for Hay's music and gave the first performance in 1921 of *Dunluce* (1920), a tone-poem which, like Harty's *The Children of Lir*, nearly twenty years later, aimed to encapsulate the four movements of a 'standard' symphony. At the behest of Sir Henry Wood, Hay conducted a London Queen's Hall Proms performance in 1925. He conducted another performance in 1933 in Belfast with the BBC's Wireless Symphony Orchestra.

Yeats's poetry was important to Hay across these years. His cantata, *The Wind among the Reeds*, dedicated 'To my wife', sets seven poems from Yeats's 1899 collection. Begun in September 1921, surely some of the music's moody bleakness was 'in the air' —a reflection of the bloody street riots and killings in Belfast in mid July and late August that year.

With the advent of broadcasting, a developing orchestral concert life, and Godfrey Brown now double-jobbing as the BBC's Director of Music in Belfast, performance opportunities were much improved for the next fifteen years. Hay wrote an orchestral *Fantasy on Irish Folk Tunes* for the opening of the new 2BE radio station.

The station's young announcer, Tyrone Guthrie no less, produced a broadcast of Yeats's *The Land of Heart's Desire* in November. It was Hay who provided the incidental music, including an atmospheric Prelude and a delicious *Faery Song*.

Another cantata, *To Wonder* (1924), for the fiftieth anniversary of the Philharmonic, was followed by more orchestral works, and, in 1930, a large-scale choral and orchestral piece, *Paean*, setting words by George Herbert. Dedicated to Godfrey Brown 'in appreciation of his interest in my works', it was performed by the Philharmonic Society in Belfast in 1931. It was also given at the Three Choirs Festival in Worcester the following year and at the Henry Wood Proms in 1934. Some performers, would-be critics, crossed out the title on their scores, replacing it with an alternative: *Pain*.

Until his death in 1943, Hay remained a highly influential, outspoken, fearless and controversial music critic, crusading for an Ulster college of music, for better school music teaching, for better standards at the BBC and for the recording of Ulster traditional music by its countryside practitioners before it vanished. How different the northern music world might have been had he been around in the post-war period.

A caricature of Norman Hay from *Radio Times*'s 2BE programme page for Thursday 2 January 1930. The orchestral programme he conducted included Stanford's *Irish* Rhapsody No 4, two items by Wagner (*Siegmund's Love Song* and *By Silent Hearth*, sung by tenor Trefor Jones), Delius's *On hearing the first Cuckoo in Spring* and *Summer Night on the River*, Hay's own *Three Irish Sketches*, songs by MacDowell, Samuel, Travers, Sheldon, Aylward and Peel, and Beethoven's *Leonore* No. 3 Overture.

HOVEN
VERDI
HANDEL
WAGNER
LISZT
GOUNOD
MOZART

1922–1951

1923

German conductor Fritz Brase comes to Ireland to establish the Army School of Music. The station's small orchestra is granted a special dispensation to include a harpist.

1924

The radio station 2BE, owned by the British Broadcasting Company, starts broadcasting from Belfast.

1925

The Abbey Theatre becomes the first state-subsidised theatre in the English-speaking world when the Minister for Finance Ernest Blythe allocates an annual subsidy of £850.

1926

The Irish Free State's first radio broadcaster, 2RN, starts transmissions on 1 January broadcasting three hours a night, Monday to Saturday, and two hours on Sunday. Its small musical ensemble is the seed from which the future RTÉ orchestras will grow.

1927

Ina Boyle completes her symphony, *Glencree (In the Wicklow Hills)*, which will wait until 1945 for a first studio broadcast and until 2016 for performance at a public concert.

The Abbey Theatre School of Ballet is set up under the direction of the Co. Wicklow-born dancer and choreographer Ninette de Valois.

1928

The Irish Free State introduces its own coinage, with the national symbol, the harp, on the reverse of each coin.

1929

The incidental music for the Abbey Theatre premiere of William Butler Yeats's play, *Fighting the Waves*, is written by American enfant terrible, George Antheil.

1930

Harold R. White's cantata *Hymn to St Patrick at Tara*, the composer's last major work, is performed in Cork.

1931

Joseph Kaye's *Victor Herbert: The Biography of America's Greatest Composer of Romantic Music* is published in new York.

1932

A massed choir of 2,000 performs before an audience estimated at one million people at a Pontifical Mass held in Dublin's Phoenix Park during the Catholic Church's Eucharistic Congress.

1933

Oxford University Press publishes *The Joyce Book*, edited by Herbert Hughes, with contributions by James Stephens, Padraic Colum and Arthur Symons, and settings of *Pomes Penyeach* by E. J. Moeran, Arnold Bax, Albert Roussel, Herbert Hughes, John Ireland, Roger Sessions, Arthur Bliss, Herbert Howells, George Antheil, Edgardo Carducci, Eugene Goossens, C. W. Orr and Bernard van Dieren.

1934

Aloys Fleischmann founds the University Orchestra, which becomes the Cork Symphony Orchestra.

1935

The Irish Folklore Commission (*Coimisiún Béaloideasa Éireann*) is set up under the auspices of the Department of Education to collect and preserve the folklore of Ireland, including music.

1936

Frederick May composes his groundbreaking String Quartet, which will wait until 1948 for a first performance.

1937

Brian Boydell gives the first performance of his Op. 1, the 1935 song *Wild Geese*, at the Cambridge Music Club.

1938

At the Gaiety Theatre in Dublin Aloys Fleischmann conducts the Radio Éireann Orchestra an all-Irish programme, the first of its kind—Ina Boyle's *Colin Clout*, Frederick May's *Spring Nocturne*, Muiris Ó Rónáin's (a pseudonym used by Fleischmann) *Trí hAmhráin* with English tenor Heddle Nash, Elizabeth Maconchy's Piano Concertino, with Charles Lynch, and E. J. Moeran's Second Rhapsody.

The Letters of Mozart and His Family, translated by Galway musicologist Emily Anderson, is published in three volumes by Macmillan.

1939

The BBC Northern Ireland Orchestra is disbanded after the outbreak of war.

The Derry Royal Opera House is destroyed by fire.

1940

Joan Trimble's *Phantasy Trio* is awarded a Cobbett Prize.

1941

The BBC opens Broadcasting House on Ormeau Avenue in Belfast.

The Dublin Grand Opera Society presents its first four-opera seasons in Dublin (Gaiety Theatre) and Limerick (Savoy Theatre), opening with Verdi's *La traviata* with May Devitt as Violetta and James Johnston as Alfredo.

1942

Baritone William Parsons with the BBC Symphony Orchestra under Adrian Boult give the first British broadcast performance of Frederick May's *Songs from Prison*.

1943

The HMV label issues Myra Hess's recording of Belfast-born Howard Ferguson's 1940 Piano Sonata in F minor.

1944

Brian Boydell promotes a concert of his own music in Dublin's Shelbourne Hotel, performing as both an oboist and singer, and with his future wife, soprano Mary Jones, also on the roster of performers.

1945

The Amalgamated Catholic Choirs of the Diocese of Dublin gives its first concert—Handel's *Messiah* under Vincent O'Brien—at the Capitol Cinema. From 1946 the choir becomes known as Our Lady's Choral Society.

1946

Arthur Duff's 1940 *Irish* Suite for strings is published by Novello.

1947

Fachtna Ó hAnnracháin is appointed music director of Radio Éireann.

1948

The newly established Radio Éireann Symphony Orchestra uses the Phoenix Hall on Dame Court as its regular concert base. Brian Boydell conducts the premiere of his *In Memoriam Mahatma Gandhi* there on 20 July.

The Music Association of Ireland is founded.

1949

The twenty-two-member BBC Northern Ireland Light Orchestra gives its first broadcast on 11 July.

1950

Michael Bowles, a key figure in the creation of the Radio Éireann Symphony Orchestra, takes up the post of resident conductor of the National Orchestra of the New Zealand Broadcasting Service.

Havelock Nelson founds the Studio Opera Group to perform chamber opera in Belfast.

The City of Belfast Orchestra is established.

1951

Austrian-born British conductor and composer Karl Rankl wins one of the prizes offered by the Arts Council of Great Britain for the festival of Britain with *Deirdre of the Sorrows*, an opera based on Synge's play, but the work is not performed.

The Wexford Festival of Music and the Arts—today's Wexford Festival Opera—takes place for the first time.

The Arts Council/*An Chomhairle Ealaíon* is set up under the Arts Act 1951. Its annual 'state endowment' for 1952 is announced as £10,000.

Ceol Siansaċ

9aḋ Meaḋon-Foġṁair, 1945 ag 8 p.m.

Cuiṁne Ċéad Blian Tomáis Dáibis agus na n-Éireannaċ Óg

Capitol Theatre

No state for music

AXEL KLEIN

The cover of the concert programme for a Thomas Davis centenary concert at the Capitol Theatre in Dublin on 9 September 1945. Three Irish composers conducted their settings of poems by Davis for baritone, chorus and orchestra—Éamonn Ó Gallchobhair's *Lament for Owen Roe*, Aloys Fleischmann's *Clare's Dragoons* (with a second soloist, Joan Denise Moriarty on war pipes) and *Songs of Thomas Davis* by Réamonn Ó Frighil (Redmond Friel).

The new Irish state was not always sympathetic to composers in its early years. But composers began to embrace modernism, and the national broadcaster, Radio Éireann, aligned itself to European cultural norms by establishing two orchestras.

The early decades after independence are a curious time in the development of classical music in Ireland. They began in a period of what literary historianTerence Brown called 'stagnation and crisis' and ended in what composer Brian Boydell in his private diaries called the 'roaring forties', making Ireland unique in a European context where the 1920s were a period of enormous artistic creativity and the 1940s a period of the most terrible destruction and feeble new beginnings.

How could the Ireland of the 1920s be such a grim period in the arts, when the successful struggle for independence should have given hope and enthusiasm to the artistic community? One might have expected a huge upsurge in creativity, deriving from national pride and the end of centuries of oppressive foreign rule. Yet, independence came with losses, the loss of lives during Easter Rising and Civil War, and the loss of six Northern Irish counties which remained part of the United Kingdom. The general mood was not enthusiastic.

A satirical proposal from the *Dublin Opinion* of December 1932. Its street of round towers, lampooning pressure within the independent Irish state for distinctive expressions of Irishness—in this case, architecture—neatly reflects the arguments in the musical world as to how Irishness through traditional Irish music should or shouldn't be reflected in the music of Irish composers. The text of the original image has been reset to make it legible.

There are two ways to read the history of Irish art music—both in general, and in particular during this thirty-year period. One is by explaining the comparative scarcity of 'great' Irish composers (in an international context) by pointing to the manifold cultural, political, religious and financial circumstances that prevented a more fruitful development. The other is to identify the personalities, works and achievements that *did* occur *despite* the unfavourable circumstances, to concentrate on the music without much attention to its background. I have often tended towards the latter because, as a sympathetic outsider, I have frequently been struck by the high quality of Irish compositions and surprised at how little known their creators are in their own country. Therefore, by removing those compositions from their context and concentrating on their intrinsic quality, a point could be made for the simple enjoyment and satisfaction that can be derived from the music itself—and then from the point of view of an Irishman, draw a measure of pride from the fact that these are works of Irish creation. Why not? I have sometimes been tempted to write a history of Irish music describing the music and nothing else, using as background the history of European classical music and nothing else. No politics. No religion. A consciously naïve approach. It is a tempting idea.

As things stand, however, we must find an explanation as to why the majority of Irish people seem to think they have no history of classical music. It is easy, and obvious, to find reasons in the history of Ireland as a British colony. Independent Ireland undertook many steps to decolonise itself after independence by removing relicts of its colonial past (think of the destruction of country 'demesnes' and Georgian architecture) and emphasising Gaelic names and customs. It is less easy to explain why, in the field of literature and drama, the names of Protestants such as Shaw, Wilde and Yeats (not to speak of Swift and Goldsmith) were reclaimed for Ireland, while in music Protestant names are still viewed with suspicion—even more so in newly independent Ireland. Imagine Irish drama without Shaw, Yeats, Synge, O'Casey and Beckett, and you arrive at the situation we have in music.

A MODEST PROPOSAL

The President of our Society of Architects has called attention to the fact that there is at the present day no distinctively Irish type of architecture, that the buildings which are being run up all over the place are merely copies of buildings in England and elsewhere, and do not reflect the genius of our race.

Something must be done to remedy this, and as a commencement, we submit our artist's conception of a terrace of middle-class houses which can be constructed at low cost and which would strike a distinctively National note. Apart entirely from aesthetic considerations, there is something about the round tower model which renders it peculiarly suitable to modern conditions. It is almost impossible for bailiffs to enter, or for writs to be served without the co-operation of the tenant, and the circular walls present an unsolvable problem to cats.

Plan of Ground Floor (18 feet in diameter).

Plan of First Floor (16 feet in diameter).

Plan of Second Floor (10 feet in diameter).

NOTE: Plans for Labourers' Cottages built on a smaller scale, and with less ornamental roofs may be inspected at our offices.

In a memorandum of the Department of Finance to the Department of the President dated 21 May 1937, on the issue of setting up a national symphony orchestra and concert hall, the (counter-)argument reads:

> [...] public attendances at Symphony Concerts, and consequently the necessity for such public concerts, has become smaller and will continue to decline. Is it any part of the State's duty to resuscitate a Victorian form of educational recreation.

Note that the question mark is missing, because the question was intended as a rhetorical one. Note also that in early 1937 the provision of symphony concerts in Dublin, not to speak of the rest of Ireland, was very limited. For a bureaucrat who is not going to offer anything it is convenient to deny necessity.

••

The years around 1922 not only marked Irish independence but were also a watershed in Irish composition. A number of leading figures of the previous two decades were dying, the present active generation was considerably less prolific, and the new generation still attended primary school. An older generation of emigrants died, including Arthur O'Leary (1919), Charles Villiers Stanford (1924) and Charles Wood (1926) in England, and Victor Herbert (1924) in the United States. Leading figures in Ireland were dying, among them Joseph Seymour (1922), T. R. G. Jozé (1924), W. H. Grattan Flood (1928), as well as the immigrants Heinrich Bewerunge (1923) from Germany and Michele Esposito (1929), who retired to his native Italy shortly before his death.

Composers whose lifetimes extended considerably into independent Ireland were either less prolific or withdrew themselves. Hamilton Harty (1879–1941) more or less stopped composing after he became conductor of the Hallé Orchestra in Manchester in 1920. His Piano Concerto of 1922 was his last major composition for many years. Robert O'Dwyer (1862–1949), Carl G. Hardebeck (1869–1945), Vincent O'Brien (1871–1948), Harold R. White a.k.a. Dermot Macmurrough (1872–1943), Geoffrey Molyneux Palmer (1882–1957)—all of them had dropped their youthful ambitions of writing large-scale operas and cantatas in favour of small-scale piano music, songs and some church music.

Composer Joan Trimble (nearer camera) and her sister Valerie were a well-known two-piano team. Australian composer Arthur Benjamin's catchy *Jamaican Rumba*, his best-known work, was written for the duo. Joan also wrote two-piano works and arrangements, and the Trimbles were regulars on Stanford Robinson's BBC Radio programme *Tuesday Serenade*. This photograph shows them in the BBC's Belfast studios with senior announcer Maurice Shillington in February 1949.

Then we have Norman Hay (1889–1943), Ina Boyle (1889–1967) and John F. Larchet (1884–1967). Hay was a presence in Northern Ireland, but his music was hardly played in the Irish Free State. Boyle had withdrawn almost completely into her abode in the Wicklow Mountains, with extremely little exposure in Dublin. Larchet, with all his commitments as music director at the Abbey Theatre, professor at the Royal Irish Academy of Music and University College Dublin, seems to have had little time for original composition, confining himself to incidental music and folk song arrangements. And of Rhoda Coghill (1903–2000), what other work of note do we have apart from her remarkable rhapsody *Out of the Cradle Endlessly Rocking* (1923), not heard complete until 1990, and then only in a broadcast of a studio recording!

One had to wait for almost fifteen years until a new generation appeared, headed by Aloys Fleischmann (1910–92), Frederick May (1911–85) and Brian Boydell (1917–2000), including, perhaps, the less prolific Arthur Duff (1899–1956), Edgar Deale (1902–99) and Joan Trimble (1915–2000), but it took years until they established themselves. May's well-known String Quartet in C minor (1936) was not performed in Ireland until 1949. Trimble

lived mostly in England and was primarily known for her career as a pianist. What's more, in these deeply conservative and non-inclusive times, all had a difficult social standing: Fleischmann with his German name, Boydell with his English accent, May as a homosexual, Boyle and Trimble as women—Ireland certainly lacked a personality that the majority of Irish people could identify with, a competent composer with an international outlook, yet strongly rooted in the traditions of his/her country, and preferably a Roman Catholic. Such a composer did not appear before the second half of the century, with Seán Ó Riada (1931–71) and Seóirse Bodley (b. 1933).

And then there was another watershed from the mid 1930s, a division between modernists and traditionalists. None of the modernists, named above, was really aligned with the European avant-garde, yet they compare well with the modestly modern approaches in other countries. But we also find composers who consciously eschewed modern compositional trends in favour of a late Romantic, light Irish style based on traditional music, such as Éamonn Ó Gallchobhair (1906–82), Redmond Friel (1907–79), Michael Bowles (1909–98), T. C. Kelly (1917–85) and Daniel McNulty (1920–96), joined by immigrant composers such as Ernest de Regge (1901–58) and Staf Gebruers (1902–70)—all technically very competent but not presentable as the Irish representatives of twentieth-century European art music.

Any survey of the time would not be complete without some English composers with Irish sympathies or family connections. These would

From left: E. J. Moeran, Frederick May, Elizabeth Maconchy and Ina Boyle, photographed in Co. Cork in 1938 by Tilly Fleischmann. The four composers along with Aloys Fleischmann (as Muiris Ó Rónáin) featured in a landmark 'all-Irish' concert in Dublin's Gaiety Theatre in October that year, with Aloys Fleischmann conducting the Radio Éireann Orchestra.

Right: The first page of Frederick May's String Quartet of 1936, a work whose modern outlook has long been seen as a turning point in Irish music. The writer Colm Tóibín, who got to know May in the 1970s, has described it as 'one of the greatest contributions to Irish beauty ever made'.

Lento espressivo.

Eilís Níc Ḋiarmada Ruaiḋ

Lamento per Strumenti a Corda

Aloys Fleischmann
do ġléas

Bunaiṫe ar ḟonn le Cearḃallán

Le ceannaċ díreaċ ón Oifig Díolta Foilseaċán Rialtais,
An Stuara, Árd-Oifig an Poist, Baile Áṫa Cliaṫ,
nó trí aon díoltóir leabar ceoil

☛ Is leis an Aire Oideaċais gaċ ceart sa bḟoilseaċán seo agus ní híníocṫa aon táille as cead cantana nó seanma

3/- a luaċ

The cover of Aloys Fleischmann's *Eilís Nic Dhiarmada Ruaidh* (*Elizabeth MacDermott Roe*). It was published in the 1950s by An Gúm, the state company which was established by Ernest Blythe in 1925 and tasked with the publication of literature in Irish. An Gúm also undertook the publication of a number of musical scores for use in schools.

include Arnold Bax (1883–1953), E. J. Moeran (1894–1950) and Elizabeth Maconchy (1907–94), who were frequently performed in Ireland during this time. In Howard Ferguson (1908–99) and Denis ApIvor (1916–2004) we have two Irish-born composers in England who did not seem to find any attention in the new state. Nor did they seem to have cared, but their music would most definitively enrich Irish concert life today. Furthermore, with Granville Bantock (1868–1946), Rutland Boughton (1878–1960) and John Foulds (1880–1939), there were three English composers sharing an Ireland-oriented Celtic consciousness that could still definitely enrich the Irish repertoire, if it would only be known. And across the big pond, the most modern Irish compositions (and this is really at the high end of the avant-garde) were written by Henry Cowell (1897–1965). There is also some very attractive, albeit considerably more conservative, music of Irish interest written by Edward Joseph Collins (1886–1951) and the Paris resident Swan Hennessy (1866–1929).

• •

Name-dropping does help to demonstrate the range and breadth of repertoire for those who go looking for it. In early independent Ireland, however, people did not look for it, with 'people' meaning audiences and the politicians responsible for cultural strategies. In studying Irish music of the twentieth century, I have often found that we are not dealing with any scarcity of repertoire for interested musicians; it is the lack of knowledge, insight and goodwill, coupled sometimes with a lack of financial resources. At the beginning, certainly, there were more urgent necessities in the Irish Free State such as the creation of an Irish economy independent of the industrialised North, a literacy programme (as a precondition for better education) and a housing programme (in 1926, almost 30 per cent of the Dublin population lived in single rooms). Yet, there is clear evidence that classical music was not perceived as an area in which the state should invest. The *Saorstát Éireann Official Handbook*, a large and richly decorated volume published in 1932 that was intended to document the achievements of the first decade of the *Cumann na nGaedheal* government coalition in the Free State, manages to ignore art music completely. There are chapters on '[…] Cultural Agencies, Education,

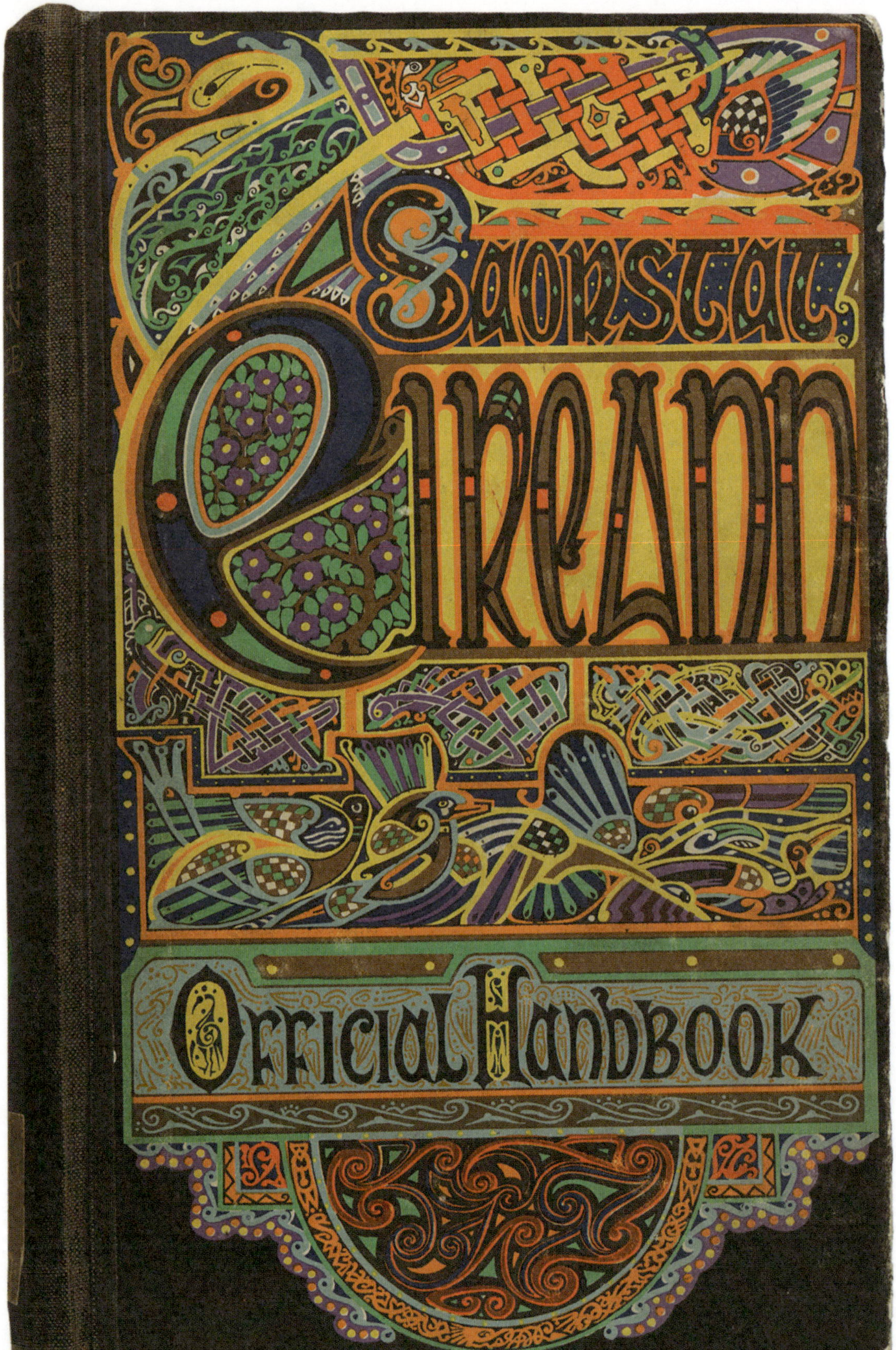
Saorstat Eireann
Official Handbook

The colourful cover of the *Saorstát Éireann Official Handbook* published by the Talbot Press in 1932. There were essays on 'The Ownership of Land', 'The Economic Problem of the Gaeltacht', 'Power Supply in the Irish Free State', 'Cultural Agencies' [The Royal Dublin Society, The Royal Irish Academy, The Irish Manuscripts Commission, The Royal Society of Antiquaries, The Feis Ceoil], and 'The Irish Language and the Linguistic Struggle'. But between 'Anglo-Irish Literature' and 'Learning in Ireland', there was only room for 'Irish Folk Music' and nothing on composers.

Libraries, Archaeology, Early Christian Art in Ireland, Modern Irish Art, Irish Architecture, the Irish Language and the Linguistic Struggle, Folklore, Irish Literature, Anglo-Irish Literature, and Irish Folk Music'. But not even the distinction between 'Irish Literature' and 'Anglo-Irish Literature' seems to have pointed the editors to the obvious parallel in music. Probably to the dismay of hundreds of musicians, for the politicians in charge at the time, an Irish art music did not exist—and this despite the fame of the annual Feis Ceoil and the presence of educational institutions like the Royal Irish Academy of Music and the Municipal School of Music at their doorstep.

It is true that before Radio Éireann enlarged the size of the station ensemble to chamber orchestra size in the late 1930s, there was little exposure to large-scale classical music in Dublin. Various attempts at establishing a regular musical life and infrastructure were undertaken without state support. Most were short-lived and confined to a small number of annual performances such as the Cork Philharmonic Orchestra (1926–37) and the Dublin Philharmonic Society (1927–36). In 1934 Fleischmann founded the University Orchestra, which would become the long-lived Cork Symphony Orchestra, in 1939. The chamber music recitals of the Royal Dublin Society were increasingly successful during the 1920s, but would a nationalist politician go to a 'royal' institution to have his mind changed about classical music? Would he not rather have experienced the same air of exclusiveness and 'high society' as in pre-independent Ireland, confirming his prejudices? In Ireland, music, the 'universal language', was more often than not perceived as a force of separation rather than unification. It seems that for many Irish politicians and large parts of the population, classical music was simply not an Irish art. There was traditional music for the Catholic majority, and classical music for the Protestant remnants of the 'Ascendancy'. This was never an accurate reflection of reality, but simplified categorisations are easier than finding an adequate response to the situation.

••

It is almost impossible to imagine the working conditions of composers in 1920s Ireland. Rhoda Coghill has told how her *Out of the Cradle Endlessly Rocking* (1923) was largely written on the grounds of Trinity College, with,

just around the corner, bullets and grenades flying, and the Four Courts going up in flames. There had been no orchestra in Dublin since the outbreak of World War I in 1914, so the composer had barely heard a proper orchestra. Yet, her score for tenor solo, chorus and orchestra to a poem by Walt Whitman became one of the most forward-looking works in twentieth-century Ireland.

Composers were still conceiving large scores, but most would give up over the course of the next few years. An operatic festival in the cultural by-programme of the Tailteann Games in August 1924 included the first performance of Harold R. White's comic opera *Shaun the Post* (1924), a new production of Geoffrey Molyneux Palmer's *Sruth na Maoile* (1923, a colourful Irish-language opera on the Celtic legend of the Children of Lir), and Stanford's *Shamus O'Brien* of 1896. As a member of the cast, the Irish singer (and music critic of the *Irish Independent)* Joseph O'Neill recounted his experience:

Middlesex-born Geoffrey Molyneux Palmer studied under Stanford in London and settled in Ireland in 1910. His entry in the fifth (1954) edition of *Grove's Dictionary of Music and Musicians* lists him as an English composer, but the latest edition of *The New Grove* describes him as Irish. His settings of poems by Joyce won the writer's praise. '30 or 40 composers at least have set my little poems to music,' wrote Joyce. 'The best is Molyneux Palmer. After him are Moeran and Bliss.'

> When the curtain rose for *Shaun the Post* ... I was so astonished at the fact that there seemed to be a greater number of people in the orchestra than in the audience, that I missed my opening lead! There was complete public apathy about this unique operatic festival.

Palmer, the composer who was so admired by James Joyce for the musical settings of his poems, originally had high ambitions in the operatic field. He had produced a nationalist comic opera in the form of a pantomime called *Finn Varra Maa* (subtitled *The Irish Santa Claus*) (1917), followed by *Sruth na Maoile (The Straits of Moyle)*. Between 1921 and 1924 he was working on a comic opera called *Grania Goes*, with a very funny plot combining the legend of the Fianna with contemporary politics. As a notice in *The Irish Times* of 28 January 1925 shows, he was by then still 'looking for a producer, and foresees a great success for this opera, as he introduces some charming Irish tunes, and also the words are witty and topical'. What he did not foresee was that at this time nobody wanted to take a financial risk in producing a new opera, witty and topical or not. Palmer even began work on a major *Cuchullain Cycle* consisting of three operas between 1925 and 1930. These never materialised because he became too ill (he suffered from multiple sclerosis), and although he handed them over for completion to Staf Gebruers, they unfortunately never saw the light of day. In the absence of an opera house in the capital, the more than limited financial resources in this period, and the predilection of Irish opera audiences towards Italian grand opera, the time was not yet ripe for contemporary opera.

Harold White, too, never wrote another opera after *Shaun the Post*. His last major work was the cantata *Hymn to St Patrick at Tara* (1930), joined at around the same time, interestingly, by a similar work by Staf Gebruers called *St Patrick's Advent in Ireland* (1932). But although these works were performed at St Fin Barre's Cathedral in Cork and at Mount Melleray Abbey respectively, there was no nationwide response to them. Both composers thereafter confined themselves to small-scale or religious music.

Ina Boyle never seems to have seriously expected that her large scores would be performed in her native country, yet she produced a seemingly endless stream of new and large works, now collecting dust in the Trinity

College Dublin manuscripts library. By all we know of her music, she really possessed great talent. Her symphony *Glencree (In the Wicklow Hills)* (1927) was performed only once in a 1945 live radio broadcast by Radio Éireann, before its inclusion in *Composing the Island* in 2016. Boyle, in fact, wrote two more symphonies, in 1930 and 1942, a violin concerto (1933), premiered in Belfast as late as 2010, and three ballet scores (between 1931 and 1939) that have never been staged. It is absolutely unbelievable how someone with her talent and with such ambitious compositions should be content with putting finished scores on the shelf and doing nothing about them. But then, this was Ireland in the 1930s, and hers was a modest and shy personality. In retrospect, she must be regarded as the most important Irish composer of the 1920s and 1930s. The process of her rediscovery, with a delay of some eighty years, can be watched 'live' at www.inaboyle.org.

Actually, the years around 1930 were a relatively good time for ballet in Ireland. Irish-born Ninette de Valois, later a leading light in international ballet, had set up the Abbey Theatre School of Ballet at the request of W. B. Yeats. Among the works she conceived during this time (1927–33) were commissions from contemporary Irish composers such as Harold White's *The Faun* (1928), Arthur Duff's *The Drinking-Horn* (1932) and John F. Larchet's *Bluebeard* (1933). Most Irish theatre historians have a blind eye for incidental music. How else should one explain that among the publications that celebrated the 100th anniversary of the Abbey Theatre in 2004, not one mentioned music, despite decades of incidental music that was specially commissioned and performed by an Abbey Theatre orchestra (well, a chamber ensemble), not to mention those really interesting ballet scores? If this music had not been an integral part of the performances, it would not have been commissioned. How can one ignore it?

The pivotal role of Radio Éireann (now RTÉ) cannot be underestimated in these formative years for twentieth-century Irish music. Its beginnings were all too modest and slow, however. It was founded in 1926, but before the erection of the Athlone transmission tower in 1933, it could not be received in all parts of Ireland. Originally it possessed a station ensemble of seven musicians. It took ten years before this was enlarged to twenty-four musicians in 1936 and to twenty-eight in 1937. For works with a larger instrumentation it was regularly supplemented with players from the Army No. 1 Band, then one of the very few regular contributors to Irish (public) musical life. At around the same time, there was a Dáil debate about the erection of a concert hall for Dublin which, like a similar public discussion during the 1960s, led to nothing.

It was not until 1938 that the Radio Éireann Orchestra gave its first (!) public concerts. These included works by contemporary Irish composers, such as the first performance of Frederick May's *Spring Nocturne* (1937) on 24 April 1938, conducted by Aloys Fleischmann—a work that already contained the germs of May's orchestral masterwork, the *Songs from Prison* (1941). Other works included Fleischmann's own *Three Songs for High Voice and Orchestra* (1937), billed as *Amhráin le Ceol-Fhuireann* by Muiris Ó Rónáin, and slightly older works such as Ina Boyle's *Colin Clout* (1921), E. J. Moeran's *Rhapsody No. 2* (1924) and Elizabeth Maconchy's Concertino for Piano and Chamber Orchestra (1928). These 1938–39 concerts were a statement. They raised awareness of a new generation of modern composers with an international outlook. And they were a wake-up call for the more conservative composers in the country.

Irish politics was far from able (or willing) to follow. The government had since 1932 been led by Éamon de Valera, by all accounts a rather distanced personality when it came to certain cultural affairs, and one who reacted with strong aversion to everything that seemed to him to belong to the Anglo-Irish part of Irish culture. He is reported as having said, for instance, that '[...] he couldn't see any reason for playing the work of foreign composers in Ireland, as we already had our own beautiful Irish music'. When the Athlone radio transmitter was inaugurated in 1933, he proclaimed what, in his opinion, constituted Irish culture. Turning to music he said:

> Ireland's music is of singular beauty. [...] It is characterised by perfection of form and variety of melodic content. [...] Equal in rhythmic variety are our dance tunes—spirited and energetic, in keeping with the temperament of our people.

And that is all. The existence and the needs of living composers completely passed him by.

••

From the mid 1930s, there ensued an extended debate about the direction Irish contemporary composition should take. It can be followed in series of articles and responses in journals such as the Jesuit periodical *Studies*, *Ireland To-day*, *The Bell*, *Envoy*, and the daily newspapers. One can only imagine what the situation may have been like in real life. This debate marked the watershed between composers of a modern, European outlook with proponents such as Aloys Fleischmann, Frederick May and Brian Boydell, and another side arguing for a renewal of Irish (art) music from sources in traditional Ireland, propagated by Éamonn Ó Gallchobhair and others. A twenty-five-year-old Fleischmann argues:

> Those who are loudest here in their advocacy of a musical revival seem to be mainly concerned with the welfare of folk-music, and widespread confusion reigns as to the distinction between these two spheres of folk-music and art-music, and their relative importance.

This seems to be underlined in an argument brought forward by James Devane:

> Will Irish music, for example, arise from an academic study of all the complexities and experiments of modern harmony and musical forms, or will it arise from Irish children saturated with our traditional melodies, from village glees, country church choirs, and peasant fiddlers?

It is an emotional argument, juxtaposing artificial 'complexities and experiments of modern harmony' and the rural joys of the Catholic countryside, the author's personal leanings being clear in the rather rhetorical question. Fleischmann, however, is convinced that:

> [...] we must remember that the task before us lies in the larger and more important field of art-music, lies in raising it from the half-baked shoddy thing it is, in establishing contact with contemporary movements, in making of music a medium for the expression of the life of present-day Ireland, by the use of present-day methods elsewhere.

Éamonn Ó Gallchobhair, pictured here with his wife, the flautist and painter Mollie Flynn, believed Irish composers should base their work on traditional Irish music. He fought a war of words over the issue in the 1930s, and was the most active stage composer of the Ireland of the mid twentieth century. His music is still in a period of protracted neglect.

Éamonn Ó Gallchobhair argues for a spiritual affinity of Irish people to their traditional music, but then comes with a strong anti-modernist point of view:

> Novelty in art is mere vulgarity, and a new thing is strong only when it has deep roots in the past. If a new music arise to express Ireland it can have as its root only the fundamental set of values that belongs to the Irish mind; and is conceivable that a great strength will lie in its atavism.

To which Fleischmann responds:

> Novelty in art, we are told, is mere vulgarity. Not only is novelty not vulgarity, it is one of the foremost essentials of art, for without novelty, that is, the reaching out after what is yet unexpressed, the utilisation of ever wider resources, art becomes a stagnant bye-pool, out of contact with the onrush of life, stale and formalised.

These views were irreconcilable. Looking back eighty years later, Fleischmann & Co. would be delighted to see that it was their view that prevailed in the end. Today, when music from the Ireland of the 1930s and 1940s is performed, it is the music of Fleischmann, May and Boydell, and there is a gradual rediscovery of Boyle. A composer yet to be appreciated and rediscovered from this particular quarter of the century is Norman Hay, whose orchestral and chamber works are as yet unperformed beyond Northern Ireland. Much of Larchet's output would merit more attention, too, for its elegant nostalgia, as well as the songs of Palmer and Coghill, and also perhaps some by Edgar Deale.

Above: Aloys Fleischmann conducting the Cork Symphony Orchestra in the Aula Maxima of University College Cork in 1938 with Charles Lynch (1906–84) at the piano. Lynch is the dedicatee of Arnold Bax's Fourth Piano Sonata (which he premiered), and he was also an important advocate of Irish music, of which he recorded an LP in 1971.

In comparison, with the exception of some violin and piano arrangements of traditional music, Ó Gallchobhair has not been performed in decades, which is as sad as it was predictable. He created huge scores: eleven ballets on folkloristic themes (1935–42), including the two-and-a-half hour production *Cathair Linn* (1942), five operettas in the Irish language (1944–63), including *Trágadh na Taoide* (1945), the performance of which was attended by, yes, Éamon de Valera. It is not that this repertoire—which includes works by Redmond Friel, T. C. Kelly and others—was not well written in terms of compositional craft and musical taste. And when it was performed, it attracted considerably larger audiences than the works of the 'modernists'. But, firstly, stylistically it comes fifty years too late—imagine what an impact *Trágadh na Taoide* would have had in 1895! And, secondly, in a canon of twentieth-century Irish compositions meriting international attention, they do not find a place.

••

Curiously enough, the years known in Ireland as 'The Emergency' and elsewhere as World War II, gradually liberated art music from its permanent state of emergency. New orchestras expanded the repertoire as well as the regional scope of music, with the Cork Symphony Orchestra, the Dublin Orchestral Players (1939) and the split of the Radio Éireann Orchestra into the Symphony and the Light (now Concert) Orchestra (1948).

The greatest boost came from an unexpected side: the Hollywood film industry. When the public symphony concerts by the radio orchestra were reintroduced in the early 1940s, the crowds could not be fully

Right: The June 1944 cover of the programme for an evening celebrating the tercentenary of the death of the Franciscan brother Mícheál Ó Cléirigh, chief of the compilers known as the Four Masters, who wrote *Annála Ríghachata Éireann* (the *Annals of the Kingdom of Ireland*). Aloys Fleischmann's *The Four Masters* Overture was written for the occasion.

Comóradh

i n-onóir

Mhichíl uí Chléirigh

bráthair bocht

Ceann na gCeithre Máistrí

Gaiety Theatre

Baile Átha Cliath

Dia Domhnaigh, 25ú lá de Mhí an Mheithimh, 1944.

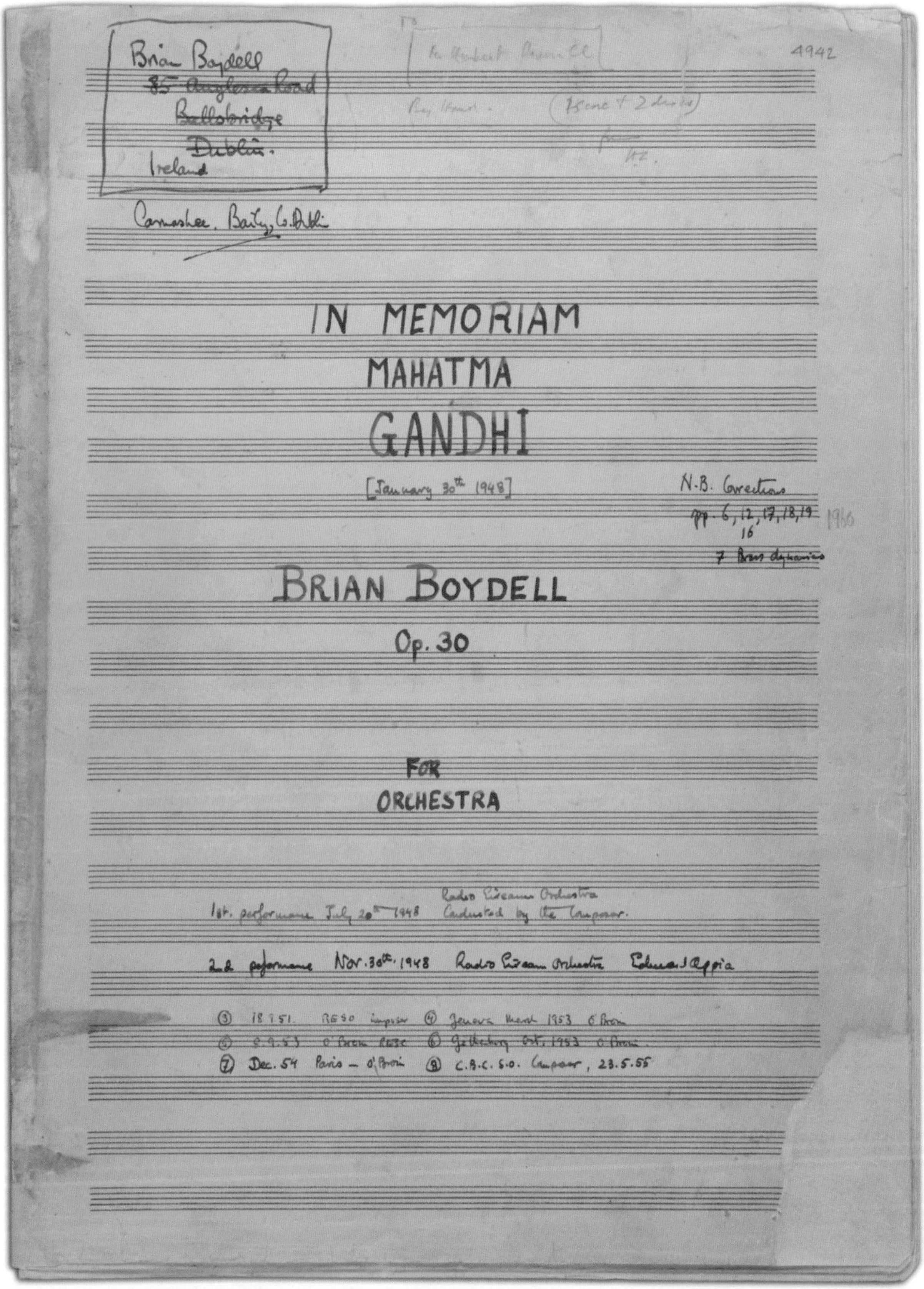
Brian Boydell
85 Anglesea Road
Ballsbridge
Dublin.
Ireland
4942
IN MEMORIAM
MAHATMA
GANDHI
[January 30th 1948]
N.B. Corrections
BRIAN BOYDELL
Op. 30
FOR
ORCHESTRA
1st. performance July 20th 1948
Radio Éireann Orchestra
Conducted by the Composer.
2nd performance Nov. 30th. 1948 Radio Éireann Orchestra Edmond Appia
7 Dec. 54 Paris – O'Broin
8 C.B.C. S.O. Composer, 23.5.55

Brian Boydell wrote two major orchestral works inspired by international issues, *In Memoriam Mahatma Gandhi* after the assassination of the Indian leader in 1948, and *Masai Mara* in 1988, named after the great game reserve in Kenya, and driven by concerns about 'ecology and people ruining the environment'. The title page of the *Mahatma Gandhi* manuscript notes performances in Europe and Canada and corrections made in 1960.

accommodated in the 800-seat Round Room of the Mansion House in Dublin. Within a few years, the attitude of the Irish musical public had changed from near-complete ignorance to well-meaning acceptance. And this included contemporary compositions. As Joseph O'Neill explains: 'Cinema-minded Dublin, through the agency of Hollywood, had become aware of the existence of the world's best orchestras, and symphonic music had lost its terrors.' Hollywood films had broadened the audiences, crossing the social and cultural barriers that existed between the followers of a traditional musical taste and 'serious' art music. American film orchestras made Irish audiences want to experience their own orchestra.

Numerous works of the international repertoire now found their way to Irish audiences. They heard four of the seven symphonies of Sibelius, works by Falla, Stravinsky and many more—largely through the efforts of Irish conductor Michael Bowles. In 1943, Radio Éireann began to commission new works by Irish composers, and while the criteria invited criticism, no doubt many composers benefited from the scheme. There was no distinction between folk song arrangements and original compositions, and the royalties were based on the length of compositions—a generous usage of repeat marks could multiply the income. Works performed included Fleischmann's overture *The Four Masters* and the cantata *Clare's Dragoons* (both of 1944), Brian Boydell's *Magh Sleacht*, Op. 29 (1947) and *In Memoriam Mahatma Gandhi*, Op. 30 (1948), Walter Beckett's *Suite for Orchestra* (1945), and also first performances of Frederick May's *Songs from Prison* (1941) and E. J. Moeran's concertos for violin (1942) and cello (1945).

For Brian Boydell, these years truly became the 'roaring forties'. In the light of May's increasing deafness (and consequent reduction in output) and Fleischmann's manifold commitments in Cork—to which one might add Boyle's and Trimble's geographical remoteness, Palmer's and Coghill's artistic withdrawals, and Beckett's and Deale's modest outputs—Boydell soon became the most significant of the modernist Irish composers in the 1940s. In January 1944, he clarified that the new 'craze' for orchestral music had not yet extended to other forms of contemporary music such as chamber music. His 'one-man show' (in the words of *Irish Times* music critic Charles Acton) was interpreted as an act of protest when he had pieces performed at the

Shelbourne Hotel like his Three Songs for Soprano and String Quartet, Op. 10 (1939), the Quintet for Oboe and String Quartet, Op. 11 (1940), the String Trio, Op. 21 (1943), and his latest, The Feather of Death, Op. 22 (1944) for baritone and flute quartet, with himself singing. This event certainly proved that some exciting chamber music was being created in Ireland. A lasting place in the repertoire was granted to Frederick May's 1936 string quartet that finally received its first Irish performance in 1949, and also to Boydell's own String Quartet No. 1, Op. 31 (1949), which was most certainly ignited by May's success. Boydell's orchestral score *In Memoriam Mahatma Gandhi* has also found its way into the canon of significant Irish works of this period, albeit not so much for its modernity as for its international perspective, its authentic expression of sympathy and its artistic sincerity.

Yet, the existence of composer's commissions by a state-run radio station, and a Department of Education-funded summer school for composers and conductors that took place annually between 1946 and 1949, did not amount to a government policy for the promotion of music, or the arts generally. As an act of self-help, composers founded the Music Association of Ireland (MAI), which undertook very valuable work in creating audiences and providing forums for composers. Repeatedly, however, composers pointed to England, where the foundation of the Council for the Encouragement of Music and the Arts (CEMA) in 1940—the predecessor of the Arts Council—had become an effective means to improve the living and working conditions of composers and musicians. It still took a few years until Ireland finally had an Arts Council. The foundation in 1947 of the new Advisory Committee on Cultural Relations meant that selected works by Boydell, Fleischmann and May were edited and published for potential diffusion abroad. In an international comparison, this support was still infinitesimally small, but at least the foundations were laid.

The long view

MICHAEL MURPHY

John Kinsella (b. 1932) and Seóirse Bodley (b. 1933) were both born in Dublin just a decade after *Saorstát Éireann*, the Irish Free State, was established in 1922. The meagre condition of musical life in Dublin was laid bare in John F. Larchet's essay 'A plea for music', which was written that same year. While other central European countries entered the twentieth century with a recognisable national tradition of composition, Ireland had practically nothing by comparison.

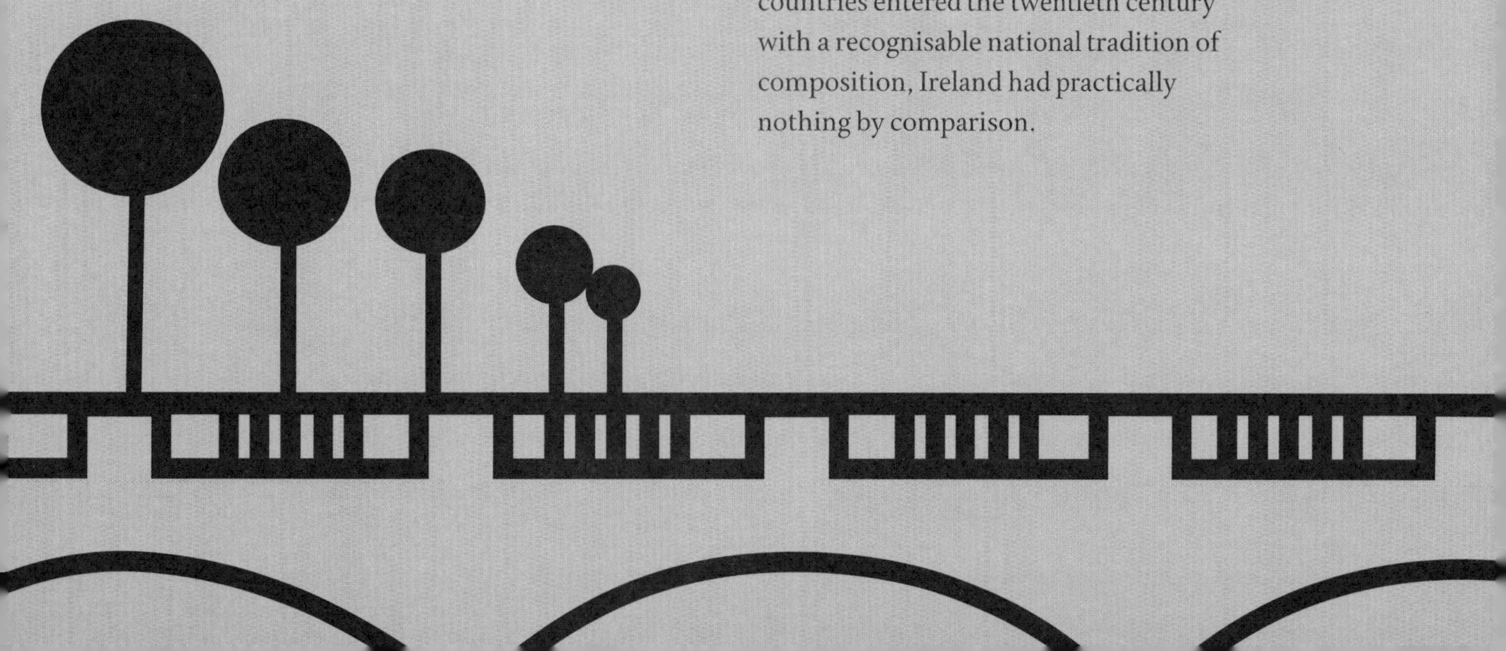

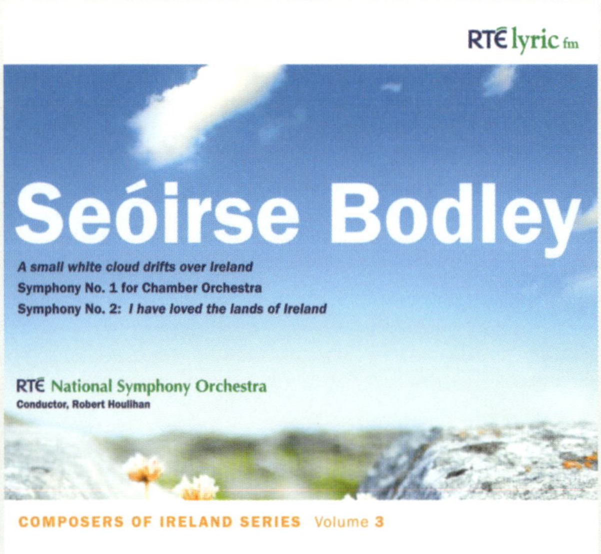

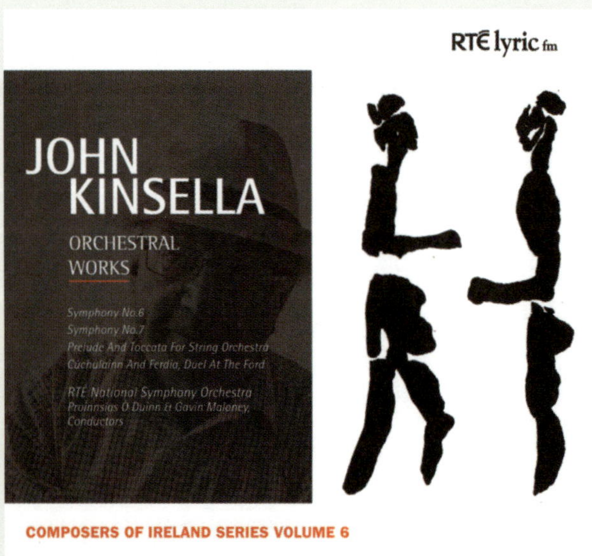

By the time that Kinsella and Bodley had started to regard composing as a personally fulfilling activity in their teenage years in the 1940s, the revival of Irish musical composition which had been sponsored by the Feis Ceoil composition competitions had long lost its momentum. Both composers made it clear that the advent of public radio broadcasting by 2RN in 1926 marked a milestone in public access to music in Ireland. The standard European concert repertoire, which both of them encountered in their early years on Radio Éireann and the BBC Home Service, laid the basis for their interest in composition. This was complemented by attending orchestral concerts in Dublin's Capitol Theatre, Phoenix Hall and, in the 1960s, the St Francis Xavier Hall. Notwithstanding the relatively poor state of music in Ireland, Dublin presented opportunities that were largely unavailable elsewhere in the country.

I met with the two composers separately and asked each of them if they believed that composers in Ireland somehow shared a

John Kinsella and Seóirse Bodley are both composers who have featured on CDs issued in the RTÉ lyric fm label's *Composers of Ireland* series, Bodley in 2009 and Kinsella in 2011.

common fate. Kinsella remarked wryly that he could not remember the last time he had seen an Irish composer. Similarly, Bodley gave the impression that the composer's lot in Ireland is a solitary one. It was clear that the history of musical life in Ireland was largely responsible for this condition of artistic isolation.

A recurring motif in my conversation with Kinsella was the importance he attached to role models. Elgar, Vaughan Williams and Stravinsky are composers whose works were of immense significance for him, and he said he admired Shostakovich's First Cello Concerto (1959) for the way it 'opened up melody again'. But his greatest admiration was reserved for Beethoven and Sibelius, in relation to whom he stated 'I love the sense of forward movement'. In general he contrasted 'goal-oriented' music with what he called 'static music', by which he meant any type of music 'which has no discernible pulse and consequently seems to be a succession of static statements'.

The La Scala Theatre and Opera House opposite the GPO on Dublin's Prince's Street North opened in 1920. It was renamed the Capitol Cinema in 1927 and sometimes called the Capitol Theatre. The success of the Radio Éireann Orchestra's symphony concerts in the Round Room of the Mansion House caused the concerts to be moved to the Capitol for its greater capacity in the 1940s. In this 1967 photograph the original La Scala lettering can be seen behind the neon tubes spelling out the Capitol name. The cinema closed in 1972 and was demolished to make way for what is now a branch of Penneys.

Not only does he delight in the linear structures of their music, but for him Beethoven and Sibelius both symbolise freedom and liberation. This is not just some abstract idea but was inextricably connected with his attempt to find an alternative mode of expression to the hegemony of serialism in post-war composition. In a nutshell, it was Beethoven and Sibelius rather than Boulez and Stockhausen who paved the way for Kinsella.

While he was excited by the earlier music of the avant-garde serialists, and deeply impressed by a visceral performance of Stockhausen's *Klavierstücke I-XI*—what was then the composer's complete piano music—by the German pianist Aloys Kontarsky in Dublin's Hibernian Hotel in 1968, he subsequently felt 'let down' by the 'dictatorial stance [Stockhausen and Boulez] both subsequently adopted'.

The advent of the Dublin Festival of 20th Century Music which ran from 1969 to 1986 provided an unprecedented stimulus for Irish composers interested in modernism. Kinsella, who had joined RTÉ as a senior assistant in the music department in 1968, was in the thick of it. 'Nobody questioned serialism,' he recalled, 'it was the thing to do'. However, when he expressed admiration for Beethoven's 'singleness of mind and his way of battering through problems', I could not help thinking that his subsequent unhappiness with the avant-garde was a problem that demanded just that type of 'heroic' response.

The avoidance of opera by Irish composers was another theme we explored. We reflected on the dearth of opera since the time of the Gaelic Revival, a cultural project which engendered a number of stage works by William Harvey Péllisier, Thomas O'Brien Butler, Robert O'Dwyer, Geoffrey Molyneux Palmer, Harold R. White and Michele Esposito. When Kinsella admitted that opera 'wasn't his thing' I could only reply that it didn't seem to be anybody's thing until the mid-century stage works of Gerard Victory, Joan Trimble and Éamonn Ó Gallchobhair. The succeeding decades saw an expansion of the repertoire by Victory, James

Wilson, A. J. Potter, Gerald Barry and others.

Bodley revealed that he had considered composing an opera to a libretto based on James Joyce's *Exiles*, but that the scant performance opportunities dissuaded him. No less dissuasive was his awareness of the likelihood that a modernist opera would be greeted with a less than positive response from an Irish audience. He recalled a reaction at the premiere of his *Configurations* for orchestra in the Gaiety Theatre in 1967, when one attendee remarked at its conclusion, 'so well they might pull down the curtain.'

The problems attending the composition of opera in Ireland were many indeed. He contrasted Ireland with Germany which, like most European countries, had an opera house tradition. In particular he recalled his experience of modern opera in Darmstadt where he studied in the mid 1960s. In the aftermath of World War II Darmstadt established a temporary theatre in the Orangeriehaus so as to maintain its operatic tradition. He recalled attending productions of Hermann Reutter's operas which, along with more modernist works, were well attended and well received. This undoubtedly planted the seed for his own unrealised stage work.

While discussing his extensive output the question of his stylistic diversity was a prominent one. Bodley, however, did not attach as much emphasis to stylistic change as perhaps might be expected. Indeed he was somewhat amused by the emphasis which critics and musicologists placed on the range of styles he was interested in exploring. 'I suppose my interests changed a bit,' he said. 'At different times I wanted to try different things and that was the way most things came about.'

Casual as this may seem, it is symptomatic of a self-actualised artist whose sense of purpose has always been unshakeable. Ireland might, after all, have some advantages for a mid-twentieth-century composer wanting to follow his own path without having to negotiate the weight of received traditions. Bodley's music reached into many aspects of Irish life, and he extended the expressive range of many genres from the congregational vocalism of the *Mass of Peace* (1976) to the high virtuosity of the extended piano work *News from Donabate* (1999).

Whether reflecting on his vocal and instrumental arrangements of Irish traditional tunes or the abstract structures of serialism, it became apparent that style was sometimes a means to an end, and other times an end in itself. In relation to his *Ceol*: Symphony No. 3 (1980), commissioned for the opening of the National Concert Hall in 1981, he remarked that he felt the need to choose a musical language that would accommodate and integrate the diversity of the performers—incorporating professionals, amateurs and children—while also enabling audience participation.

By contrast, stylistic issues were at the heart of *The Narrow Road to the Deep North* (1972), for two pianos, commissioned by the Belfast Festival at Queen's, a work to which Bodley attached much significance. In a number of his works he wished 'to put together two things that don't mix,' which in this case was a traditional Irish *sean-nós* type melody of his own composition set against 'a dissonant and jarring background'. When it was first performed in the Whitla Hall in Queen's University, 'half the audience went one way,' he recalled, 'and half went the other'. This is a rather telling remark as it raises a number of issues relevant not only to the issue of style.

While he agreed that there were political connotations to the work, not least because of its title, the location of its premiere and its composition at a time when the 'Troubles' in Northern Ireland were already entrenched, he admitted that he 'didn't intend them to be primary'. The allusion to *sean-nós* melody invokes the notion of voice and its narrative potential, which is ripe for political interpretation in this context. But perhaps the greatest political element to this work is not so much the contrasting nature of the material but the fact that there is no synthesis between the melody and the texture.

As a narrative device, unresolved conflict is resonant on many levels, in this case invoking ideas about the ancient and the modern, or the difference between that which is Irish and European, or between folk and art cultures. Each of these dichotomies is central to the history of music in Ireland, and Bodley himself is central to that history, not only as a composer but also as a thinker about that history. Around the same time as he composed this work he was invited to write an introduction to the Irish University Press's republication of the third (1913) edition of W. H. Grattan Flood's *A History of Irish Music.* In his introductory article, Bodley demonstrated an awareness of the historiographical problems that attend the musicological discourse of Ireland's musical past.

That book was published in 1970, a year prior to his chairmanship of the newly founded Folk Music Society of Ireland, which sought to come to terms with the burgeoning interest in Ireland's traditional music. When he composed *The Narrow Road to the Deep North* he was keenly aware of the breadth of its address and its depth of expression. I suggested to him that perhaps the most challenging aspect of the work was that it flew in the face of a central principle of art music (and folk music no less), namely the precept of 'unity'. Bodley replied that the avoidance of unity is yet another option for the composer if done in 'full awareness'. Here, as elsewhere, it was clear that Bodley's compositional intelligence is paralleled by an equally multivarious intellect.

I was curious to know how both Bodley and Kinsella regarded the various institutions that sponsored, promoted and rewarded artistic creativity in Ireland. Certain organisations were valued for their practicality above all else. The Contemporary Music Centre was rated highly by both composers, not only for its archival resources and production of scores and CDs but also for its advocacy of Irish composition. Both composers also converged on the notion that Radio Éireann (forerunner of RTÉ) was the single most important institution for stimulating composition in Ireland. This was not surprising as both composers were fortunate enough to

have enjoyed the patronage of the national broadcaster on many occasions.

Kinsella expressed very strong views on the role which RTÉ should play in sponsoring Irish composers, namely that the broadcaster should keep before the public a 'canon' of works by Irish composers. He recalled the time when Victory and he programmed weekly, hour-long orchestral radio broadcasts on Friday nights, regularly featuring works by Irish composers. He received correspondence from listeners in Britain and elsewhere, testimony to the importance of the national broadcaster in promoting Irish composition abroad and not just within the broader context of musical life in Ireland.

Kinsella's abiding concern with canonic composers was evident again when he related the provenance of his orchestral work

John Kinsella (above left) and Seóirse Bodley (opposite) were born just a year apart, in 1932 and 1933, respectively, but their careers took very different trajectories. Kinsella had very little formal training and developed late. Bodley developed early and was trained thoroughly in the heart of Europe, in Germany. Both composers engaged with the techniques of the European avant-garde and moved on to more personal stylistic accommodations in later life.

Cúchulainn and Ferdia: Duel at the Ford, which was commissioned by RTÉ for the sixtieth Anniversary of the National Symphony Orchestra in 2008. The programme of that gala anniversary concert included Beethoven's Piano Concerto No. 4 along with excerpts from Richard Strauss's *Salome,* two works which Kinsella regarded as having 'heroic' themes, namely the supposed Orphic programme in the central movement of the concerto and the tragedy of John the Baptist in the opera. Kinsella therefore felt it appropriate to compose a 'heroic' piece on an Irish theme which would exploit the larger than usual orchestra at his disposal on that occasion. If he had previously rejected a major part of the European tradition (serialism) as it was 'getting him nowhere', this was another opportunity to express his sense of belonging to that tradition while addressing an Irish audience.

Kinsella has recently completed his latest work, Symphony No. 11, for

which he expressed hopes of a Finnish premiere. It too is embedded in a specific aspect of the European symphonic tradition, namely the special aura that surrounds a composer's 'lost' work. In this case the work that inspired Kinsella was Sibelius's 'lost' Eighth Symphony. He told me about touching the fireplace where Sibelius allegedly destroyed sketches of that symphony, and that three fragments of sketches believed to be of that work were edited by Timo Virtanen and subsequently recorded by the Helsinki Philharmonic Orchestra. It was these sketches which Kinsella found so inspirational for his Eleventh Symphony. Given the sensitivities surrounding copyright, he was adamant that he wasn't 'completing' Sibelius's lost symphony in the manner in which Barry Cooper had 'composed' Beethoven's unfinished Symphony

John Kinsella in rehearsal with the RTÉ Vanbrugh String Quartet (from left, Christopher Marwood, Keith Pascoe, Simon Aspell, Gregory Ellis) in the library of Bantry House during the 2009 West Cork Chamber Music Festival.

No.10 from the remaining sketches. Moreover, it seemed to me that Kinsella's new Symphony No. 11 involved a sense of spiritual completeness by deepening his own affinity with Sibelius' music. Sadly, Bodley's current compositional project also involved lost music, in this case because of the impossibility of retrieving the digital score of a song cycle which he was composing on his computer. The inspiration for these songs came about when Bodley and his wife, Dr Lorraine Byrne Bodley, happened to meet the poet Brendan Kennelly in Dublin's Dawson Street. Shortly after they repaired to a coffee shop, Kennelly disappeared only to return promptly with a copy of his *Reservoir Voices*. Bodley immediately responded to Kennelly's notion of 'envoicing' otherness (i.e. ordinary objects outside of himself), and promptly started to set certain of the poems. While the vagaries of computer technology led to the total loss of his working score, Bodley expressed his resolve to compose his cycle anew having completed three songs already.

Notwithstanding the high status which both composers enjoy, they both spoke with disarming modesty. As Kinsella noted, while composing has 'been a lifetime's work, I still regard myself as a novice after all this time. I'm always finding new ways of doing things, and better ways of doing things.' Bodley intimated that he was still discovering what it meant to be a composer. Neither gave the impression that his work was done.

1952–1969

1952

The Cirulli Quartet give the first performance of Brian Boydell's String Quartet which won the Radio Éireann Chamber Music Prize in 1949.

1953

Dresden-born Hans Waldemar Rosen becomes conductor of a new ten-member chamber choir, the Radio Éireann Singers.

Milan Horvat becomes the first principal conductor of the Radio Éireann Symphony Orchestra (RÉSO), and the orchestra starts its Sunday evening concerts at the Gaiety Theatre in Dublin. Éimear Ó Broin becomes the orchestra's assistant conductor.

1954

The first International Choral Festival is held in Cork.

1955

Brian Boydell conducts the Canadian Broadcasting Corporation Symphony Orchestra in a programme of Irish music on 23 May.

1956

The American Decca label issues two LPs of music by Irish composers—Brian Boydell, Frederick May, Seóirse Bodley, A. J. Potter, T. C. Kelly, John F. Larchet and Arthur Duff—in performances by the Radio Éireann Symphony Orchestra under Milan Horvat.

Dublin violinist Hugh Maguire is appointed leader of the London Symphony Orchestra.

1957

Éimear Ó Broin, assistant conductor of the RÉSO, shares the London Philharmonic Orchestra's Young Conductor's Prize with Colin Davis.

Carlo Franci conducts the RÉSO in the first performance of Seán Ó Riada's *Hercules Dux Ferrariae*.

Joan Trimble's *Blind Raftery*, one of the first television operas, is broadcast by the BBC.

1958

The first complete Irish performance of Bach's *St Matthew Passion* is given by the St James's Gate Musical Society at the St Francis Xavier Hall in Upper Sherrard Street.

1959

George Morrison's documentary film about the Easter Rising of 1916, *Mise*

Éire (*I am Ireland*), with music by Seán Ó Riada, is screened at the Cork Film Festival. It is the first feature-length film in the Irish language.

The new Cork-based Radio Éireann String Quartet (Roger Raphael, Brendan O'Reilly, Peter Sermon, Gwenda Milbourn), formerly the Raphael Quartet, gives its first concert in August.

1960

Two Irishmen, John Beckett and Michael Morrow, found the influential Musica Reservata early music group in London

1961

Tibor Paul is appointed principal conductor of the RÉSO and also becomes music director of Radio Éireann a year later.

Telefís Éireann begins transmission at 7.00 p.m. on 31 December.

1962

The RÉSO gives its last concert at the Phoenix Hall, Dame Court, and establishes the St Francis Xavier Hall on Upper Sherrard Street as its Dublin concert base.

The Arts Council of Northern Ireland is established as a successor to the Council for the Encouragement of Music and the Arts.

The Cork International Choral Festival holds its first Seminar on Contemporary Choral Music.

1963

Sheila and Gerald Goldberg establish a series of lunchtime recitals at the Crawford Gallery in Cork.

Paddy Moloney founds the traditional Irish music ensemble The Chieftains.

The Radio Éireann Festival of Music 1963 includes a concert at Dublin's Adelphi Cinema with Igor Stravinsky conducting his own *Chorale variations on Bach's Vom Himmel hoch* and *Symphony of Psalms*. The festival also includes the Irish premiere of *The Rite of Spring*.

1964

Festival '64—which later becomes the Belfast Festival at Queen's—is held for the first time, with Michael Emmerson as director.

Irish businessman Ronan O'Rahilly creates the pirate radio station Radio Caroline, which broadcasts pop music from a ship anchored in international waters off the coast of Essex in England.

1965

Irish National Opera, specialising in the performance of piano-accompanied opera in English, gives its first production, of Mozart's *Marriage of Figaro*, in Athlone.

The German label Harmonia Mundi Schallplattengesellschaft issues a record of *Irische Volkslieder* (*Irish folk songs*), arrangements by T. C, Kelly, Carl Hardebeck, Seán Ó Riada, John F. Larchet, Redmond Friel, Éamonn Ó Gallchobhair, Fachtna Ó hAnnracháin, Gerard Victory, Seóirse Bodley, Edgar Deale and Charles Villiers Stanford sung by Der Kammerchor von Radio Dublin (Irland) (the Radio Éireann Singers) under their conductor, Hans Waldemar Rosen.

1966

The Ulster Orchestra is founded in Belfast.

The RTÉSO gives its first concert outside Ireland at the Royal Festival Hall in London under its conductor Tibor Paul. No work by an Irish composer is performed.

1967

The first ROSC Exhibition of International art is held in Dublin.

1968

Composer Gerard Victory is appointed director of music at RTÉ.

1969

The RTÉ Singers and their conductor Hans Waldemar Rosen undertake a European tour of Germany, Switzerland and the Netherlands, with repertoire that includes Brian Boydell's *Madrigals* and Gerard Victory's *Kriegslieder*.

The Dublin Festival of 20th Century Music is held for the first time.

James Wilson's *Twelfth Night* is presented as a fringe event at Wexford Festival Opera by Irish National Opera.

Getting into gear

KEVIN O'CONNELL

To readers beyond the island of Ireland, the dates that bookend this chapter may seem somewhat arbitrary: no world wars began or ended, no major treaties were signed. But to Irish eyes they have their own significance. The key facts are the signing into law of the Arts Act in 1951 which established *An Chomhairle Ealaíon* (the Arts Council) and the first Dublin Festival of 20th Century Music in 1969. The period defined by these dates permits leakage at both ends and I have made some attempt to contain it, but not, I hope, at the expense of musical sense and continuity.

The overworked word 'transitional' applies to the period as it does to any: the 1950s left behind one era of Irish culture and the 1970s opened another. My task is to explain as best I can the nature of the transition. This task is complicated by a number of considerations. Several of the main personalities were musically formed in the pre-war years. And some are still happily productive today. How, for example, to discuss John Kinsella (b. 1932), a composer of the generation of several others treated here? 'By talking about his symphonies,' an Irish listener will correctly and impatiently answer. But Kinsella's prolific symphonism (he has so far written eleven) is a late development in his career; his First was completed in 1984 when he was fifty-two. Thus even a generous treatment here is bound to offer at best a partial view of his development. The same might be said of Seóirse Bodley's (b. 1933) career as a symphonist. Readers are requested to keep in mind this chronological untidiness.

A list of the composers who helped define the period must include Seóirse Bodley, Ina Boyle (1889–1967), Brian Boydell (1917–2000), Aloys Fleischmann (1910–92), John Kinsella, Séan Ó Riada (1931–71), A. J. Potter (1918–80), Joan Trimble (1915–2000), Gerard Victory (1921–95) and James Wilson (1922–2005). These composers formed no school and promulgated no unified theory for the direction of Irish music. Like most composers, they were too busy with their own work to bother much with such matters. But areas of common interest and occasional conflict nonetheless emerged.

The situation for composers in the 1950s remained professionally precarious but was greatly improving. Principal among the improvements was the establishment of the Radio Éireann Symphony Orchestra in 1948 (now the RTÉ National Symphony Orchestra). By the early 1950s Dublin was at last behaving like a musical capital city, and audiences could hear the classical repertoire played regularly and professionally. Northern Ireland had been rather better served. The BBC's Wireless Symphony Orchestra, later renamed the BBC Northern Ireland Orchestra, had begun providing concerts in the 1920s. It was disbanded in 1939 and a new BBC Northern Ireland Light Orchestra started work in 1949. The Ulster Orchestra was founded in 1966, and the two orchestras were merged in 1981. The resulting loss of orchestral positions was partly balanced by the possibility of performing larger works.

The Music Association of Ireland (MAI) was founded in 1948 with the purpose of heightening public awareness of classical and especially Irish music. Boydell, Frederick May (1911–85) and Fleischmann were involved from the beginning, and in 1953 a separate MAI composers' group was set up with Boydell as chairman and A. J. Potter as chief organiser. The concerts of new Irish work promoted by the group formed the seed of the Dublin

Opposite: The Gathering Ireland 2013 was a high-profile tourism-led project aimed at drawing the Irish diaspora back to the home country. It had a forefunner in 1953, in a three-week Easter festival, *An Tóstal*, aimed at Irish exiles and friends of Ireland from everywhere—the word means pageant, muster, array or display. For 1954 *An Tóstal* established a number of new festivals, including a choral festival in Cork, now the Cork International Choral Festival. Still under the umbrella of *An Tóstal*, the Cork Film Festival followed in 1956, when the city's celebrations included a concert by the Vienna Philharmonic Orchestra under André Cluytens. The orchestra also played in Limerick, but could not perform in Dublin due to the lack of an adequate hall.

Festival of 20th Century Music and international guests were invited to give lectures. In September 1956 Henry Cowell talked at the Royal Irish Academy of Music about modern American music. Less successful was the MAI's campaign for a concert hall for Dublin, a goal that it would take another thirty years to achieve.

The period under review neatly encompasses the first heady phase of the traditional music revival that has been so crucial for Irish music generally. The revival is too big a subject to discuss in any detail here, but it is worth recording that its success was not, in the increasingly urbanised Ireland in the 1950s, a foregone conclusion. Its inception is often dated to the publication of Donal O'Sullivan's great work, *Carolan, The Life and Times of an Irish Harper*, in 1958. In fact this publication was little noticed at the time.

The attitude of Irish composers to wider musical influences can perhaps be classified into three broad areas. Frederick May, Brian Boydell, Ina Boyle, Joan Trimble, James Wilson and A. J. Potter were born at the time of or before Irish independence (1922); they were all trained in England (Boyle commuting from Wicklow to study with Vaughan Williams in London) and felt no pressing sense of separation from the neighbouring culture, as witness the importance of Vaughan Williams for Boydell, Boyle, May and Potter, of Bax for Trimble and of Britten for Wilson.

A certain amount of religious and social conditioning was doubtless part of this; Wilson was English by birth and Trimble and Potter were Northern Irish. If early formation is vital to an artist's identity, Elizabeth Maconchy (1907–94) is as Irish as any composer discussed in this chapter. But family circumstances dictated that she would contribute to England's rather than Ireland's musical culture. The same might be said of Belfast-born Howard Ferguson (1908–99), though efforts are being made in Northern Ireland to reclaim this gifted composer. The reverse path could also be taken: James Wilson was English-born but settled permanently in Ireland in 1948.

A second thread is represented by Seóirse Bodley (b. 1933), whose predilections, reflecting a different but equally strong Irish bias, were more European than British. Bodley in the early 1960s visited the Darmstadt Summer School, the hothouse of avant-gardism of the period, and the results can be heard in *Configurations* (1967), a startling piece of 1960s Irish modernism. This piece is a marker in Irish music in the same way that Liberty Hall (1963) or Busáras, the Dublin Central Bus Station (1953), are markers in Irish architecture. In its uncompromising angularity and experimentation with performer choice in the manner of execution, *Configurations* declared that modernism-without-apology had arrived in Ireland. The music of Gerard Victory also reflected a strong Darmstadt influence. Both composers would adapt the lessons learned there to their own very personal ends.

The third strand, the traditional music one, found its main representative in the dynamic figure of Séan Ó Riada.

Busáras, Dublin's central bus station, designed by Michael Scott and built between 1947 and 1953, was the first monument of modern architecture built in post-war Dublin.

Looming over this generation was the shade of Frederick May (1911–85). There was once an ill-advised attempt to draft May into the European mainstream on the flimsy enough evidence of an abortive attempt to study with Berg in Vienna. His one major work of the post-war era, the tone poem *Sunlight and Shadow* (1955), is full of deftly beautiful touches in harmony and orchestration, but the debt to Vaughan Williams is sometimes overwhelming, Vaughan Williams representing the dangerous phenomenon of a great composer who is a bad model. Brian Boydell, a friend of May and admirer of Vaughan Williams, showed a keener awareness of the dangers and kept an independent voice, nowhere more than in his three string quartets. To dramatise the personal tragedy of May's later life (deafness, alcoholism) into the ostensible tragedy of Irish music, as some have been tempted to do, is to make too much of the matter. May's demons were personal enough to render such generalisations suspect, and several of his contemporaries like Boydell, Wilson and Trimble pursued long, productive careers.

Seán Ó Riada (1931–71) was the only composer of the era to attain the status of a household name. By a peculiarly Irish circumstance though, he is representative as much in his contradictions as in his achievements. He started with an interest in the avant-garde and European modernity, spending some time in Paris. With the traditional music revival he took on a new identity and thereafter rode both horses, the traditional and the 'classical'. The problem about this stance, both from his own point of view and that of his listenership, was that the horses were riding in different directions. His classical audience had some awareness of the traditional Ó Riada; his traditional audience for the most part cared little for the classical composer. Here Ó Riada ran up against a wall: in an atmosphere where 'classical' music, tainted with the legacy of west-Britonism, held a questionable place, his very success was suspect, for the better you are at doing something of which people are suspicious, the more suspicious they become.

His most ambitious concert piece is *Nomos* No. 2, a work which evolved over six years (1957–63) and is scored on a large scale for baritone soloist, chorus, orchestra and harpsichord. The work sets some of the most despairing texts from *Oedipus at Colonus,* and shows not only the young Ó Riada's appetite but to some extent his capacity for the large-scale statement. The choral writing is often starkly unison or octave-based, while the orchestral writing features the composer's characteristically hard-driven ostinati. These technical means can seem meagre for a forty-minute work, and the invention is sometimes thin, but Ó Riada shows something of Bruckner's capacity for weaving large paragraphs from small motifs.

The most controversial movement is the last, where direct quotations from the repertoire surface only to be dissonantly rejected in a grim parody of the finale of Beethoven's Ninth. (Ó Riada here incidentally anticipates by a decade Michael Tippett's similar use of the Ninth in his Third Symphony.)

Igor Stravinsky, whose 1913 *The Rite of Spring* helped shape the course of music, was the greatest composer to conduct in Ireland during the twentieth century. He rehearsed in the St Francis Xavier Hall in Upper Sherrard Street (demolished in 2006) and conducted the Radio Éireann Symphony Orchestra in his *Chorale Variations on Bach's 'Vom Himmel hoch'* and *Symphony of Psalms* in 1963 at the Adelphi Cinema on Dublin's Middle Abbey Street, on the site now occupied by the exit from Arnott's car park. The concert also included the Irish premiere of *The Rite of Spring* conducted by Robert Craft. He is here seen in an audience with President Éamon de Valera.

Seóirse Bodley has observed that this movement needs a sympathetic conductor to bring it off in performance, and at some moments the discourse threatens to grind to a halt entirely. A transitional fugue brings this bleak work to its final climax. Ambitious it is, and perhaps recklessly so. But ambition by itself has a strong appeal, and one understands the effect that this misfit of a work seemed to have on Ó Riada's contemporaries. There is nothing else quite like it in Irish music.

Neither this work nor the other *Nomoi* (the central pillars of his original achievement) could resolve the tensions that bedevilled Ó Riada's creative struggles. The break in his career comes with the film score *Mise Éire* of 1960. This score turned the composer into a national figure. One cannot but be aware of how different it is from his concert music. By the 1960s, traditional music was becoming increasingly important to him, with his miniature folk orchestra Ceoltóirí Chualann functioning as the standard-bearer of the folk revival. In these circumstances, it is no exaggeration to talk of a pre- and post-*Mise Éire* Ó Riada. It is by no means to belittle his later achievements

Above: Seán Ó Riada (originally John Reidy) became a national figure through a film score, for George Morrison's *Mise Éire* (*I am Ireland*). He became even more celebrated as the man who created the traditional music ensemble, Ceoltóirí Chualann, forerunner of The Chieftains. His achievements in traditional music have come to outshine his work as a composer.

Opposite: The great Irish contralto Bernadette Greevy in a still from the 1981 RTÉ programme *The Classical Ó Riada*.

to lament that this change came so early, while there was so much exploring still to be done. Listeners are left with a strange picture in which all of the probing efforts, including much of *Nomos* No. 2, are the work of a composer still in his twenties.

The resulting conflicts are traced with a certain tragicomedy in the book *Integrating Tradition: The Achievement of Séan Ó Riada*, edited by Bernard Harris and Grattan Freyer, a 1981 essay compilation which was effectively a posthumous Festschrift for the composer. It is to be hoped that a publisher will reissue this book, for in its very provisionality and attempt to make sense of a career cut tragically short, it is one of the indispensable documents of modern Irish music. The contributions from Victory and Bodley are among the most interesting, the former detailing the key role of the RTÉ orchestral and arts structure in furthering Ó Riada's career. But the exchange with *Irish Times* critic Charles Acton, reproduced in full, is the key one.

Acton had adversely criticised one of Ó Riada's traditional concerts, accusing him of throwing away his talent on ephemeral activity. Ó Riada, breaking with composerly etiquette, answered his critic with an ad hominem attack upon Acton's Protestant, classical, 'west British' assumptions. At this point the tensions of two decades exploded, the critic insinuating that the composer was prostituting himself to public taste, the composer accusing the critic of promoting effete gentility. It was as if a family row had spilled across the front pages of the tabloids, the home truths flying like shrapnel. The exchange (also reproduced in Tomás Ó Canainn's study of the composer) was terminated by Ó Riada's sudden death in 1971, and still makes gripping reading.

One cannot leave this remarkable figure without recording something of his wider impact. Gael Linn's recording of the concert at the Gaiety Theatre, *Ó Riada sa Gaiety*, which turned out to be among his last, captures something of the electricity that he generated. The performance of *Marcshlua Uí Néill (O'Neill's March)* retains its hellraising quality; for Irish listeners who lived through that era it is as iconic as any number by Louis Armstrong or the Beatles. The art form that had been consigned to Hell or Connaught had returned with a vengeance.

Ó Riada did not live to resolve these tensions, and his contemporaries were left to sort out his treacherous legacy. The composer who more than

The Gaiety Theatre on Dublin's South King Street, photographed in 1968. Opened in 1871, the theatre has been an important venue for opera. For many years, in spite of its extremely dry acoustic, it was home to the subscription concerts of the Radio Éireann Symphony and later RTÉ Symphony Orchestras. It also hosted the 1971 Eurovision Song Contest.

any other attempted to address the issues was Seóirse Bodley. The sense of shock at the emergence of pieces like *The narrow road to the deep north* for two pianos (1972, arranged for solo piano in 1977) and *A small white cloud drifts over Ireland* for orchestra (1975) was for some younger composers (the present writer among them) tinged with a feeling of abandonment: here was a flag-flyer for the avant-garde not only assuming the Ó Riada mantle, but recklessly mixing his ingredients, traditional and avant-garde, in a way that Ó Riada had only hinted at.

These works lie beyond the brief of this essay, but they very much reflect the complications of the 1960s. The pages of Harris and Freyer's book are much peppered with the slippery word 'synthesis', which was the direction that Ó Riada appeared to be taking at the end of his life. However one assesses the success of these works in combining radically different elements, Bodley was addressing in almost gauchely provocative terms a problem that persists. What is an Irish composer actually supposed to be doing? The traditional role that confined the composer to arranging jigs and reels for the RTÉ Light Orchestra or the BBC Northern Ireland Light Orchestra was rightly seen as hopelessly inadequate. But was worshipping at the modern European shrines so different from the Brahms-epigonism of Stanford and earlier Irish composers?

This matter has remained stubbornly relevant. The question 'What are Irish composers doing?' too easily changes into 'What are Irish composers nowadays reacting to?' That major centre of the avant-garde, the Darmstadt International Summer Course for New Music, is itself part of history, and it has become clearer with time that the acolytes of high-profile international movements can too often end up serving as the burnt offerings also. The Bodley works, rather than attempting to synthesise the alien elements, appeared to set them side by side in a kind of either-or relationship: traditional/modernist, Dublin/Darmstadt. The listener is left to decide between them.

Perhaps the Irish work of the 1960s that comes closest to Bodley's *Configurations* in its radical language is *Favola di Notte* (1967) by Gerard Victory. Victory had recently returned from Darmstadt and the experience clearly left its mark on this *montage sonore* of divisi string textures and strident brass writing. The effect is very bracing, even if it suffers, like much avant-gardism, from an unwillingness to give the listener's attention some breathing room.

This remarkable work shows nothing of Victory's talents as a composer of light music. Less puritanical in this respect is A. J. Potter, whose *Sinfonia "de Profundis"* (1969) seems determined to embrace every genre of music including the waltz and jig. The work is in five movements that owe little to sonata procedures, though the second is a recognisable scherzo. Another original feature is the use of the hymn 'Remember God's goodness, O thou man', which runs through the work in a combination of variation form and

Opposite, left: Composer Gerard Victory at his desk in RTÉ in 1968. In spite of holding down a demanding job as RTÉ's director of music, he was extremely prolific. His output runs to over 200 works, including operas, symphonies and a mammoth requiem cantata, *Ultima Rerum*. His taste ran from avant-garde to mainstream to light music. He never forgot seeing the revues and pantomimes of the 1920s and declared his earliest role model to be Ivor Novello, not just for his musical skills, but also on account of his material success.

Opposite, right: Belfast-born A. J. Potter studied under Vaughan Williams in London and fought in World War II in Europe and Asia. After a stint in a managerial job in Nigeria he resumed his musical studies in Birmingham and returned to Ireland to make a living through music, singing in the choir of St Patrick's Cathedral, Dublin, and teaching at the Royal Irish Academy of Music. He was a prolific choral and orchestral arranger for Radio Éireann in the 1950s, and is celebrated for his colourful orchestration. One of his most searching and deeply personal works is the *Sinfonia "de Profundis"* of 1968.

idée fixe. The tune appears most strikingly in the scherzo, as low woodwinds state it against an obsessive jig in the strings. From this moment the scherzo builds up to a climax of Ivesian cacophony. In the third movement *Adagio* Potter hints strongly at the personal crisis that gave rise to the *Sinfonia*. But there is always something menacing even in the most jubilant moments of this teeming farrago of a score, which created a public sensation at its 1969 Dublin premiere. It tempts one to see in this northern Presbyterian who studied with Vaughan Williams an Irish Charles Ives. The exceptional orchestral métier has perhaps not been equalled by any Irish composer; the musical substance is of bewilderingly variable quality. In its inventive power and unresolved stylistic tensions, the *Sinfonia* joins the long list of mid-century Irish works that suggest paths opened up but never completely explored.

The contribution of Aloys Fleischmann (1910–92) to Irish music as composer and scholar was enormous. His ballet score *An Cóitín Dearg* (The Little Red Coat) (1951) shows a comprehensive mastery of mid-century orchestral resources. So assured is the work that one wonders what Irish composers lost by the lack of a viable Irish film industry, for Fleischmann is no fastidious abstainer from delicious orchestral effects, though the viola and harp scoring in the Intermezzo (No. 6 from the orchestral suite) shows him capable of delicacy too. His confidence in handling the orchestra is equally evident in *Cornucopia* for horn and orchestra of 1970. This two-movement concerto is more restrained in its colouristic effects than the ballet. The need to make the solo instrument heard is clearly important, though perhaps something of the austerity characteristic of much Irish music of the 1960s influenced Fleischmann also. The first movement is split by a solo cadenza which gives way to a haunting berceuse-like passage beautifully scored for strings, harp and the solo horn. The second movement is a true quick Rondo, not an easy formal challenge to bring off in a modern harmonic idiom.

The large output of James Wilson includes seven operas, making him one of the Irish pioneers of the genre. These works are not easy to discuss in a general essay, covering as they do forty years of creative activity. Many of them suffered the fate of so much modern opera, enjoying a successful first run but failing to enter the repertoire. Such was the fate of his first opera *The Hunting of the Snark* (1963). *A Passionate Man* (1995), treating a short but crucial period in the life of Jonathan Swift, shows some of the mature Wilson's strengths and weaknesses as a dramatic composer. The libretto, adapted from Bruce Arnold's play *A Most Confounded Tory*, treats Swift's complicated love life, but also deals with the political intrigues of the period. The attempt to explore a political theme is courageous. But it is not clear how the intrigues of the Duke of Marlborough and his opponents are to be made dramatically interesting for a modern audience. The most lyrically telling music is given to Swift's young love, Vanessa, suggesting that the love interest was Wilson's real interest as well. Elsewhere the vocal writing lapses into the colourless arioso too typical of much modern opera, expertly judged to convey the words, but less than compelling to listen to. Modern Ireland has failed to provide a dependable platform for native opera, and it is difficult not to see in James Wilson's operatic career a reflection of this sad reality. The theatre composer more than any must hone his craft in front of a living audience, and this too often was what Wilson and other opera composers lacked.

The operatic career of Joan Trimble (1915–2000) also took root in stony soil. Trimble's *Blind Raftery* (1957), a BBC commission, was one of the earliest

Opposite: Cork-born Havelock Nelson trained in medicine and music in Dublin, where he founded an amateur orchestra, the Dublin Orchestral Players. He spent most of his life as staff accompanist for the BBC in Belfast, where he also established new performing groups. He is best remembered for his songs.

Joan Trimble was anything but prolific, and after her 1957 television opera, *Blind Raftery*, the first by a female composer, the demands of family life kept her silent but for two works, an Air for two Irish harps in 1969 and *Three Diversions* for Wind Quintet in 1990. Both concert posters are by Marcus Patton.

television operas. The work tells the story of the blind poet's marriage to the mysterious Spanish woman Hilaria. Trimble's traditionalist language finds ample outlet in Cedric Cliffe's libretto with its opportunities for arias, duets and comical turns. The pedlar's sales pitch for his fraudulent financial schemes in scene two is very deftly blended into the one large ensemble, set in a tavern, where the dark truth of Hilaria's past is revealed. Trimble incorporates many jigs and reels almost to the point of cloyingness, but contrives contrasting colours also; Hilaria's first-scene aria is accompanied by a guitar, and the Spanish element conveyed by a sinuous cor anglais. Much of Raftery's most personal music is in five-eight time, a simple but effective method of suggesting the blind poet's intense inner world. This work does not suggest a major operatic talent, but shows a gift for dramatic pacing, compression and characterisation. It was the last significant work that Trimble was to write for decades.

Opposite: Brian Boydell holding a long-obsolete instrument, a bass ophicleide, in a still from the television series *Music in the Making*, produced by Anne Makower, and broadcast in 1964.

Any full assessment of the later output of Ina Boyle (1889–1967) must await a staged performance of her opera *Maudlin of Paplewick* (1966). The entire score can be viewed on the website of the Manuscript and Archives Research Library of Trinity College Dublin, www.digitalcollections.tcd.ie. Like many composers discussed in this chapter, Boyle had a strong literary bent, and her late vocal style can be sampled in *Three Songs of Walter de la Mare* (1956). The third song, 'Moon, Reeds, Rushes' is one of the most affecting by an Irish composer.

The tradition of Irish light music was carried on by such composers as Arthur Duff (1899–1956), John F. Larchet (1884–1967) and T. C. Kelly (1917–85). These composers cultivated a consciously conservative idiom with high values of musical crafstmanship. Their work, with its frequent use of Irish tunes, defined for many listeners what Irish classical music sounded like in the same way that Paul Henry's landscapes of Achill Island defined Irish painting. Duff's *Echoes of Georgian Dublin* (1955) and Larchet's *By the Waters of Moyle* (1957) are fine examples of their work. Northern representatives of this group included Cork-born Havelock Nelson (1917–96) and Redmond Friel (1907–79), and Trimble's *Ulster Airs* are a fine contribution to the genre.

These composers worked at a historical moment that saw composers of serious intent almost stop producing lighter works, a development for which we are the poorer. And their often Church of Ireland or Protestant background is interesting; the painter Paul Henry, for example, was an Ulster Baptist. The romanticising of the west of Ireland, notionally the uncorrupted heartland of authentic gaeldom, was in fact a largely non-Catholic cultural phenomenon, and resulted in the curious circumstance of Catholic artists looking to Europe or America for inspiration, while Protestant artists sought to establish an Irish identity as traditionally conceived, with revival of the Irish language and of the folk tradition in music and mythology as mainstays.

The output of Brian Boydell (1917–2000) is best viewed through the medium of his three string quartets, the works that the composer himself

considered his finest achievements. The First (1949) was evidently his attempt to match Frederick May's Quartet, and is a considerable achievement in its own right. But it should not overshadow the excellence of the other two. The Second Quartet (1958) encapsulates the mature Boydell style in its terse two-movement structure. The first movement crosses a G minor tonality with Boydell's preferred octatonic melodic and harmonic formulations. This technical resource, alternating tones and semitones, owes nothing to Messiaen, the young Boydell having discovered octatonicism for himself. Intriguing in this movement is the strongly Irish inflection of the main theme. The second movement is a scherzo that shows Boydell's mastery of intricate rhythm (in this respect he perhaps surpasses May) and the vaulting counterpoint that is another hallmark of his style.

Brian Boydell was an indefatigable proselytiser for music, on radio, on television, in education and in the corridors of power. He is shown above in 1967 introducing a television programme, *The Music of Swift's Dublin*, with Hugh Maguire (violin), Edward Beckett (flute), John Beckett (harpsichord) and Betty Sullivan (cello).

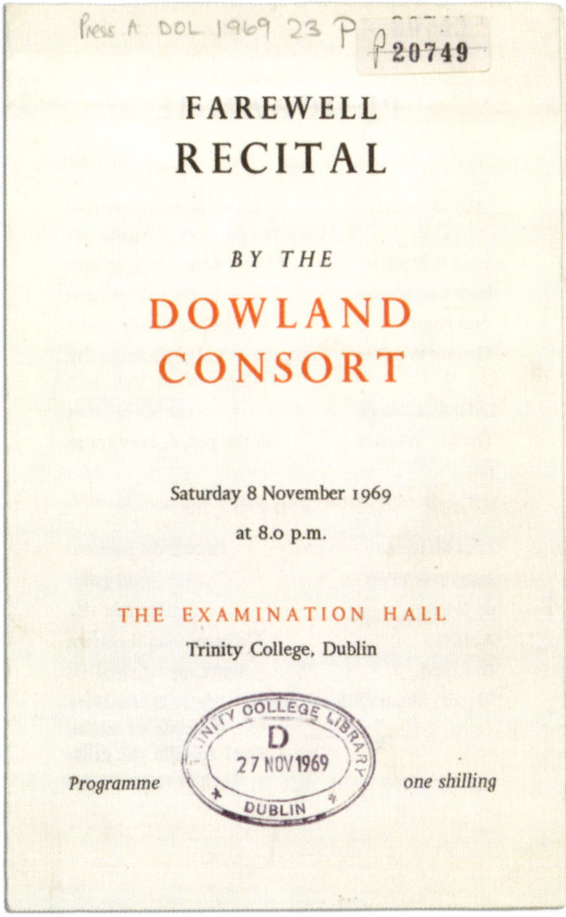

FAREWELL RECITAL

BY THE

DOWLAND CONSORT

Saturday 8 November 1969

at 8.0 p.m.

THE EXAMINATION HALL

Trinity College, Dublin

Programme *one shilling*

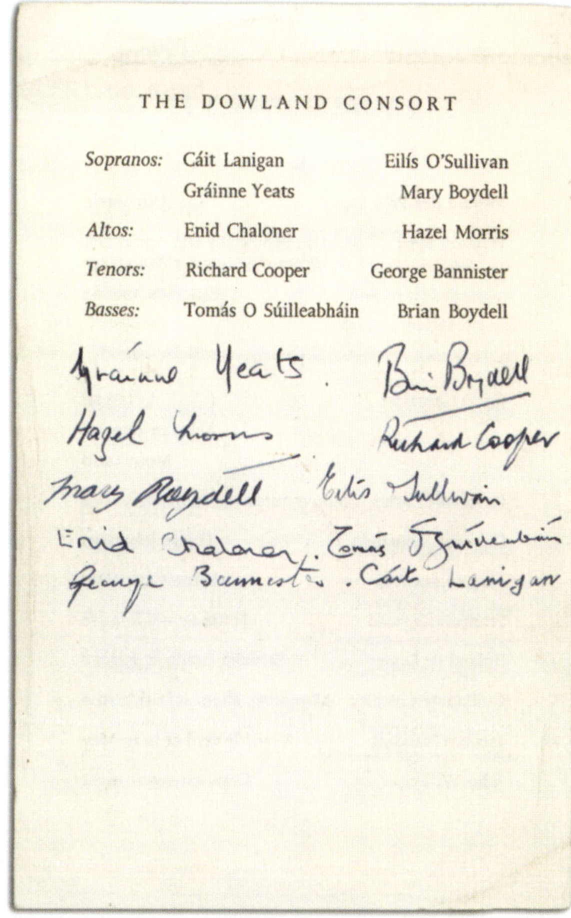
THE DOWLAND CONSORT

Sopranos:	Cáit Lanigan	Eilís O'Sullivan
	Gráinne Yeats	Mary Boydell
Altos:	Enid Chaloner	Hazel Morris
Tenors:	Richard Cooper	George Bannister
Basses:	Tomás O Súilleabháin	Brian Boydell

In 1958 Brian Boydell formed the Dowland Consort, specialising in the vocal music of the sixteenth and seventeenth centuries, and performing seated around a table to evoke the manner in which madrigals were originally sung. The group, which was broadcast by both RTÉ and the BBC, gave its first concert in 1959, recorded an LP for the English Alpha label in 1965, and gave its farewell concert in 1969.

The Third Quartet (1969) lays some claim to be Boydell's finest achievement in abstract musical construction. A first glance at the score reveals a disconcertingly spartan musical substance: a trill on one note, and four notes descending in a pattern of interlocking fourths. But Boydell proves himself a master of the terse motivic language of one of his heroes, Sibelius, and the discourse, embracing a final movement fugato, adds up to much more than the sum of the parts.

Boydell's productivity flagged after this work. Clearly his Trinity College professorship took its toll on his time. His enormous energy found outlets in many artistic endeavours including the founding of the Dowland Consort (1959–69), which can claim to have effectively launched the early music revival in modern Ireland. Reluctant to produce inferior work and scornful of fashion, he became a figure of conscience for a new generation

The Dowland Consort performing in the Examination Hall, Trinity College Dublin. The singers are, left to right, Richard Cooper, George Bannister (tenors), Eilís O'Sullivan, Cáit Lanigan, Gráinne Yeats, Mary Boydell (sopranos), Enid Chaloner, Hazel Morris (altos), Tomás Ó Súilleabháin and Brian Boydell (basses).

of composers. The orchestral work *Masai Mara* of 1988, which includes recorders in the orchestration, shows his still restless, exploring spirit.

Like Boydell, John Kinsella (b. 1932) approached the modernist challenge in a personal, non-doctrinaire way. His *Two Pieces for String Orchestra* (1965) and Second String Quartet (1968) engage more with the classic modernism of Webern and later Stravinsky than with Darmstadt. The Quartet, cast in four movements, shuns the colour-effects of the avant-garde in favour of a severe, almost geometric expressivity. The work's texture often divides into the classical 'double-duo' format, the austere two-voice discourse allowing for few sensuous effects. But the third-movement *Lento* features a triadic climax marked *affetuoso*, echoed by the A major 6/4 chord which brings to an end the stormy finale. This movement incidentally is not the only music discussed in this chapter that shows the influence of Shostakovich. *Two Pieces for String Orchestra* similarly shows a composer not afraid to go his own way, with the first piece having an exposition repeat. The second piece shows Kinsella's awareness of late Stravinsky: one passage ornaments a chorale-like theme in the lower strings with violin cantillations. These works wear their modernist credentials lightly, but they favour objective utterance over emotional effect. This objectivising trait in Kinsella's music of the 1960s is most clearly seen in his *Rondo for Orchestra* (1969), which ends with an extended solo for the timpani. What links all the works here discussed is a concern with extended form that prefigures Kinsella the late-flowering symphonist.

The 1950s was the last creative decade in the long life of Howard Ferguson (1908–99). But he produced some of his best music during these years, including the brilliant short song cycle *Discovery* (1951), setting the bitter-sweet poems of Denton Welch. In the course of their eight minutes, the songs match the moods of the poems with an astonishing aptness both in vocal line and pianistic figuration (Ferguson was himself a brilliant pianist). The song *Jane Allen* tells its sardonic story in less than forty seconds. The recording of these songs by Kathleen Ferrier has been reissued on the Decca label.

In 1969 the north-east corner of Ireland erupted in a prolonged and intermittently savage conflict over matters of national identity, as a large Catholic minority expressed dissatisfaction with its secondary status in a series of civil rights marches which were met with strong official opposition and sometimes violence. The launch in that year of the first Dublin Festival of 20th Century Music was, to put it no more strongly, a suggestive coincidence. As the Republic looked outwards, the North appeared to recede into tribal conflict.

The reality was not so simple. If some pre-1969 formulations of the compositional problems suddenly appeared provincial and out of date, the post-1969 declaration of a musical free state with its liberties and iconoclasms could, from a Northern perspective, seem unanchored in reality. The aggressive anti-nationalism of the revisionist movement in the Republic left bereft a Northern Catholic population that felt its cultural existence, to a great extent affiliated with the the Irish language and music, severely threatened. Nor did the revisionist movement, driven like so much in Irish culture by a kind of political-literary engine, address musical problems convincingly. What role for musical iconoclasm in a society that had so few musical icons? The initial impact of the Troubles, as they euphemistically came to be called, was culturally negative, for conflict sends people retreating to their heartlands and annihilates nuanced argument.

In this unpromising ground a school of composers was to take root and flourish. As this essay has already hinted, Northern Ireland is aesthetically more conservative than the rest of the island. Almost the first thing that reviewers noticed about the school of Ulster poets finding international recognition in the 1960s was not 'innovation' but the emphasis on traditional verse discipline. This trait is also to be found in the school of Northern composers that began to emerge in the 1960s. The careers of David Byers (b. 1947) and Philip Hammond (b. 1951) as administrators, decisively influential as they have been, have sometimes unhappily overshadowed their activity as composers. They were alert to European developments (Byers studied with Henri Pousseur) while exemplifying a bias that might be taken as a particularly Ulster one in favour of solid technique as the basis of original statement. Hammond's *Thanatos* (1977) for large-scale forces including an electronic score, and Byers's *Pholypony* for wind quintet (1975) suggested new directions for Northern Irish music that were later to find institutional embodiment in the Belfast Sonorities Festival, first held in 1981.

Howard Ferguson was the most successful Northern Irish composer of the twentieth century. He studied composition in London with R. O. Morris and Vaughan Williams, piano with Harold Samuel and conducting with Malcolm Sargent. His output is small, his style conservative, but the quality of craftsmanship is high, and his works have been performed and recorded by leading international performers, including Isaac Stern and Jascha Heifetz. He worked with Myra Hess on the daily recitals in London's National Gallery during World War II, and after he stopped composing in 1959, he turned to the editing of keyboard music. His editions are known to generations of piano students.

BBC
Invitation Concert
HOWARD FERGUSON
90TH BIRTHDAY
ULSTER ORCHESTRA
ADRIAN LEAPER conductor
PHILIP MARTIN piano
CHRISTOPHER MALTMAN baritone
Music by FERGUSON & GERALD FINZI

The Dublin Festival of 20th Century Music represented a change of direction in Irish music, and several of the composers discussed here would take a leading part in it. Some mysteries remain. Why, for example, did Irish composers respond so readily to innovations in pitch and sonority, but so little to the rhythmic challenges of modernism? Perhaps standards of performance at the time needed to catch up with composers' imaginations. The composers of the 1950s and 1960s have become for later composers a parental or grand-parental generation, and the reactions of these younger composers, if sometimes critical, have softened with time, as they generally do where parents are concerned. At bottom lingers the sense of wonder at a generation that worked so hard and accomplished so much.

Belfast-born composer David Byers working outdoors as a choral conductor on the BBC's *Songs of Praise*. An organist himself, he is also one of the most prolific Irish composers of organ music. As a music producer with the BBC he was a skilled programmer, specialising in lesser-known repertoire with the Ulster Orchestra. He has worked to encourage stronger links and greater understanding between north and south.

Pianos, festivals and the puzzle of a contemporary music ensemble

JANE O'LEARY

It was a dark time of year when I arrived in Galway from the U.S. in December 1972. I knew little about the musical life of the country, but I had heard that Stravinsky was a guest here some years earlier (actually nearly ten years before) and that there was an important festival of new music in Dublin. I soon realised that Ireland was a very small island, that travelling outside the country was dependent on either a very expensive flight or a tortuous boat journey, and that travelling within the country took much longer than the number of miles would imply.

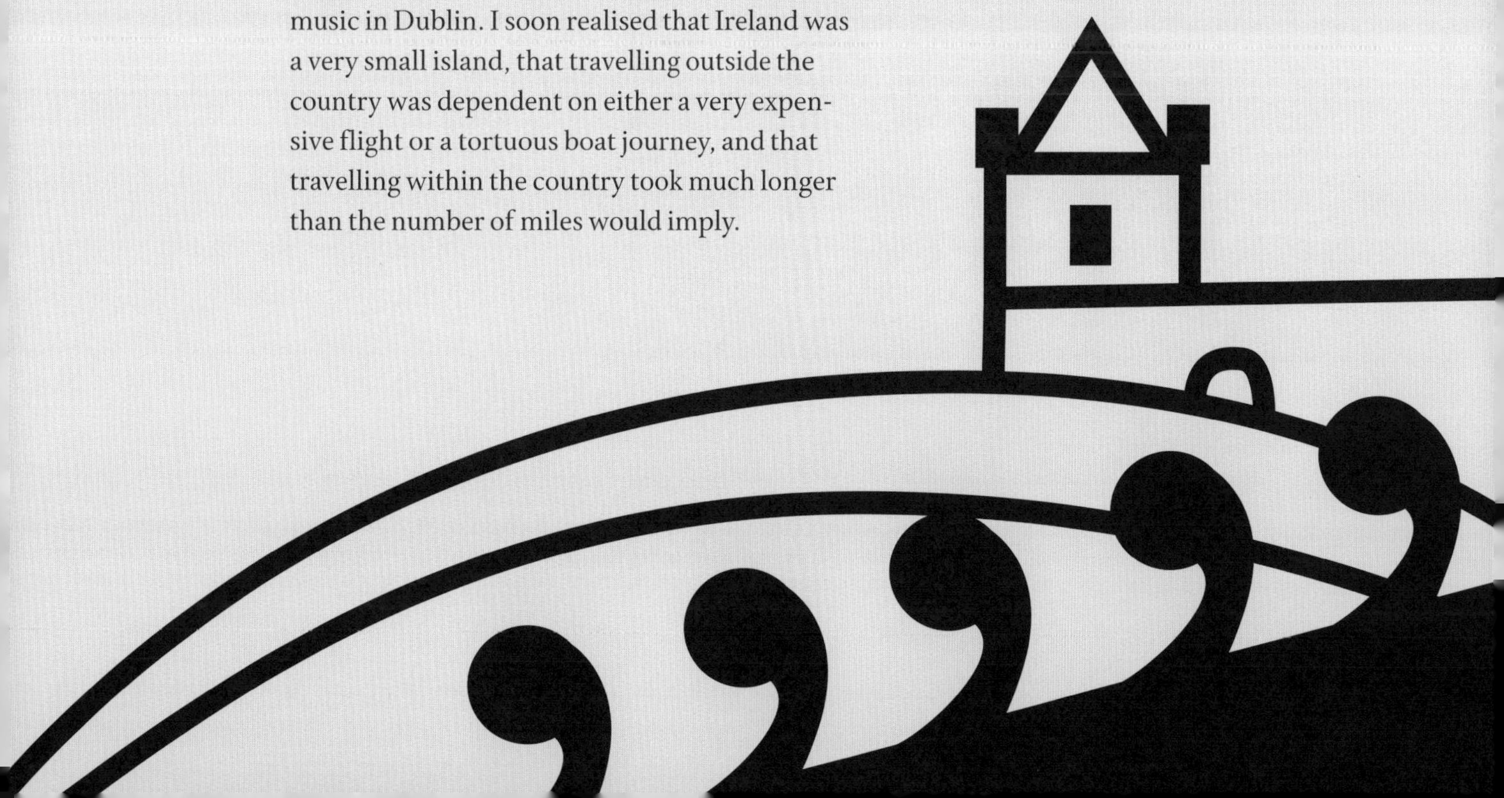

I have recollections of searching for a piano to practise on in the university and finally finding an upright ensconced in the 'ladies' club'. This memory evokes flashes of later experiences with pianos around the country—performing in the Music Association of Ireland's regional recitals on pianos which were so out of tune that we had to abandon ensemble pieces, listening to Míċeál O'Rourke performing on a badly maintained upright piano in Connemara, watching the only grand piano in Galway literally fall apart before our eyes at a concert in a school hall.

But almost everyone had some sort of piano in their home, and there was no shortage of people requesting lessons. There was an eagerness to learn amongst the university

Opposite: An early photograph of Jane O'Leary's contemporary music ensemble, Concorde. In the photograph are, left to right, seated: Brighid Mooney (cello), Madeleine Berkeley (flute); standing: Alan Smale (violin), Jane O'Leary (piano), Anne Woodworth (mezzo soprano) and Helmut Seeber (oboe). The group's 353 concerts have taken them to 13 countries, with repertoire that included 239 world premieres, 212 of them of works by Irish composers.

community in particular. I soon began giving evening courses on 'the art of listening' which were immensely popular and spread around the county through the 'adult education' scheme. My memories include the university language lab which generously facilitated me in converting excerpts from LPs onto cassette tapes, and the midnight 'mail train' back from Athlone where I gave lectures for the Gramophone Society.

Piano teaching had its mysteries: I had never heard of a system of 'grade exams'—why would you need to pass an exam in piano playing? Surely, it was about developing a love of music, communicating through public performances, learning to enjoy music in a broadest sense? No, I was told. Fingers were struck by rulers if you played a wrong note. If you didn't pass exams, how could you rate your progress?

Concerts too were a strange phenomenon. Promoted by 'private clubs' or 'societies', there was an air of exclusion about them. One felt there was a dress code, possibly even a 'class' code, and an assumption that you should 'know something about music' before you could enjoy listening to it. I remember arriving at Castletown House with a few friends from the west for one of the early Festival in Great Irish Houses concerts. Having spent the day touring around, we were eyed with suspicion as we walked in—somewhat 'underdressed' apparently.

Ireland seemed to be obsessed with festivals—a rather strange idea to me at the time—but one of the most significant was the Dublin Festival of 20th Century Music, organised and promoted by the Music Association of Ireland. It offered a chance to hear an outstanding array of contemporary classics, meet the most distinguished composers of new music in Europe, and experience newly commissioned pieces by Irish composers. It offered a starting point for discovering just who these Irish composers were. Apparently, they were all men. Some years after arriving in Ireland, I prepared a talk for an international conference on women in music. It was a major challenge to find even a few examples from Irish composers for illustration.

Attending the 20th Century Music Festival in 1974, I was impressed to see that there was encouragement for young Irish composers in the form of a designated concert. As the diverse group of young composers got to know each other, and also performers with an interest in their music, the Association of Young Irish Composers came to life.

But I was deeply puzzled and upset that this opportunity to hear new music—something I was used to, something I needed in my life—seemed to be restricted to the festival. A gap of two years between festivals seemed inordinately long. I began talking to my colleagues in the performance area—would they be interested in performing new music more regularly, would they take that risk, would they enjoy learning music that had never been done before?

Soon, a small group of willing performers gathered and came up with the name Concorde—the supersonic plane was also born around that time and seemed to symbolise the modern era. The aim was to present new (and newish) music from around the world to audiences on a regular, continuous basis. It seems strange now to think that although supersonic flights existed (admittedly not in Ireland!), it was next to impossible to obtain a new telephone line in Galway before 1979, when a papal visit brought phone lines to the west.

Full of enthusiasm, our committed group of musicians approached the Arts Council to see if they would give funding towards a couple of concerts in 1976. I had chosen American repertoire. It was the bicentennial year, and I was familiar with many compositions which had never been performed in Ireland. We were met with a total lack of comprehension—they did not know what a 'contemporary music ensemble' was. My models were several New York ensembles formed in the 1960s and 1970s—the Group for Contemporary Music, Da Capo Players, Speculum Musicae. But this was a new concept for Ireland. There was no funding offered. However, they said 'give the concerts and we'll see'. So we did. And here we are forty years later—still enjoying our engagement with new music—in a completely different musical environment!

Filling in the blanks

HILARY BRACEFIELD

I arrived to live in Northern Ireland in 1976. Before that time, I had hardly thought about the music scene in Ireland. From childhood I knew about the Londonderry Air, John McCormack records and Thomas Moore melodies, and had some idea of Irish traditional music. A favourite song was 'I dreamt I dwelt in marble halls' from Michael Balfe's opera *The Bohemian Girl*—but I knew that from a Laurel and Hardy film, even though the opera was toured in my native New Zealand in the nineteenth century. Composers like Stanford and Wood I just assumed were English; and living in Birmingham, the only addition to the above catalogue was John O'Conor after he gave a piano recital there.

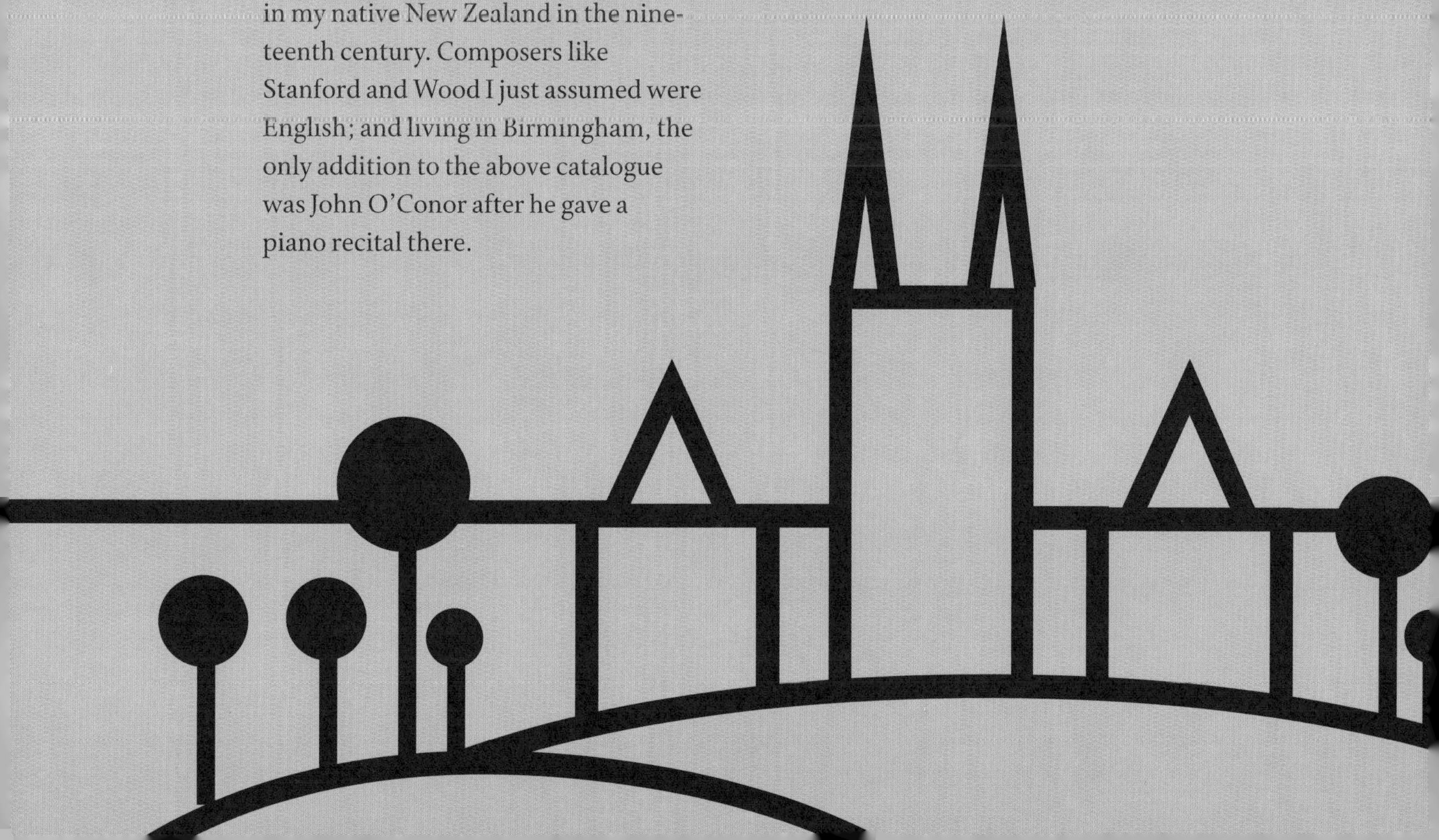

But 1976 was not the ideal time to experience music in Northern Ireland. Many artists refused to come (the usual excuse was 'my wife won't let me'), and many residents did not venture out at night. Thus I remember the regular concerts of the British (now Belfast) Music Society, an institution since 1921, held on Sunday afternoons in a packed Whitla Hall. And in fact, chamber music has endured the whole century in both Dublin and Belfast; a form considered elitist, with audiences becoming increasingly white-haired, but where artists, both established and up-and-coming, continue to travel the world, and where audiences never quite die out.

Next most enduring, and also always apparently threatened with extinction because of cost, is opera. I have seen a huge number of different operas over the years by both local and visiting companies, and not just the standard repertoire. My first actual experience of music in Ireland was being sent to review the opera season in Belfast in early 1976. Firstly the hotel in which I was to stay was blown up the day before, and then there was a spectacular car chase ending on the steps of the ABC Cinema, widely covered on television. The operas were being staged in the cinema because the Frank Matcham-designed Grand Opera House was closed. It had just been bought by the Arts Council, and would be restored and reopened in 1980.

My first experience of opera in Dublin was in 1983: the umpteenth production there of *Rigoletto.* The sets and chorus seemed all pushed to one side of the stage—so that the President of Ireland could see the action from his box, someone told me. Thankfully, the old Dublin Grand Opera Society with its Verdi and Puccini warhorses is no longer, and though companies continue to come and go and finance is a constant problem, opera also still continues and Ireland has produced what looks like an opera which will become a standard in Gerald Barry's *The Importance of Being Earnest.*

During the 1970s and 1980s the only event to which Belfast people turned out in droves was the annual festival begun by Queen's University in the 1960s. My first was in 1976, and the festival still continues although Queen's has now pulled out of sponsorship. I first heard the RTÉ Symphony Orchestra at the Festival in 1978, with the enticement of Bruckner's Seventh Symphony. Sadly, many members of the orchestra were not keen to travel north, even for an evening, and sent deputies. It was not an amazing occasion. Even more unsettling were the performances of both Northern Ireland orchestras in their concerts at various Queen's Festivals. Neither the BBC Northern Ireland Orchestra nor the Ulster Orchestra were full strength, so players were borrowed as required, not always with happy results.

One famous performance of Tchaikovsky's Fourth Symphony boasted the sight, obvious to the audience, of rival brass players brawling on stage. The orchestras merged in 1981 and the fullish strength Ulster Orchestra is still clinging on financially today. The RTÉ National Symphony Orchestra still sees no need to travel north, but performances I have heard in Dublin have been of pleasing quality.

Irish contemporary composers may not think it, but they have more opportunities for performance than in many other countries. The Dublin Festival of 20th Century Music, for example, ran from 1969 to 1986. I attended the 1982 version, in a sudden January snowfall which paralysed the country. Half of the guest performers could not get out of Europe, the RTÉ orchestral players could not all get to rehearsals in the city centre in Dublin, and the advertised performance of *Inori* conducted by Stockhausen himself, in the new National Concert Hall, opened in 1981, had to be cancelled. Stockhausen allowed us to hear it from a tape edited together from noisy LP pressings purchased in Dublin, and his son Markus played the trumpet piece *Aries*. My impression of the Irish music heard in that festival was of middle-of-the-road competence, although the editor of my review took two words from separate parts of the article and headlined it 'Stagnant Backwater?'

Apart from the 20th Century Festival, composers continue to have their works programmed by both of Ireland's symphony orchestras, by string quartets in residence, by Jane O'Leary's indomitable Concorde since 1976 and Crash Ensemble from 1997. The Tyrone Guthrie Centre, opened in 1982, gives composers and other artists a retreat in which to compose, and the Contemporary Music Centre, established in 1986, really helps bring Irish composers to the world. In the North, the Sonorities Festival began in 1981 and carries on, though mainly now as an electronic music festival. Both Northern Ireland and the Republic of Ireland tried early music festivals in the 1980s, but curiously these have disappeared in the North: perhaps early music has just entered the mainstream.

Two things I have discovered since being in Ireland have had profound effects on music in the country in this century of music. Firstly, in 1916 Ellen O'Byrne began producing Irish music records for the expatriate community in New York. After World War I these began to be brought back to Ireland, including those of the great Sligo fiddler Michael Coleman and his compatriots. He had gone to New York in 1921, and his records began to appear from 1924 onwards, thus spreading the Sligo style countrywide. And the opening of the 2BE radio station in Belfast in 1924 and of 2RN in Dublin in 1926—its first director, Séamus Clandillon, was a traditional singer and folk song collector—brought Irish local music over the airwaves eventually to everyone.

Looking back, I can see that by arriving in 1976 I was coming into an era of expansion and change in the 1980s, quite an exciting time for music in Ireland. Now I am established here it is harder to reflect on the current scene and what may be yet to come in an era

Marcus Patton's poster for the first Sonorities Festival in Belfast, bringing an Irish slant to twentieth-century composers from Satie, Schoenberg and Stravinsky to Cage, Stockhausen and Messiaen.

N ASSOCIATION WITH THE ARTS COUNCIL OF NORTHERN IRELAND & THE DEPARTMENT OF MUSIC QUB

SCHOENBERG AND SOME COLLAGUES PREPARING FOR THEIR VISIT TO THE FESTIVAL

SONORITIES

NORTHERN IRELAND'S FESTIVAL OF 20TH CENTURY MUSIC

24-27 APRIL 1981 AT QUEEN'S UNIVERSITY BELFAST

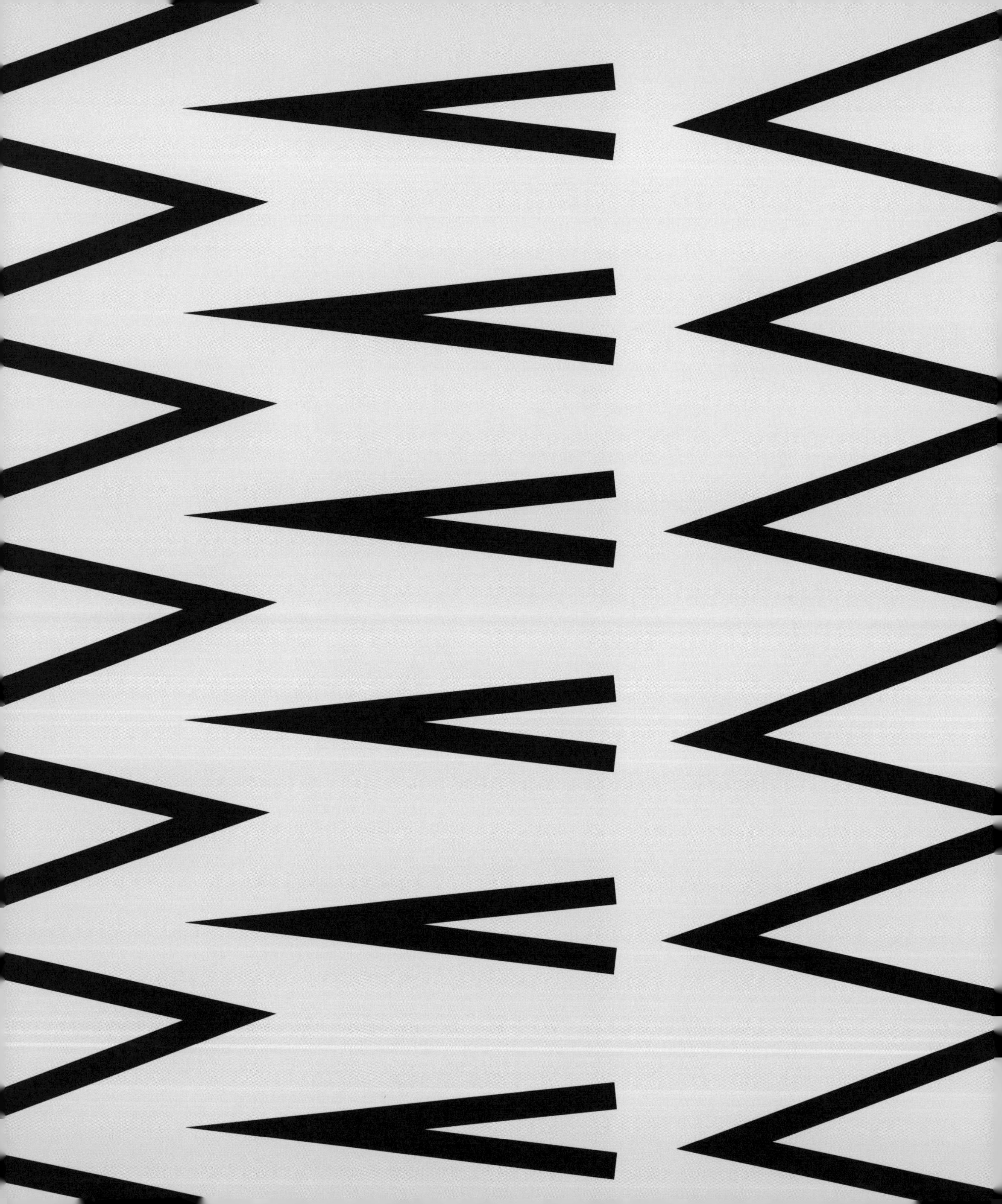

1970–1989

1970

The New Irish Chamber Orchestra (today's Irish Chamber Orchestra), founded by Lindsay Armstrong and André Prieur, gives its first concert.

Ireland wins the Eurovision Song Contest for the first time, with Dana (real name Rosemary Brown) performing 'All Kinds of Everything' by Derry Lindsay and Jackie Smith.

Brian Boydell's First String Quartet and Seóirse Bodley's String Quartet are given their first UK broadcasts on BBC Radio 3 in performances by the RTÉ String Quartet, taped at the 1969 Dublin Festival of 20th Century Music.

1971

The Rippen piano factory in Shannon goes into receivership after facing a tax judgment of £61,479 from the Revenue Commissioners and experiencing pressure from creditors. The factory claims to have been supplying 6 per cent of the pianos sold in Europe.

Decimal currency is introduced.

1972

The New Irish Recording Company issues its first LPs, including works by Seóirse Bodley, Brian Boydell, Aloys Fleischmann, John Kinsella, Gerard Victory and James Wilson.

The Association of Young Irish Composers presents its first concert.

1973

The New Irish Chamber Orchestra under André Prieur gives the first UK broadcast performance of Seán Ó Riada's *Hercules Dux Ferrariae* in a BBC Radio 3 relay from the Nantwich Festival.

1974

The first Kilkenny Arts Week is held, featuring a programme with a strong representation of music.

1975

The Arts Council/*An Chomhairle Ealaíon* appoints Colm Ó Briain as its first full-time director. With a total staff of eight, its state grant-in-aid rises to £200,000.

EMI issue an LP of recordings of violin sonatas by E. J. Moeran and Howard Ferguson, played by Geraldine O'Grady and Charles Lynch.

In a favourable review of Frederick May's String Quartet in *Gramophone* magazine, Felix Aprahamian writes 'when it comes to music, the Tonga Isles seem less remote than Erin.'

1976

Composer Jane O'Leary founds the contemporary music ensemble Concorde.

Summer Music at Carrolls, a new series of free chamber music concerts adventurously programmed by Colman Pearce, takes place in the Dublin offices of tobacco company P. J. Carroll.

1977

The BBC Northern Symphony Orchestra under Albert Rosen performs an all-Irish programme on BBC Radio 3 on 6 April, Frederick May's Scherzo, Gerard Victory's Second Piano Concerto (with Philip Martin) and Brian Boydell's *Symphonic Inscapes*.

1978

English composer George Newson is appointed the first composer-in-residence at Queen's University Belfast.

The Academica Quartet becomes RTÉ's string quartet in residence.

The European Economic Community Youth Orchestra, founded in 1976, makes its first tour and features nine Irish musicians among its 135 players.

1979

Ciarán Benson's report, *The Place of the Arts in Irish Education*, is published by The Arts Council/*An Chomhairle Ealaíon*.

1980

The six-week-long *A Sense of Ireland* festival takes place in London.

The RTÉSO goes on its first European tour, with repertoire including Brian Boydell's *In Memoriam Mahatma Gandhi*, A. J. Potter's *Rhapsody under a High Sky* and Gerard Victory's *Olympic Festival* Overture.

1981

The National Concert Hall (NCH) opens in Dublin.

The Sonorities Festival of Contemporary Music is held in Belfast for the first time.

A. J. Potter's *The Wedding* is produced at the Abbey Theatre by Irish National Opera.

The first issue of *Soundpost* magazine is published by the Music Association of Ireland.

1982

Bernard Harrison's *Catalogue of Contemporary Irish Music* is published by the Irish Composers' Centre.

1983

Composer John Buckley founds the Ennis Composition Summer School in Co. Clare.

Composer John Kinsella is appointed head of music at RTÉ.

1984

Bryden Thomson succeeds Colman Pearce as principal conductor of the RTÉ Symphony Orchestra, becoming the first musician to hold conductorship positions with the RTÉSO and the Ulster Orchestra.

RTÉ creates the RTÉ Chamber Choir.

1985

Donald Herrron's *Deaf Ears?*, a shaming report on the provision of music education in Irish schools, is published by the Arts Council.

The first issue of *Music Ireland* magazine is published by Amadeus Publications.

1986

The newly founded Opera Theatre Company presents its debut production, Britten's *The Turn of the Screw*.

A new music development and touring agency, Music Network, is founded.

The Vanbrugh String Quartet becomes RTÉ's quartet in residence.

Belfast-born Barry Douglas becomes the first Western pianist since Van Cliburn in 1958 to win outright the gold medal at the Tchaikovsky Piano Competition in Moscow.

1987

Impresario Noel Pearson presents a three-day Ó Riada Retrospective at the National Concert Hall.

1988

The first GPA Dublin International Piano Competition is won by French pianist Philippe Cassard (26). The competition commissions its first test piece from Philip Martin.

1989

The music of Howard Ferguson, a symposium edited by Alan Ridout, with a memoir by the composer, is published by Thames Publishing.

Growth and consolidation

MARK FITZGERALD

Overleaf (detail on left): In June 1981 three composers living in Cologne, Gerald Barry, Chris Newman and Kevin Volans, came up with an alternative to 'new music'. They held a meeting and issued a manifesto to bring into being the Society for Newer Music. The news was reported in the October/November 1981 issue of *Soundpost* magazine.

The 1970s and 1980s brought an array of strikingly individual composers, Ireland's first new music ensemble, the National Concert Hall and the Contemporary Music Centre.

The period 1970 to 1989 marked a decisive shift in Ireland's contemporary music scene both in terms of the development of infrastructural supports and also in the emergence of a radical new generation of composers. In 1970 there was no National Concert Hall and no Contemporary Music Centre. The Music Association of Ireland, long one of the lynchpins of musical events in Ireland, was in decline over this period and various of its functions were gradually taken over by different new organisations. A second edition of Edgar Deale's *Catalogue of Contemporary Irish Composers* from 1973, incorporating composers from Northern Ireland as well as the Republic, was able to muster up a mere thirty names, of whom four were dead, two were English (Elizabeth Maconchy and James Wilson, the latter not yet having taken Irish nationality) and one Scottish (John Purser).

New Music Superseded

Readers may be interested to hear that New Music has been superseded in Europe. THE SOCIETY FOR NEWER MUSIC was founded recently in Cologne by three composers: Gerald Barry, Christopher Newman and Kevin Volans, and has published the following introduction and manifesto:

'The term "New Music" has been in popular use now for thirty years, and has come to denote an historical style, rather than serve as a description of a characteristic of the music: the adjective "new" has little meaning when applied equally to, say, the music of the early fifties as well as the eighties.

'Our recent work bears no relation aesthetically and stylistically to most of what is termed New Music. Another description of our music is therefore called for in order not only to set it apart from New Music, but also to point to the optimism with which we view it.

'We sought a name which did not contain any reference to style, technique or aesthetic, but which places the music in historic sequence. The name Newer Music seemed appropriate. In order to mark the occasion of our adopting this name, we decided to found an informal society and to set down a brief account of our aims. Thus began

THE SOCIETY FOR NEWER MUSIC
(SNERM)

First meeting held 25 June, 1981, Wallräf-Richartz Museum, Cologne.

'The main aim of the society is to promote work and activity possessing an understanding and knowledge of artistic freedom. Such work would manifest itself in a diversity of media and forms. Such work would not necessarily be bounded by any particular historical style. Such work would be distinguished by a certain recklessness, the consequence of true integrity. Such work would therefore be personal, would not excuse itself, would abhor security. Such work would necessitate a direct view of the world, stripped of sophistication, and rooted in a sense of wonder. Clearly, such work could draw freely from all available sources. The Society applauds diversity, quality and imagination. Such work is, in effect, indefinable.'

A week of Newer Music will be held in January at the Theater am Turm in Frankfurt. To mark the occasion, a book will be published containing articles and scores by the composers involved.

Left (detail on right): The New Irish Recording Company advertised its arrival in *Gramophone* in October 1972. All the records were welcomed by the magazine's reviewers. Felix Aprahamian wrote of Charles Lynch's record of works by Fleischmann, Victory, Wilson, Boydell and Bodley that 'This record comes as a timely reminder that London is not the only capital city within the British Isles where new native music, ranging from the conservative to the speculative, may be heard; and anyone with a particular interest in new piano music other than that of the "way-out" variety should find it interesting enough to buy.' Max Harrison wrote of Kinsella's Quartet, 'Perhaps his is not a remarkably individual musical personality, but I should like to hear more from him.' Trevor Harvey described Victory's *Miroirs* as 'a piece that whets the appetite for further acquaintance with Victory's music'. And Stanley Webb called Gerard Gillen 'a refreshing newcomer to organ recording'.

Paradoxically, the underdevelopment of the contemporary music scene had its advantages for senior composers. Partly because there were so few of them active, they were used to having their large-scale work taken up by the RTÉ Symphony Orchestra and a significant proportion of works received repeat performances. It was doubtless a great help that one of these composers, Gerard Victory (1921–95) was the Director of Music at RTÉ from 1967–82 while another, John Kinsella (b. 1932), was a senior assistant and later Head of Music after Victory's retirement.

Irish composition was, however, almost completely unknown outside of this island, one of the stumbling blocks being the complete lack of the necessary infrastructure for the dissemination of contemporary music. There was no publication house in Ireland that would take on Irish composers' work, and those who tried to find publishers abroad almost invariably met with a lack of success. Throughout this period composers were lucky if they got a publishing house interested in a single piece or a particular genre, as for example happened with James Wilson (1922–2005), who secured publication for his Accordion Quintet (1967) and Accordion Studies (1969), and Gerard Victory, who managed to get some of his wind band and orchestral music published. Gerald Barry (b. 1952) was the first composer to buck the trend when his work was taken on by Oxford University Press in 1985.

If composers wished to try to interest performers, publishers or institutions abroad in their music they would have to either send their original score or cover the high costs of having copies of the score made; until the advent of a fund from the Performing Right Society, costs for making copies beyond the premiere had to be borne by the composer. Scores performed by RTÉ were held by their library and had to be obtained on loan if they were to be sent abroad. There was also a cost involved in obtaining copies of a recording of any performance that RTÉ might have, while the recording of pieces played in other contexts presented logistical problems of sourcing appropriate equipment.

Commercially available recordings could have been a potentially effective means of gaining a new audience and attracting the interest of performers at home and abroad, but here again Irish composers were at a disadvantage. A major advance on this front seemed at first to have been made at the beginning of the 1970s with the formation of the New Irish Recording Company,

Music Diary

January 1971

RTE Symphony Orchestra

8 Friday 8 pm
Studio Concert*
St. Francis Xavier Hall, Dublin
György Ligeti: Lontano
Bruno Maderna: Oboe Concerto No. 2
Seoirse Bodley: Yeats' Song Cycle, 'Never to have lived is best'
Igor Stravinsky: Rite of Spring
Veronica Dunne, soprano
Lothar Faber, oboe
Pierre-Michel Le Conte, conductor

12 Tuesday 8 pm
Studio Concert*
St. Francis Xavier Hall, Dublin
Penderecki: Threnody for the victims of Hiroshima
John Kinsella: Montage II
Ole Schmidt: Fantasy and Allegro
Shostakovitch: Symphony No. 10
Mogens Ellegaard, accordion
Proinnsias O Duinn, conductor

Presented for the Dublin Festival of Twentieth Century Music.

17 Sunday 8 pm
Public Concert
Gaiety Theatre, Dublin
Proinnsias O Duinn: Symphony No. 1
Shostakovitch: Cello Concerto No. 1.
Mahler: Symphony No. 1 in D.
Erling Bløndal Bengtsson, cello
Proinnsias O Duinn, conductor

18 Monday 8 pm
Public Concert
City Hall, Cork
Programme as on 17th

24 Sunday 8 pm
Public Concert
Gaiety Theatre, Dublin
Schumann: Overture, Manfred
Tchaikowsky: Violin Concerto in D
Debussy: Prelude à l'après midi d'un Faune
Debussy: La Mer
Igor Ozim, violin
Eimear O Broin, conductor

26 Tuesday 10.30 and 2.30
Schools Concerts
St. Francis Xavier Hall, Dublin
Organised by Ceol Chumann na nOg
Douglas: Meet the Orchestra
Haydn: Slow movement from Surprise Symphony
arr. James Bolger: Three Irish Dance tunes
Gounod: Faust Ballet music
Sibelius: Overture Finlandia
Colman Pearce, conductor

31 Sunday 8 pm
Public Concert
Gaiety Theatre, Dublin
Buxtehude-Chavez: Chaconne
Jean Martinon: Irish Symphony
César Franck: Symphonic Variations
Schumann: Symphony No. 4 in D minor
Gabriel Tacchino, piano
Jean Martinon, conductor

RTE

Tickets for Public Concerts from RTE Ticket Unit, McCullough Pigott, 11/13 Suffolk St., Dublin 1.

Tickets for Studio Concerts are obtainable free of charge, from Reception Desk, RTE, Henry Street, Dublin 1.
Postal applications *must* be accompanied by a stamped addressed envelope.

Programmes are subject to alteration.

Above: The *RTÉ Music Diary* for January 1971.

Opposite: The state opening of the National Concert Hall on 9 September 1981 featured the RTÉSO under Colman Pearce, with (left to right) Aindréas Ó Gallchóir (speaker), Violet Twomey (soprano), Bernadette Greevy (mezzo soprano), Louis Browne (tenor) and William Young (bass-baritone). The main choirs in the balcony are Our Lady's Choral Society and the RTÉ Chorus, with the Choristers of St Patrick's Cathedral (right) and the RTÉ Singers (left).

which issued recordings of string quartets by Victory and Kinsella, orchestral music by Victory, Seóirse Bodley (b. 1933) and Arthur Duff (1899–1956), and an LP of piano music by Bodley, Victory, Wilson, Brian Boydell (1917–2000) and Aloys Fleischmann (1910–92). However, the company was dissolved before other recordings could be released, although some further pieces such as Bodley's First String Quartet (1968) had already been recorded. Another venture in 1985 resulted in three cassettes of chamber music by Bodley, Kinsella, Wilson, John Buckley (b. 1951), Raymond Deane (b. 1953) and John Gibson (b. 1951).

Throughout the 1970s the main Dublin performance venue for the RTÉ Symphony Orchestra was the St Francis Xavier Hall in Upper Sherrard Street, one of several inadequate stopgap solutions to the problems posed by a city with no suitable concert venue. A 1964 government decision to build a new hall, designated as a memorial to the U.S. President John F. Kennedy, was debated and postponed for a decade. In 1974, the Fine Gael–Labour coalition government decided to abandon the idea of a purpose-built hall in favour of converting the pre-existing Great Hall on University College Dublin's Earlsfort Terrace site.

Overleaf: In January 1964 the government announced that Ireland's state memorial to the assassinated U.S. President, John F. Kennedy, would be a concert hall built in Dublin and carrying the president's name. The decision was made on the advice of the Arts Council. The hall was designed by Raymond McGrath, principal architect of the Board of Works, but no definitive site was ever chosen before the project was killed off.

The National Concert Hall opened in 1981 with a gala concert featuring Seóirse Bodley's specially commissioned *Ceol*: Symphony No. 3, a work which included audience participation. The venue quickly became the primary home for classical music despite the extreme limitations of its stage in 1981 (since enlarged), an auditorium size that made it more difficult to cover the cost of visits by expensive international performers, its problematic acoustic and lack of suitable space for chamber music events. The existence of the hall was a major benefit to the RTÉSO, but the more adventurous programming associated with the free concerts in the St Francis Xavier Hall was abandoned by administrators who felt a more cautious approach was necessary now that all concerts had an admission price. This was to impact not just on Irish contemporary composers but also reduce audiences' exposure to the latest music from abroad.

The lack of direct contact with what was happening in contemporary music around the world had been a key element shaping how music had developed in Ireland over the course of the twentieth century. Irish composition in the

Raymond McGrath '67

JOHN F. KENNEDY MEMORIAL HALL

Ussy
2.5.73

Dear Mr Barry
You have my per-
mission to use the
text of <u>Lessness</u> in
performances &
broadcasts of this work
as set to music by you.
You will also require
the authorisation of
Calder & Boyars. I
have written asking them
to attend to the matter.
Yours sincerely
SB.

MS

2a

74 Old Cabra rd.,
Phibsboro,
Dublin 7.
April 26th '73.

Dear Mr. Beckett,

Thank you so much for your letter concerning the copyright fees for the first performance of "Lessness". It was an overwhelming success. I am sorry to have to bother you again, but there is a problem about the copyright. I wrote to the publishers Calder and Boyars in connection with the drawing up of an

Opposite: A letter from Gerald Barry to Samuel Beckett about the use of the writer's *Lessness* in a work for contralto and orchestra. Beckett's reply, written on Barry's original letter, grants the permissions requested. *Lessness* had three performances in Dublin before the composer withdrew the work.

first half of the century could be described essentially as a close relation of the English compositional school. Many Irish composers looked to English examples for inspiration and the Irish musical establishment demonstrated a similar detachment from the radical European avant-garde. Bartók, Sibelius and Hindemith were for many the epitome of modernism.

In the 1960s there had been a belated engagement with some of the ideas of European modernity, most notably in the serial pieces composed by Seóirse Bodley. However there was always a sense of the most 'advanced' Irish composers being at least ten years behind their European counterparts, with the majority lagging some considerable distance behind that. The most important blow dealt against Irish conservative insularity was provided by the Dublin Festival of 20th Century Music, which ran between 1969 and 1986. This was an international festival which at its peak provided audiences (and Irish composers) with a musical experience which has not been replicated by any organisation in the Republic since. It confronted Irish composers with the very latest music from other countries and exposed their own music to critics and musicians from abroad.

The festival was however not entirely devoted to the promulgation of the avant-garde or the contemporary. Indeed, the first festival began somewhat unpromisingly with an open forum at which the chair, Brian Boydell, proposed the motion that contemporary music was 'further removed from the understanding of the ordinary listener than ever before,' while the programme included composers such as Rawsthorne, Martinů, Kodály and Hindemith alongside more modernist works. Among the latter was a concert devoted to LPs of electronic music by Stockhausen, Berio and others. Electro-acoustic music had not received any serious attention from Irish composers at this point, and it was only in 1971 with Roger Doyle's (b. 1949) first tape pieces *Obstinato* (1970) and *Why is Kilkenny so Good?* (1970, rev 1974) that a real engagement with new technology occurred. The festival also included a lunchtime concert of pieces by young composers, including Derek Ball (b. 1949), Philip Martin (b. 1947), Eric Sweeney (b. 1948), and the fifteen-year-old Raymond Deane. This eclectic approach to programming was probably due to the mixed aesthetic outlooks of those involved in its organisation, and it continued to be a feature of later festivals. But it was the increased inclusion of contemporary works by foreign composers that was to have the greatest impact on reducing the time-lag between compositional developments abroad and what Irish composers were doing.

Just as performances of Messiaen's early music by Jean Martinon with the Radio Éireann Symphony Orchestra in the late 1940s had profoundly influenced composers such as the now reactionary Boydell, the appearances at the festival of composers such as Peter Maxwell Davies (1934–2016) in 1974, Olivier Messiaen (1908–92) in 1976, Witold Lutosławski (1913–94) in 1978, Elliott Carter (1908–2012) in 1980, Karlheinz Stockhausen (1928–2007) in 1982 and Mauricio Kagel (1931–2008) in 1984 fed into the work of Irish composers.

James Wilson for example, whose new opera *Twelfth Night* had been premiered by Irish National Opera during the Wexford Festival in 1969, found himself completely re-evaluating how one could approach writing stage works after witnessing the performance of Maxwell Davies's *Eight Songs for a Mad King* conducted by Seóirse Bodley in the 1974 festival. This work and also *Miss Donnithorne's Maggot,* performed by the Fires of London under the composer in 1978, fed into his ideas for stage works composed in the 1980s.

John Buckley first appeared as composer of his Cor Anglais Sonata (1973) in the 1974 festival, which began with a performance of Lutosławski's Second Symphony. This work demonstrates Lutosławski's limited use of aleatoric writing; all pitches are carefully notated, but the exact rhythmic alignment in certain sections of the work is left to the performers, with the conductor indicating the beginning and end of sections. The impact of Lutosławski's music on Buckley can be clearly heard in his 1977 four-movement composition *Taller Than Roman Spears*. The third movement (*Bealtaine*) (the Irish for May) contains a central aleatoric section in which eight groups of instrumentalists overlap with each other, the conductor indicating the point at which each group enters and ceases. Lutosławski appeared in person at the 1978 festival, which included performances of *Mi-Parti* and the Cello Concerto. Buckley was to study his music more formally in ensuing years influencing not only his use of aleatoric techniques in the 1980s, but also his approach to harmony and orchestration.

The inclusion in the festival of a concert of music by young composers gave some of these composers the idea of hosting a concert of their own outside the auspices of the festival. The success of this venture led a group of them—

Opposite: John Buckley was the first of the generation of Irish composers born around 1950 to win official recognition. He was commissioned by the Department of the Taoiseach in 1979 to write music for the Irish Ballet Company as part of the Pearse Centenary celebrations, and shortly thereafter commissioned by the Cork International Choral Festival and the New Irish Chamber Orchestra. He is the Irish composer who has taken the most interest in the display of orchestral virtuosity, an interest which is fully displayed in his Organ Concerto of 1992.

Raymond Deane, Gerald Barry, Brian Beckett (b. 1950), Derek Ball and John Gibson—to form the Association of Young Irish Composers in 1972 in order to promote their work and find new performance opportunities. In this context it is not surprising that when young composers felt similarly excluded from opportunities at the beginning of the twenty-first century, composer David Flynn used the AYIC as inspiration to form the Irish Composers' Collective (originally called the Young Composers' Collective).

While it is clear that there was a definite differentiation in the early 20th Century Festivals between the young composers, slotted into a lunchtime or afternoon space, and the senior composers, who were featured in evening concerts and whose works were given to distinguished visiting performers,

the situation for young composers in the early 1970s was in fact better than it would be by the late 1980s.

The Dublin Symphony Orchestra, an amateur orchestra founded in 1967, had instigated a Young Irish Composers' Competition. Derek Ball won the 1970 prize for his *Four Chimerae*, which was premiered by the DSO in 1970, and performed by the RTÉSO under Colin Block in 1971. Roger Doyle won second prize for his Four Sketches for Orchestra which the DSO performed in 1971, followed by an RTÉSO performance in 1973. In 1972 the prizes were given to Gerald Barry's *Lessness*, Raymond Deane's *Sphinxes* and Derek Ball's *Wormwood*. *Lessness* and *Sphinxes* were then performed on two occasions each by the RTÉSO in the ensuing years, while the list of performances of Irish composers for the period 1969–78 given in Richard Pine's *Music and Broadcasting in Ireland* demonstrates that they also performed works by John Buckley, John Gibson and Eric Sweeney, all of whom were in their twenties. By contrast, the list for 1979–88 contains no composers in their twenties. There was substantial press coverage for the AYIC, with articles about their formation as well as reviews of their concerts. Indeed, *The Irish Times*'s critic Charles Acton (1914–99), who disapproved of their initiative in forming a new organisation and ignoring the Music Association of Ireland, commented in 1974 'At times lately I have felt that young composers are having more opportunities and exposure than their output merits.'

Like Bodley before them, many of these young composers spent time abroad studying composition. Raymond Deane signed up for studies with Gerald Bennett (b. 1942) and Isang Yun (1917–95) and briefly Karlheinz Stockhausen. Gerald Barry studied with Peter Schat (1935–2003), Stockhausen and Mauricio Kagel. Frank Corcoran (b. 1944) studied with Boris Blacher (1903–75). Jerome de Bromhead (b. 1945) and John Buckley took advantage of international summer schools in composition with de Bromhead taking a course with Franco Donatoni (1927–2000) and Buckley attending one run by John Cage (1912–92) and Merce Cunningham (1919–2009). Buckley also spent a more protracted period studying with Alun Hoddinott (1929–2008). Apart from the desire to encounter new musical horizons this also reflects the severely limited opportunities to study composition within Ireland at this time.

In 1983 Buckley founded the Ennis Composition Summer School (now the Irish Composition Summer School), an annual venture which he continued to

Previous pages: A scene from Anne Makower's RTÉ television production of James Wilson's opera *Letters to Theo*, subtitled 'The Life of Vincent van Gogh in his own Words'. It was filmed in November 1986 with John Cashmore, right, in the role of the painter.

run throughout this period with the assistance of his former teacher James Wilson. As the course became more established, visiting composers were invited as tutors, at first mainly Irish composers and then increasingly composers from abroad. The school became an important centre for aspiring composers; those who attended over the years included Rhona Clarke (b. 1958), Stephen Gardner (b. 1958), Marian Ingoldsby (b. 1965), Gráinne Mulvey (b. 1966), Elaine Agnew (b. 1967) and Siobhán Cleary (b. 1970).

In contrast with the frequently self-taught and sometimes amateur efforts to grapple with modernity in Ireland in earlier years, several of the generation of the 1970s experienced high modernism from the inside. Unlike the previous generation, which was trying hard to catch up with what had happened in Europe some time before, this was a generation which was conscious that the days of heroic modernism were over. New movements had sprung up; minimalism, new simplicity, new complexity and various other isms, which were eventually bundled under the all-encompassing title of postmodernism. Composers were not just influenced by the latest developments in composition but also by such things as the performance techniques being used by the emerging early music movement. Simple dichotomies between tonality and atonality were no longer seen as tenable by many.

Sometimes compositional decisions were of course dictated by more practical considerations. With no dedicated new music ensemble in Ireland and limited experience for most musicians in the performance of more avant-garde works, a composer like Raymond Deane felt it was necessary in his early chamber works to write in a style that would not present insurmountable problems for performers unaccustomed to contemporary music. The simplicity of the material in a work like *Embers* (1973) resulted in music with a type of structural focus that was to be the foundation of Deane's music from the 1990s onwards. His music from the 1980s by contrast tends to contain a greater proliferation of material and overall complexity, as well as a more systematic use of techniques derived from serialism. An exception to this is the First String Quartet (*Silhouettes*) (1981), which was written as a relaxation from the composition of *Enchaînement* (1981–82), a large-scale work for an orchestra of Mahlerian proportions.

The engagement with new ideas from abroad was not something that sent all composers in the same direction. During the 1970s Bodley undertook a

journey from being the most avant-garde of Irish composers to rejecting modernism in favour of a neo-romantic language tinged with stylised elements of Irish traditional music. The first indication of this departure was to be heard in his 1972 composition *The Narrow Road to the Deep North*, originally scored for two pianos and later rearranged for solo piano.

The original inspiration for the work came from an encounter with Bernd Alois Zimmermann's *Monologe* for two pianos (1964), which collides quotations of Bach and other composers with highly dissonant material. Bodley's work juxtaposes atonal blocks of material with tonal blocks and ideas inspired by *sean-nós* music. There is no overt integration of these different elements. This idea was explored further in his orchestral work *A Small White Cloud Drifts Over Ireland* (1975), premiered at the 1976 Dublin Festival. Again the work features the juxtaposition of fragments of different material including stylised gestures from Irish traditional music, though the more dissonant material of *The Narrow Road* has been omitted.

Opposite: Dmitri Shostakovich, the greatest composer of the Soviet Union, visited Ireland just once, to receive an honorary Mus. D from Trinity College Dublin in 1972. He attended a concert at St Patrick's Cathedral in which the Irish Chamber Orchestra played his Chamber Symphony under André Prieur, and he and his wife visited the home of fellow composer Brian Boydell, where this photograph was taken. Pictured, left to right, are Barra Boydell, Irina Antonovna Shostakovich, Mir Filatov (USSR Embassy, London), Cormac Boydell, Ron Hill (Department of Russian, TCD), Dmitri Shostakovich, Jacqueline Hill, Brian Boydell and Mary Boydell.

The highly positive critical reaction in retrospect seems to have been motivated more by misguided obsessions with the nature of some of Bartók's less challenging works and the erroneous belief that Ó Riada's compositions had achieved a synthesis of modernism and traditional music that was in some way different from the *Irish* Rhapsodies of Stanford. What Bodley was initially trying to achieve—to find a way of escaping the regularity of the irregularity inherent in his serial compositions—was overlooked, as were the potentially more radical implications of a work like *The Narrow Road*. Bodley himself was to move away from these implications in the works which followed in the 1970s and 1980s. Pieces such as the song cycle *A Girl* (1976) and the avowedly 'postmodern' Second Symphony (*I have loved the lands of Ireland*) (1980) embraced a more conservative neo-romantic sound-world.

Bodley had consolidated his position as one of the senior figures in Irish music during this time. He was chair of the Dublin Festival of 20th Century Music until 1980, and when the government set up Aosdána, an academy for creative artists, in 1981, he was selected as one of the founding members. The other composers selected were Aloys Fleischmann (1910–92), Frederick May (1911–85), Gerard Victory, James Wilson, John Kinsella, Frank Corcoran and Jane O'Leary (b. 1946). Of these Fleischmann and May represented the first generation of twentieth-century composers along with Brian Boydell who, as one of the selectors, was not eligible to join immediately; he became a member in 1984.

May had ceased to compose decades previously and Boydell had also greatly reduced his compositional output, with many of his post-1970 works being occasional music. The significant exception is his orchestral work *Masai Mara* (1988), an evocation of the eponymous national park in Kenya. It is also a work intended to convey an ecological message, Boydell's interest in ecological matters being somewhat ahead of their more widespread acceptance in Ireland—the Green Party first won a seat in the Dáil in 1989. Fleischmann was the most active of these three composers completing a number of substantial works in the 1970s and 1980s including the second movement of his *Sinfonia Votiva* (1977), his ballet *The Táin* (1981) and *Song Cycle from 'Tides'* (1973). While Fleischmann divested his voice of the romantic elements noticeable in early works such as his Piano Quintet (1938) in favour of a sparer style, he did not embrace the new techniques emanating from Europe.

Opposite: The RTÉSO and Albert Rosen on the stage of the Gaiety Theatre in 1975. Orchestral concerts completely disappeared from this acoustically dry and physically cramped venue after the opening of the National Concert Hall in 1981.

The youngest founding members of Aosdána were allied to a more modernist stance in 1981. Frank Corcoran was, like Buckley, influenced by Lutosławski and György Ligeti (1923–2006), as well as being interested in the idea of ancient Celtic Ireland. However, the application of these ideas is very different from what is found in Buckley's music. His aleatoric macro-counterpoint, first demonstrated in his Piano Trio of 1978, consists of independent lines using different time signatures and tempo markings superimposed on each other, resulting in unpredictable vertical (harmonic) combinations. From 1980 onwards he lived in Germany and was appointed as lecturer at the Staatliche Hochschule für Musik und Darstellende Kunst in Hamburg in 1983.

Jane O'Leary was born in the United States and had studied with Milton Babbitt (1916–2011) at Princeton University before relocating to Galway in 1972. She found the musical scene in Ireland somewhat behind the times but also felt a certain hostility to her music and to her personally as an outsider. However, this potentially damaging atmosphere only encouraged her to become more involved in the dissemination of contemporary music by Irish and international composers, and in 1976 she founded the new music ensemble Concorde. Based around a core group of voice, flute, clarinet, violin, cello, piano, and adding other performers to the group as required, the ensemble has commissioned and given repeat performances of works by most significant Irish composers. O'Leary's own music was to undergo a transformation in the early 1980s, moving away from the more rigorously serial work of her early instrumental pieces to a more intuitive approach to structure with a greater emphasis on sonority.

The middle generation, in which one can group Victory, Wilson and Kinsella, had a more problematic relationship with the challenge posed by Bodley's modernist phase and the increased exposure to modern music from abroad. Each of these composers felt the need to accommodate some of the technical procedures of European modernism such as serialism even if they themselves were not entirely sympathetic to atonal let alone serial writing. Most of these composers claimed to use a 'freer' form of serialism, or in other words one that could accommodate overt tonal references, usually citing Berg as the inspiration for this approach.

Kinsella's Third String Quartet (1979) is a notable example of a piece which claims its origin in the exploration of the intervals of a twelve-note row

Above: Composer Gerard Victory, RTÉ's Director of Music (left) with Austrian conductor Albert Rosen, principal conductor of the RTÉSO, in the departure lounge at Dublin Airport, waiting to catch a flight to Edinburgh for the start of the orchestra's three-week, thirteen-concert European tourof 1980.

in a 'free' version of serialism, yet the resultant piece sounds like it could have been composed in the 1920s. It is not surprising therefore that in the 1980s Kinsella was to follow Bodley in abandoning a modernist stance in favour of a more neo-romantic language. The shift also signalled the enthusiastic embrace of the symphonic form with Kinsella composing eleven symphonies in the ensuing years. The younger Eric Sweeney was to follow a similar path, moving from serially composed works in the 1970s and 1980s, such as the string orchestra work *Circles* (1985), to a new language forged from a combination of influences from American minimalism and Irish traditional music. He later commented of his earlier work that 'I didn't really believe in it, so I can't imagine why anyone else would believe in it!'

Victory and Wilson both similarly incorporated serial elements into their compositions, but in their huge outputs such pieces sit alongside works composed in a more deliberately 'light' style. A. J. Potter (1918–80) was another figure whose output was similarly varied. All three composers also devoted time to the composition of operas despite an almost complete lack of opportunities for performance in Ireland. The main Irish opera company of the time, the Dublin Grand Opera Society (1941–2010), mounted just a single short work by an Irish composer, Victory's *The Music Hath Mischief* (1960), which was performed in 1968. To this day, despite hefty Arts Council funding, Wexford Festival Opera disdains to perform the work of living Irish composers, preferring to showcase minor contemporary American composers. Only Irish National Opera, founded in 1964, a company which specialised in touring small-scale productions of opera around Ireland, generally just with piano accompaniment, was willing to engage with Irish composers, mounting productions of Wilson's *Twelfth Night* (1969) in 1969 and 1970 and Potter's *The Wedding* (1979) in 1981. Irish National Opera ceased to be funded by the Arts Council in 1985 as the Council began to reorganise and 'professionalise' elements of the Irish music infrastructure. Victory and Wilson found that they had to rely on either ad hoc performances in Ireland, frequently in less than adequate circumstances, or performances abroad.

The operas of these composers are all quite conventional in form and content. By contrast, Gerald Barry's *The Intelligence Park*, which he worked on through the 1980s, left its first audiences in 1990 as puzzled as they were exhilarated by the high-voltage music, with Paul Griffiths commenting in *The Times* of the premiere by Almeida Opera in London, 'Never mind what the piece is about: it just quite shockingly is [...] The gestation has been long—almost ten years—but the child can be pronounced in rude good health, even if it looks like nothing one has ever seen.'

Barry had already demonstrated his theatrical flair in *Things that Gain by Being Painted* (1977), premiered at the 1980 Dublin festival. This was allied to a musical language which, as Raymond Deane noted, seems untouched by the nineteenth century. The opening of the opera, which forms the basis of the orchestral piece *From The Intelligence Park* (1986), had its inspiration in the idea of 'a provincial Italian opera band, blasting forth from the pit' and demonstrates key facets of Barry's style at this point: parts moving in rhythmic unison, unexpected lengthy silences, abrupt switches from one block of material to another and a strong emphasis on melodic line.

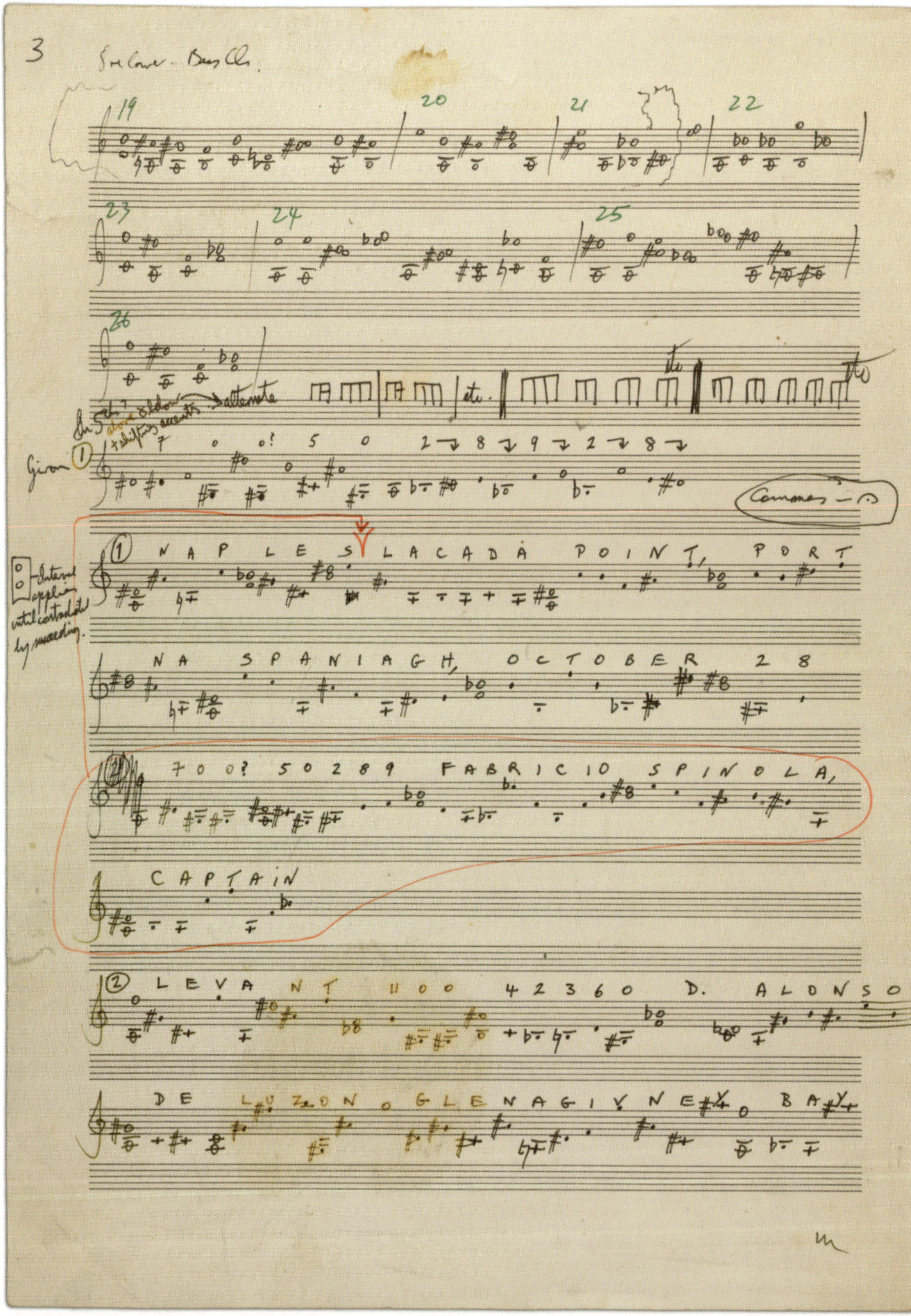
3
19
20
21
22
23
24
25
26
etc.
alternate
Giron
NAPLES LACADA POINT, PORT
NA SPANIAGH, OCTOBER 28
700? 50289 FABRICIO SPINOLA,
CAPTAIN
LEVANT 1100 42360 D. ALONSO
DE LUZON GLENAGIVNEY BAY

Opposite: In 1988 Gerald Barry became the first modern Irish composer to be commissioned by the BBC's Henry Wood Promenade concerts in London. He was asked to write a piece for the Ulster Orchestra celebrating the quatercentenary of the defeat of the Spanish Armada. As an Irishman from Co. Clare, he demurred from the celebration but kept the commission. The title of the work, *Chevaux-de-frise*, literally Frisian horses, is the name of a medieval anti-cavalry defence of stakes or spiked objects. There's an example outside the Dun Aengus Fort on the Aran Islands. The sketch, opposite, shows how Barry generated pitch material for the piece using names and locations associated with Armada shipwrecks off the Irish Coast taken from Niall Fallon's *The Armada in Ireland*.

The pianist in the premiere of *Things that Gain by Being Painted* was the South African-born Kevin Volans (b. 1949) who was to relocate to Ireland in 1986, later taking Irish citizenship. Like Barry he had studied with Stockhausen and Kagel and had reacted against the dogmatic aspect of the New Music movement in Cologne. With Barry and the English composer Chris Newman he founded a Society for Newer Music (SNerM), whose only output was a manifesto calling for a music that would be free to draw on all available sources. During the 1980s Volans's own music was centred on a project to Africanise Western art music, at first by transcription and then by more elaborate incorporation of elements of African music (structure, patterning and gesture) into his own musical language. *White Man Sleeps* (1982; version for string quartet 1986) represents the earlier stages of this project, which for Volans was not just a rediscovery of the country from which he came but also a political gesture in protest against the apartheid state.

Volans was composer in residence at Queen's University Belfast from 1986 to 1989. At this time several new voices were emerging from the North including Kevin O'Connell (b. 1958), who first came to prominence when he won the composition section of RTÉ's Young Musician of the Future competition in 1982, and Michael Alcorn (b. 1962), whose first electro-acoustic work, *Hanging Stones,* was composed in 1985. The Sonorities Festival, founded in 1981, was initially held every second year, and mostly curated by the resident composer at Queen's. It provided focused programmes of new music, notably Volans's festival of American experimental music in 1989.

In the Republic the landscape for composers was changing again, and not entirely for the better. By the mid 1970s the AYIC had become the Association of Irish Composers embracing composers of all generations. In an attempt to tackle the lack of publication opportunities they had begun a project of producing basic mass copies of select compositions. In 1983 these ideas were expanded with the formation of the Irish Composers' Centre, which was set up as a limited company with James Wilson and Bernard Harrison as its first directors. It was intended to act as an archive for scores and recordings of Irish composers' music.

In 1985 the Arts Council decided to cut funding to the Irish Composers' Centre and founded in its place a Contemporary Music Centre (CMC). It was envisaged that the centre's remit would include the promotion of both

Above: The Vanbrugh String Quartet (pictured here at Russborough House, Blessington, Co. Wicklow, with its original membership, Gregory Ellis, Elizabeth Charleson, Simon Aspell, Christopher Marwood in 1989) was RTÉ's quartet in residence from 1986 to 2013. The Vanbrugh have been consistent advocates of Irish composers on disc—beginning with a recording of works by Walter Beckett, Brian Boydell, John Kinsella and Ian Wilson for Chandos in 1994—and in concert, particularly through their work at the West Cork Chamber Music Festival.

national and international contemporary music. In 1987 it hosted a new music weekend at the Project Arts Centre and arranged an exchange with Swedish composers, while other events hosted by CMC included performances by Singcircle of Stockhausen's *Stimmung* and music by Jonathan Harvey (1939–2012) and Frederic Rzewski (b. 1938). In the ensuing years, however, CMC narrowed its focus to concentrate solely on Irish contemporary music with an emphasis on the creation of a library, holding hard copies of scores of any Irish composer who had successfully applied for representation (though this sometimes meant excluding younger composers until they had met specific criteria) and a recording library supplemented by cassette copies of tapes from the RTÉ archive.

The decision to abstain from the promotion of international contemporary music when coupled with the sudden demise of the Dublin Festival in 1986 greatly reduced advocacy for the performance of international contemporary music. Irish composers had also lost an important international showcase for their music and the opportunity for contact with international performers. Composers were to find that once again people in positions of importance were succumbing to an increasingly provincial mindset. James Wilson noted privately to a colleague that his attempts to invite performers from abroad to perform Irish music were 'met with "We've got our own performers," which is great for preventing the popularising of Irish music abroad'. It seemed for a time that after a period of rapid infrastructural improvement and the emergence of an array of strikingly individual voices, a certain stagnation had set in as the 1980s came to a close.

The ethnic orchestra

PROINNSÍAS Ó DUINN

After spending some years abroad in both North and South America it was interesting to return to Ireland in the early 1970s. The home of the RTÉ Symphony Orchestra was the St Francis Xavier Hall in Upper Sherrard Street. The orchestra gave regular weekly concerts there, with seasons of special Prom concerts in the Gaiety Theatre. The acoustics of both venues were challenging, and the facilities cramped. On the plus side, the music department in RTÉ was able to schedule a wide range of repertoire for its regular Friday concerts. These were free to the public and at the same time afforded invaluable experience to young Irish artists.

Two pages from Seóirse Bodley's *A Small White Cloud Drifts over Ireland* showing music for the strings composed in traditional Irish style set against avant-garde gestures from the brass.

The home of the RTÉ Light Orchestra was in a badly ventilated space over the toilets of the CIE Club in O'Connell Street until it moved to the studios in the new Radio Centre in Montrose in 1971. With very few exceptions the orchestra spent its time recording for radio programmes. Again, the setup afforded young Irish artists the opportunity to gain experience of performing with an orchestra. The orchestra itself, however, seldom appeared in public. My first priority after being appointed its principal conductor in 1978 was to change this. There was a change of name, to the RTÉ Concert Orchestra, and it took a sixty-three concert, seventy-five-day tour of the USA to prove to both orchestra and authorities in RTÉ that the Concert Orchestra was indeed a valuable artistic entity and should be performing live to audiences.

The RTÉ Singers, ten in number, which I conducted from 1974 to

1978, were based in the Portobello Studios but were disbanded within a decade. The RTÉ Symphony Orchestra moved base from the St Francis Xavier Hall to its new home in the National Concert Hall in 1981.

My first reconnect with these groups was a Prom concert in the Gaiety and a Dublin Festival of 20th Century Music concert in St Francis Xavier Hall with the Symphony Orchestra, two radio recordings with the Light Orchestra and a recording with the Singers in Portobello—all within two weeks. Whereas all of the groups performed with enthusiasm, all of them were understaffed for purpose when compared with international norms and did not always have the ideal mix of tone colours within sections.

Audiences today have become familiar with concerts in which traditional musicians share the stage with professional orchestras. It may be difficult for some of today's listeners to realise the impact in the mid 1970s of Seóirse Bodley's (b. 1933) *A Small White Cloud Drifts over Ireland* (1975). Bodley didn't bring traditional musicians into the orchestra, but incorporated the idiom and accent of traditional music in a way that simply bypassed the conventions of traditional arranging techniques.

He was up to date with the newest developments and writing techniques—the use of 'duration of sound' rather than 'beaten bar lengths', for example—and he had his own clear voice in his creative writing. Orchestras and conductors had become accustomed to interpreting novel techniques, personal codes and footnotes used by contemporary composers. Deliberately setting out to ask classically trained orchestral musicians to imitate in a large ensemble the sounds and style of a particular ethnic traditional music and musicians is a different matter, and was new in this country at the time.

The subtle question of style in the medium is also something that is difficult for the composer to indicate in the printed score. The sounds made by our traditional fiddle players is achieved with a peculiar hold of the instrument and bow along with a unique view of note values, rhythms and rubato. Bodley had to rely on the performer interpreting the printed note values and performing them with the knowledge and insight of the intended style. 'Do you read music or are you talented?' is a quip I heard from a trad player around that time. It just about summed up the two schools. There were a number of Irish musicians in the RTÉSO who were fully aware of traditional Irish music, but it did take more verbal clarification at rehearsal than usual.

A Small White Cloud was an early example of the marriage of traditional shapes and colours mixed in a symphonic structure. Bodley writes always with an understanding of his forces. Unfortunately, it was never the policy in RTÉ to allow for immediate repeat performances that would enable both the musicians and the audience become truly familiar and relaxed with new compositions.

Others, like Aloys Fleischmann (1910–92), had worked in the field of marrying traditional and classical instruments. But the real breakthrough in featuring traditional players—who could not necessarily read music—with complex ensembles involving detailed and specific structures, came later. It was the introduction of computer-generated material on tapes and CDs that allowed traditional players learn the music by ear while hearing the orchestral context in which they would find themselves in the actual performance. Composers like Bill Whelan (b. 1950) and Shaun Davey (b. 1948) capitalised on this. Meanwhile, the formal education of musicians in the colleges and academies incorporated the study of ethnic music into the content of their courses. The developments of the last four decades have not followed any path suggested by *A Small White Cloud*. In short, there's no other Irish piece for orchestra quite like it.

Elephants, giraffes, insects

DAVID HARRINGTON

I first encountered the music of Kevin Volans in 1984 when Kronos performed at the Darmstadt International Summer Course. Normally I find it difficult to attend concerts when I'm on tour, but for some reason this night was different. At that particular concert I fortunately heard the music of both Kaija Saariaho (b. 1952) and Kevin Volans (b. 1949) for the first time. Both composers have gone on to shape the music of Kronos in dramatic ways.

Kevin's compositions played that night in Darmstadt sounded unlike any other concert music I had heard before. I remember his music immediately immersing me into a sound world I had hoped for yet until then had never found. I've been a collector of distinctive musical experiences for as long as I can remember, and with the music of Kevin Volans it was clear that something was happening in the world of music that could give us new ways of thinking about life.

I introduced myself to Kevin and we began to talk about a new piece for Kronos. The way he spoke of music led me to conclude that he could make something beautiful for Kronos. Later that year the score and parts to *White Man Sleeps* arrived in San Francisco. In a certain way I think that African string quartet music began as a result of that encounter with Kevin Volans in Darmstadt.

Our first rehearsals of *White Man Sleeps*—especially of Dance #1, the first of the five dances/movements—had to be done at an extremely slow tempo. We had never played this kind of hocketing before, where each member of Kronos has to hold on for dear life to every other member, and respond naturally. For us ever to feel comfortable playing this music it needed to become second nature.

Slowly over many weeks *White Man Sleeps* began to emerge. Eventually we premiered the piece at the Cotati Cabaret, a nightclub just outside Petaluma, California. Not too long after that performance, Kevin heard us play it for the first time. I remember those early rehearsals with incredible happiness. The kinds of things Kevin said to us were unlike what any other composer had ever said to us before.

I recall thinking about the flexible arc of music Haydn set in motion at the Esterháza Palace with his string quartets. Now, in 1984, this young composer who grew up in South Africa and lived in Ireland was asking us to think about the gaits of elephants and giraffes, the sounds of insects—to actually create these sorts of images in his music. In Dance #5 there is a fantastic alteration of the sound because of a radical retuning of the viola and cello; what an unbelievable sound

Opposite: South African-born composer Kevin Volans moved to Europe in the 1970s and became associated with the *Neue Einfachheit* (New Simplicity) movement in Germany, where he studied and lived. He settled in Ireland in 1986, was composer in residence at Queen's University Belfast from 1986 to 1989, and took Irish citizenship in 1994. His breakthrough work was *White Man Sleeps*, originally written in unequal temperament for two harpsichords, viola da gamba and percussion, which became an international bestseller in the arrangement for the Kronos Quartet. He is also a fine pianist, and is pictured here at the piano in 1992.

is revealed almost magically. Our imaginations expanded; the world of our music grew. *White Man Sleeps* is the first piece in the musical mosaic that would, by 1992, become our *Pieces of Africa* album. *White Man Sleeps* occupies a unique place in the work of Kronos. In sound, feel, tonality and imagery, this piece announces a new place for concert music. Kevin Volans wrote three other distinctive works for Kronos: *Hunting : Gathering, The Songlines* and *Black Woman Rising*.

I will always be grateful to Kevin Volans for giving Kronos the extraordinary body of music that began with *White Man Sleeps.*

1990–2000

1990

The RTÉ Symphony Orchestra is expanded in size and renamed the National Symphony Orchestra, with George Hurst succeeding János Fürst as principal conductor.

Brian P. Kennedy's *Dreams and Responsibilities, The State and the Arts in Independent Ireland*, is published by the Arts Council.

1991

British organist Peter Hurford inaugurates the National Concert Hall's Kenneth Jones organ in a concert with the National Symphony Orchestra under Proinnsías Ó Duinn.

1992

John Buckley writes his Organ Concerto for the new instrument at the National Concert Hall.

1993

Labour TD Michael D. Higgins, who will be elected President of Ireland in 2011, becomes the first Minister for Arts, Culture and the Gaeltacht, the first minister for arts to be a full member of the cabinet.

The 1,000-seat University Concert Hall opens on the campus of the University of Limerick.

1994

Gerard Victory's 100-minute cantata, *Ultima Rerum*, is released on CD by Marco Polo as the start of an Irish Composer series, funded by RTÉ and the Arts Council.

1995

The Irish Chamber Orchestra relocates from Dublin to Limerick, and reforms as a group of contracted musicians.

1996

Axel Klein's *Die Musik Irlands im 20. Jahrhundert* is published by Georg Olms Verlag.

The West Cork Chamber Music Festival, with an active policy of commissioning new work from home and abroad, is held for the first time in Bantry.

The report of the ministerially appointed PIANO review group (Provisional and Institutional Arrangements Now for Orchestras and Ensembles) recommends that the National Symphony Orchestra 'should be established by law under an independent Board answerable directly to the Minister for Arts, Culture and the Gaeltacht.' The recommendation is not implemented.

1997

Composer Donnacha Dennehy, conductor, composer and pianist Andrew Synnott and clarinettist Michael Seaver found the Crash Ensemble.

The 2,234-seat Waterfront Hall opens in Belfast.

1998

Harry White's *The Keeper's Recital: Music and Cultural History in Ireland 1770–1970* is published by Cork University Press.

1999

The new national arts and music radio channel, RTÉ lyric fm, starts broadcasting on 1 May.

The Vogler Quartet from Berlin become Sligo's quartet in residence.

The first issue of *Classical Ireland* magazine is published by Lacethorn.

2000

David Fennessy's string quartet, *graft*, is shortlisted for the Gaudeamus Music Week prize in the Netherlands.

Jennifer Walshe wins the Kranichsteiner Musikpreis at the Internationale Ferienkurse für Neue Musik in Darmstadt.

RTÉ lyric fm holds a five-day Gerald Barry Festival, the national broadcaster's first extended concert celebration of the work of a living Irish composer.

In the time of the Celtic Tiger

MICHAEL DUNGAN

Gerald Barry in a photograph by the American philanthropist and photographer Betty Freeman, a great supporter of contemporary music. She commissioned Barry's piano piece *Le Vieux Sourd*.

The 1990s, the decade that gave birth to the Celtic Tiger economy, was when I first started interviewing Irish composers. Naturally I didn't like every composer's music equally, but every one of them—there was, honestly, no exception—was highly engaging and had illuminating things to say about music, opera, art, literature, performance and life. Knowing their views affected the way I heard their music. Oh, I know, in theory we are supposed to appreciate music on its own merits. But reality is different: things you know about a composer are likely to inform how you hear what they compose.

The 1990s was a good decade for the composition of Irish music, yet one composer stood out. Gerald Barry seemed then (as now) imbued with a particular authenticity which derives from what always struck me as an exceptional concordance between the sound of his music and any outward aspects of personality that he was ready to share with the public—his enthusiasms and opinions, his sense of the ridiculous, the breadth of his reading and other interests, his single-mindedness, his fresh take on things. You could, of course, have a composer who enjoyed exactly such a concordance but whose music was hard to listen to nonetheless. Not so with Barry. On its own his music has an immediate and distinctive appeal, but it's an appeal that grows further with any glimpse you catch into how truly the music reflects the man who wrote it.

A page from the typescript of Meredith Oakes's libretto for Gerald Barry's opera, *The Triumph of Beauty and Deceit*, with amendments by the librettist and changes and annotations by the composer. The work was commissioned by Channel 4 in the UK (the television production was directed by Donald Taylor Black) and is a reworking of Handel's last oratorio, *The Triumph of Time and Truth*. Although Channel 4's original vision was that the operas they commissioned should not be experienced other than as television, Barry's work was performed in concert a number of times, and made it to the stage in 2002.

••

Gerald Barry was born in Co. Clare in 1952. By his late twenties he had already attracted what would prove lasting and important attention, notably in London. It was there in 1979 that the earliest piece he now acknowledges—*Things that gain by being painted* (1977) for singer, speaker, piano and cello—made a positive impression. Oxford University Press signed him up in 1985, and the BBC commissioned a large orchestral piece for the 1988 Proms. This was the aggressive and relentlessly energetic *Chevaux-de-frise*, described in the Proms programme as 'a belligerent toccata'. Infamously, in the silence before the applause at the premiere, someone shouted, 'Rubbish!'

The shouter must have represented a minority view: the piece received an enthusiastic welcome and caused a stir. At first *Chevaux-de-frise* even seems to derail its own expectations, opening with an angry plodding tread in the brass and then suddenly giving way to jaunty strings. Phrases repeat until abruptly abandoned, and it can all seem rather random—a wilful, or perhaps mischievous evasion of expectation—until a pattern emerges of notch-by-notch jumps of increasing energy-levels, as though a cartoon mad professor is slowly advancing the dial on his evil machine. Features like these were about to come to even greater prominence in a project that had all but monopolised Barry's creative energies throughout the 1980s and would launch him into the new decade with its premiere at London's Almeida Festival in 1990: his first opera, *The Intelligence Park*.

The Intelligence Park was a collision involving a complex libretto (by the zealously polymathic Joyce scholar Vincent Deane), a classic, operatic love-triangle (with a twist), a historic setting in eighteenth-century Dublin, and music like a tireless, unlimited engine of high-speed ideas. And it was a collision that generated something that worked, in large part owing to the impression of an irrepressible life force, boundless and reckless. Barry said

Pleasure: Don't look. It brings bad luck (getting out of the bath)

Time: (to Pleasure) Persuasive Puck, what can alarm you?
Why should that mirror harm you?

Truth: (to Beauty) Doting boy
Whose foolish joy
Lies in his mirror's fond employ,

Leave your mirror,
Mine is clearer,
Free of flattery, free of error.

Crumbling weight
Of man's estate;
In my mirror see your fate.

Beauty: In the midst of our enjoyment
Curious thought will find employment,
Asking what is still to see.

Pleasure: Do not turn your head from Pleasure,
Do not bargain, ~~weight~~ weigh and measure,
Love and thrift do not agree.

Beauty: Mirror show me left and right,
Beauty's first and second sight,
Am I still from blemish free?

Pleasure: If you ~~arrest the moment~~ stop as you are flying,
Heartless eyes on Beauty spying,
~~Appetite~~ Ardour turns to apathy.

Beauty: Am I every heart's desire?
Are my glances full of fire?
Say if Time has damaged me.

Deceit: Cold and glassy,
Hard and nasty
By his mirror Truth is known.

He will fashion
Love and passion
Into covenants of stone.

3/10/91

at the time that he favoured texts which allowed for 'careering at tangents'—a wonderful, apt image.

How does he do it? His music includes some fairly conspicuous components: high tempos subject to abrupt changes; rapid, almost minimalist-style repetition; and long runs of jagged unisons between instruments and voices. The end result is a distinctive sound, way more than the sum of its describable parts, and easily identifiable by the listener.

What are *not* readily identifiable for listeners are the source materials Barry draws from and the techniques he uses to fashion them into music. Perhaps not surprisingly, his earliest technical experimentation goes back to his childhood and long predates the almost ten years he spent abroad studying composition with members of the European avant-garde: a year with Peter Schat in Amsterdam and the rest divided between Karlheinz Stockhausen and Mauricio Kagel in Germany. During a pre-concert interview that I carried out with him in 2009 he recalled the first time he composed a piece that ended up being seen by someone else. It happened at a piano competition in Ennis when he was fourteen. The first of his two competition pieces was a Chopin nocturne, but the second was a work of his own, derived from a Mozart sonata that he had physically cut up into small fragments and then reassembled to his own design. Interestingly, a point that he returned to twice when telling the story was *not* that a child had written a piece this way. Rather, it was that the child was oblivious of the fact that anyone might consider his compositional procedure unusual.

In the decades that followed he continued to employ similar strategies, generating music by using a range of techniques whose evolutionary line is traceable to youthful ventures like the chopped-up Mozart. In the graphically titled '———' (1979) he re-deployed notes extracted from those whooshing, orchestral scales Tchaikovsky uses as climactic flourishes. Similarly, in the 1980s, working on *The Intelligence Park*, he tabulated all the fleeting chords created by passing-notes in fifty Bach chorales. He used these tables to generate material not only for the opera, but also for various instrumental and vocal pieces that he created from moments within it. These included a ninety-second toccata for solo piano, *Swinging Tripes and Trillibubkins* (1986), and *From The Intelligence Park* (1986, originally titled *Of Queens' Gardens*) for chamber orchestra.

Opposite, left: A flyer for the 1990 Almeida Music Festival production of Gerald Barry's opera, *The Intelligence Park*. After its London run of five performances, Michael Colgan brought the production to the Gate Theatre in Dublin for a further four nights.

Opposite, right: Gerald Barry featured on the cover of the July/August 1990 issue of *Music Ireland* magazine in connection with an interview about *The Intelligence Park* with Adrian Jack. Jack, himself a composer, was director of the musicICA new music series at the Institute of Contemporary Arts in London, and it was he who commissioned the opera.

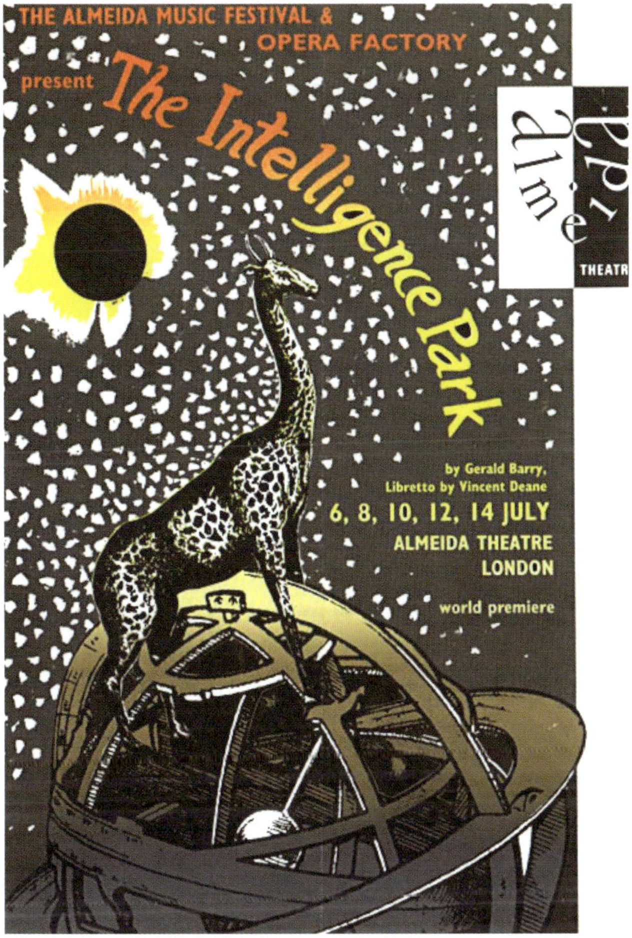

More opera followed immediately. In 1991 Barry was one of six composers commissioned by Channel 4 to write fifty-minute operas for television. His new piece reprised much of what had characterised *The Intelligence Park*—including energy, music subverting text, an element of absurdity—and prescribed an all-male cast to bring to life a libretto by Meredith Oakes based on Handel's final oratorio, *The Triumph of Time and Truth*. Barry emerged well from what Jennifer Barnes calls 'the Faustian pact' that composers make with television. 'In exchange for only one chance to screen their work,' she says in her book, *Television Opera*, 'they will receive an increased profile, a magnificent production budget, and, according to the blunt way in which we obtain viewing figures, a single audience far in excess of any production run.' The opera—*The Triumph of Beauty and Deceit* (1991–92)—was broadcast on Channel 4 in March 1995, released on CD in 1998, staged in Aldeburgh, London and Berlin in 2002, and also performed in concert in Los Angeles, Paris, and New York.

Barry's Britten-like nose for unearthing delight in little-known texts was evident in his next BBC commission in 1995: *The Conquest of Ireland* for bass soloist and orchestra, premiered by Stephen Richardson and the BBC Symphony Orchestra under Matthias Bamert in London in January 1996. The text's strangely detailed descriptions of individual soldiers come from the book of that name by the twelfth-century Welsh clergyman, historian and prolific writer, Giraldus Cambrensis, whose name can be translated as Gerald de Barry.

During the 1990s Barry received within Ireland the kind of acclaim he had already established abroad. This was nicely illustrated at the tail-end of the decade when RTÉ devoted a five-day festival to his music in Dublin in June 2000. The national broadcaster—which had had difficult times in the 1990s because of constraints imposed by the Broadcasting Act 1990, and management conflicts with principal conductors of what's now the RTÉ NSO—here chose to celebrate the first birthday of its new twenty-four-hour classical radio station, RTÉ lyric fm, by devoting its performing groups and resources to an exciting, large-scale celebration of the country's leading composer, which was shared across Europe via broadcast by the EBU.

Raymond Deane was the first real *enfant terrible* of modern Irish music, startling listeners with his debut, performing his own piano piece *Format* at the 1969 Dublin Festival of 20th Century Music. The following summer, aged sixteen, he attended the Darmstadt summer school, and he has colourfully documented the ups and downs of his life in the 1970s and 1980s in a frank 2014 memoir, *In My Own Light*. He is also a political activist, and was one of the founders of the Ireland Palestine Solidarity Campaign. This 1992 drawing by Gerald Mangan reflects the composer's deep interest in chess.

• •

Raymond Deane (b. 1953) was born less than a year after Gerald Barry, also in the west of Ireland, in Galway. Similarities continue: both knew from an early age that they wanted to be composers, both attended University College Dublin before continuing their studies in Germany, where both had stints with Stockhausen. When you meet either man, you feel immediately in the presence of a lively and very formidable intellect.

Given so much overlap of time, place and formation, it is in some ways a wonder that their music sounds so utterly different. That it does is immediately apparent in both composers' first big works of the decade: Barry's *The Intelligence Park* and Deane's *Krespel's Concerto* for violin and orchestra. While both of these pieces completed in 1990 have narrative origins, the frenetic subversion of the libretto in Barry's opera is in sharpest contrast with the

LIFE OF A MEDIUM:
Raymond Deane orchestrates an overture

ASSOCIATION OF YOUNG IRISH COMPOSERS

Concert

works by

DEREK BALL, RAYMOND DEANE

on

Saturday 14th April 1973

at 8 p.m. in

Examination Hall T.C.D.

TICKETS AVAILABLE AT McCULLOUGH-PIGGOTT

ADMISSION 60p
STUDENTS 30p

The Association of Young Irish Composers was a loose collective formed in 1972 by Derek Ball, Gerald Barry, Brian Beckett (secretary), Sally Ann Bryan, Raymond Deane, John Gibson (president) and Niamh O'Kelly. Its declared aims were 'the profitable performance of works by young Irish composers and the general furtherance of the performance of twentieth-century music in this country.' The association promoted concerts of its members until 1975 when it merged with the Composers' Group of the Music Association of Ireland to form the Association of Irish Composers.

more traditional if not programmatic approach to storytelling of the concerto, a reworking by Deane of a radio opera commissioned by RTÉ in 1983.

Where Barry embeds and conceals musical sources such as his Bach-derived chords, Deane imports them and displays them. In this case, the Krespel of the title is the character from an E. T. A. Hoffmann story who appears—with his daughter Antonia—in Offenbach's *Les contes d'Hoffmann*. To introduce the character of Antonia in his concerto, Deane quotes the aria Offenbach wrote for her ('*Elle a fui, la tourterelle*'), and in his programme note suggests that the whole work can be seen as a set of variations on this aria. And however you care to nail down the impression of madness in the Barry—via related descriptions such as anarchic or reckless, or, a word he himself uses, vertiginous—there is no such suggestion of *that kind* of madness in the Deane, not even when there is actual madness in the story (Krespel's, prompted by Antonia's death). Perhaps it boils down to the difference between simply sounding mad in the Barry and the goal of depicting madness in the Deane.

Depicting *anything* in music often requires the use of musical language that offers at least some common ground between composer and listener. For example, the first of Deane's little set of *After-Pieces* for piano (1990) alludes to the French folk song '*A la claire fontaine*' and evokes the play of fountain water with delicate right-hand notes near the top of the keyboard. It may be a trope, but using a trope means that there is the presence of vocabulary shared by composer and listener.

Features that are characteristic of his orchestral and piano music in the 1990s also appear in his chamber music from around that time. Mid decade he completed a trio of chamber works loosely connected by a single idea: a mocking irreverence towards death. On the one hand, Deane recognises formative influences—such as Stravinsky and Bartók from the first half of the century, and Berio, Boulez, Stockhausen and Xenakis from the second—which he has fully assimilated into his own voice. On the other hand he imports other music directly and explicitly as part of his overall reflection on the single idea, the irreverence towards death.

For example, in the second of the two pieces—*Catacombs* of 1994, for clarinet, violin, cello and piano—he quotes and distorts passages easily recognisable from the 'Catacombs' of Mussorgsky's *Pictures at an Exhibition*.

Something similar happens in the final piece, *Seachanges (with danse macabre)* for flute, violin, piano, cello and percussion, the first of the set to be composed. Here he sets the *Dies irae* plainchant within the context of a range of percussion instruments chosen to recall the *mariachi* music he heard during a visit to Mexico.

Other pieces are more independent of extramusical references and ideas, such as his second string quartet, *Brown Studies*, composed in 1997 to a commission from the Vanbrugh String Quartet. Unlike *Krespel*, nothing is depicted here. Unlike both *Krespel* and, for example, *Catacombs*, there is no prominent musical quotation. Musical allusion seems to be confined to things like the presence of a fugue (in the third movement), perhaps in reference to the quartets of Beethoven or Haydn. The piece otherwise gains a different kind of intensity by being inward-looking. Deane states that he wrote the initial sketches while completing his opera, *The Wall of Cloud* (1997), whose 'positive assertions' he intended the quartet to offset 'with negation and ambiguity in a manner more typical of my work as a whole.' If you take this idea, and the inward intensity of *Brown Studies*, and expand it to an orchestral context, you have the 1994 Concerto for Oboe and Orchestra commissioned by the RTÉ National Symphony Orchestra, with its now-tender, now-hostile treatment of the soloist as a somewhat undersized hero-in-exile.

••

The 1990s also saw the continuing output of an older generation of Irish composers, among them those born before or during World War II. John Kinsella (b. 1932) had emerged from personal and artistic crisis in the 1980s to dedicate his creative life to the writing of symphonies. His inspirations included Bruckner, Mahler and, above all, Sibelius. His endeavours were ideally supported by a golden handshake from RTÉ when he retired as head of music in 1988. Having written his first and second symphonies in 1984 (aged fifty-two) and 1988 respectively, his retirement package from the broadcaster included the commissioning of the next four.

Kinsella's Symphony No. 3 (1990) parades a deep and unabashed affection for its antecedents. For example, Bruckner is a constant presence in the third-movement *Adagio tranquillo*. With its two long movements framed and joined by short interludes, the symphony is unconventionally structured as well as masterfully crafted to convey the essence of its subtitle, '*Joie de vivre*'. At the other end of the decade Kinsella effectively paired his Seventh Symphony (1997) with that of his hero, Sibelius, the connections audible, again unapologetically. In between, the Symphony No. 4 (1991) attempts to take account of Irish identity, by allusion either to the Irishmen unsafely convicted for the Birmingham pub bombings of 1974—the work's original subtitle was *The Birmingham Six*—or to Irish geography after Kinsella renamed the work *The Four Provinces*.

The question of Irish identity is something Seóirse Bodley (b. 1933) has approached from a variety of angles over the course of a long creative career. Following a youthful appropriation of Irish traditional music in the 1950s and an immersion in serial and other avant-garde techniques in the 1960s, he determined in the 1970s to bring these two components together, notably in *A small white cloud drifts over Ireland* (1975). In the years that followed, however, much of his music gravitated away from serialism and back towards tonal style.

In the 1990s this change was clear in the last two of his five symphonies, both premiered in 1991, both with specifically Irish elements that are more integrated than overt. There is extramusical background to No. 5, subtitled *The Limerick Symphony*. It was commissioned to commemorate the passing of 300 years since the Treaty of Limerick had brought an end to the Williamite War and to the siege of the city. It is not programmatic music but rather was intended as a reflection on the experience of these events. The sound is tonal and traditionally symphonic in colour and style. Sometimes an Irish element escapes 'integration' to rise and break the surface for a brief moment of prominence before vanishing, for example near the beginning of the third movement (just a few bars after a really obvious reference to Mahler's *Resurrection* Symphony). But by the end of the 1990s he was composing non-orchestral music that reflected a return to serialism and which contained no Irish elements at all, for example in *News from Donabate*, a fifty-minute piece for solo piano from 1999.

Within the 1990s output of Frank Corcoran (b. 1944) there appear side-by-side certain works based on Irish connections and others that are devoid of any. His single-movement Symphony No. 3 (1994), for example, is driven by a purely musical preoccupation with just six notes. The result, typically for Corcoran, is a wild, chaotic sound-world, a product of his particular notion of macro-counterpoint whereby the flowing together of various streams of musical lines generate harmony, sometimes aleatorically. Prominent among his works with a strong Irish background is his series of pieces inspired by the colourful character of Mad Sweeney (*Buile Suibhne*), a minor Irish king of the seventh century. The Irish connection is extra-musical, and the series variously includes works for chamber ensemble, for ensemble plus voices, for piano solo, and for tape in the case of *Sweeney's Vision* from 1997, for which he won the Bourges International Electro-acoustic Music Competition in 1999.

Opposite: Frank Corcoran, from Borrisokane in Co. Tipperary. He came late to music, not hearing his first symphony concert until the age of nineteen, his first string quartet at twenty. He trained in Dublin, Rome and Berlin, and he worked as a music inspector for the Department of Education for eight years in the 1970s. His music is unique among Irish composers in the way it connects with the ancient and primitive. He likes to be provocative, and his conversation can be multi-layered enough to be difficult to follow in real time. Once asked what he might have been had he not been a composer, he answered 'A thinker, tinker, philosopher, theological traveller.'

••

In Northern Ireland the 1990s was the decade that saw the peace process gather momentum and reach a watershed in the Good Friday Agreement of 1998. By then, however, many Northern Irish composers had already absorbed the experience of conflict with great immediacy, and some were writing music that consciously reflected this experience.

Among those who have written about this is Hilary Bracefield, whose *The Politics of Silence: The Northern Ireland Composer and the Troubles* presents a snapshot sampling of Northern Irish composers in the mid 1990s. It includes Kevin O'Connell (b. 1958), who is also the subject of a study by Jennifer McCay. Her focused analysis of his orchestral work *North* (1997) aims to demonstrate that, beyond whatever O'Connell may or may not have meant by it, the title he gave the piece and how he uses his motivic material may produce unintentional results. She presents a persuasive array of evidence to support this, not excluding the most obvious, that he borrowed the title from Seamus Heaney, whose poem and collection with that name (*North*, 1975) openly address the Northern Ireland conflict. Once aware of this connection a listener would be hard pressed *not* to associate the agitation, the sometimes bleak intensity and wide-ranging colours of O'Connell's post-serial orchestral work with some kind of personal response to the Troubles.

Other major works of the period show no outward connection to the conflict. For example, his 1997 chamber opera *My Love, My Umbrella* is an exploration of human relationships based on the John McGahern short story, while the forty-six-minute String Quartet (2000) is absolute music that inhabits a taut, unflinching sound-world.

Music by other Northern composers offers insight as to just how complicated is the relationship between influences and creativity. The first orchestral commission received by Belfast-born Stephen Gardner (b. 1958) was from the BBC, who wanted a piece for the Ulster Orchestra's St Patrick's Day concert in 1992. The result was *Wanting, not Wanting*. But it would be another three years before Gardner revealed how he had been influenced by two sectarian murders as he worked on the piece.

Like Kevin O'Connell and Stephen Gardner who both left Northern Ireland, Deirdre Gribbin (b. 1967) left Belfast—where she had grown up on the Falls Road—and in the 1990s lived variously in Denmark, New York and England. She came late to composing but enjoyed success at an accelerated rate, for example becoming associate composer of the Orchestra of St John's, Smith Square, London, in 1998, the same year in which her first opera, *Hey Persephone!*, commissioned by Almeida Opera, was premiered at the Aldeburgh Festival. She was just thirty. She was attracting attention with chamber pieces such as the delicate piano trio *How to make the water sound* (1997) and, for large ensemble, *Tribe* (1997), a hard-hitting response to the tension surrounding the annual Orange marches through Drumcree outside Portadown. Gribbin's music draws much on extramusical reference, only some of which relates to Northern Ireland, *Tribe* being the first overt example.

Ian Wilson (b. 1964) wasn't even thirty when early works—such as his first string quartet, *Winter's Edge* (1992), later recorded by Chandos, and the languidly meandering yet neatly unified orchestral work *Rise* (1993)—were earning him a profile. He drew inspiration from a wide variety of sources including painting, his religious faith and literary texts. By 1998 he was busy with commissions from the BBC (his concerto for alto saxophone, *Who's afraid of Red, Yellow and Blue*), the Irish Chamber Orchestra (*Limena*, a

Deirdre Gribbin is one of a number of Northern Irish composers whose work has directly responded to the social and political troubles she has lived through. She studied in her native Belfast with Kevin Volans, in London with Robert Saxton, and in Copenhagen with Per Nørgård. Her *Unity of Being* opened the UKWITHNY Festival in New York, the city's first international arts event after 9/11. She had great success with her 1998 Opera, *Hey Persephone!*, which won an Arts Foundation Award, and her recent work has sought to bring theatrical elements into normal concert environments.

Ian Wilson is one of several Northern Irish composers who have chosen to move south into a more nurturing cultural environment, not least because of the support available to members of Aosdána. He is an adaptable composer who has broadened his compositional practice to work with musicians from jazz and traditional Irish backgrounds, has explored cross-fertilisation with Indian music, worked on projects involving improvisation, and has increasingly engaged with electronics.

concerto for piano and strings), the London Mozart Players (*Near the Western Necropolis*) and, for RTÉ in 1999, his first violin concerto, *Messenger*. This last drew on his experience of living in Belgrade, a city he eventually fled with his wife and young son after four days of NATO bombing in 1999 near the end of the war in Kosovo. The irony of someone from Belfast having this experience was not lost on him.

Wilson and Gribbin were part of a new wave of Northern Irish composers born in the 1960s who began to emerge in the 1990s. Their cohort also included Elaine Agnew (b. 1967) who would blossom later but enjoyed early success with works such as *Philip's Peace* for cello and piano (1994) and *Strings A-stray*, commissioned and recorded by the Irish Chamber Orchestra (1994 rev. 1998). Michael Alcorn (b. 1962) had a commitment to electro-acoustic music that took root during his undergraduate years. By 1989 his early success in the genre had earned him a post in Queen's University Belfast, where he later became director of the Sonic Arts Research Centre (2001) and subsequently professor of composition (2004). Interestingly, it's in one of his few purely orchestral and non-electro-acoustic pieces—the now-raging, now-grieving *Macha's Curse* of 1997—that he first gave open expression to his response to the Troubles.

••

The real godfather of Irish electro-acoustic composition is Roger Doyle (b. 1949). For Doyle the 1990s were dominated by his single largest work, the epic six-hour, five-CD box set *Babel*. It presents his original concept of a vast, science fiction-inspired tower-city, all brought to life by a blend of live and electronic music, and in which different CD tracks represent different locations. Some of the discs explore rooms and places within the city. This involves cross-connections whereby sounds featured on one track—or in one 'room'—are distantly audible in the presentation of others, through the wall, as it were, or down the corridor. Two of the discs are devoted to broadcasts from Babel's internal radio station, KBBL.

Opposite: Roger Doyle, pictured here in 1990, was Ireland's pioneer in the field of electronic music. He performed in rock bands, most famously Supply, Demand and Curve, and studied composition with A. J. Potter. His first tape compositions in the early 1970s launched him as Ireland's first electronic composer. He later studied in Utrecht and Helsinki, and in spite of working in a country without an electronic studio, won his first international prizes for his work in 1981. He has also written for films and theatre and formed the music-theatre group Operating Theatre with the actor Olwen Fouéré. He famously appeared onstage playing incidental music at the piano for Steven Berkoff's Gate Theatre production of Oscar Wilde's *Salomé* in 1988.

Michael Alcorn, Seóirse Bodley and Kevin O'Connell were among the composers who made long-term commitments to teaching composition in third-level institutions. Although much of Kevin Volans's (b. 1949) teaching was private, the 1980s included third-level posts in his native South Africa (the University of Natal) and at Queen's University Belfast (where he was composer-in-residence), followed in 1992 by a year in Princeton University in New Jersey. His teaching trump card, perhaps, arose during his own study in Cologne, where he coincided with Gerald Barry in the mid 1970s. There he became Stockhausen's teaching assistant, succeeding Richard Toop. But after he declined an invitation to take up the post full-time, Stockhausen never once spoke to him again. The long list of Irish composers who studied with him includes Elaine Agnew, Siobhan Cleary, Deirdre Gribbin, Andrew Hamilton, Deirdre McKay, John McLachlan and Jennifer Walshe. Volans, who became an Irish citizen in 1994, balanced his teaching with composing, adding three more string quartets (Nos. 4, 5, and 6) to the three which were recorded by the Kronos Quartet in the 1980s, including *White Man Sleeps* (1986), which earned him a wide international profile. Some of his other increasingly post-minimalist works include *Cicada* for two pianos (1994) and The Concerto for Piano and Wind Instruments (1995).

John Buckley (b. 1951) had been a secondary school teacher before turning to composition full-time in 1982. The pedagogical drive stayed with him, however, and in 1983 he co-founded (with James Wilson) the important Ennis Composition Summer School (now the Irish Composition Summer School), and in 2001 he would take up a lecturing post in St Patrick's College in Drumcondra. Over the course of the 1990s his output included concertos for organ (1992) and alto saxophone (1997), solo piano music, and a massive work for soloists, choir, and orchestra, *Maynooth Te Deum* (1995). But the piece that best drew together his teaching and composing strands was the 1983 Sonata for Unaccompanied Violin. After it was prescribed as a set-piece for the Leaving Certificate music syllabus (up to 1998), it offered a gateway to contemporary music for a generation of Irish schoolgoers and showed them that not all composers were dead.

The public performance of new music in general and of new Irish music in particular was subject to many challenges and disappointments in the 1990s. Not least of these were those arising from the threatened and actual disbanding of music-performing groups within RTÉ as it worked through the consequences of legislatively induced earning caps. The absence of a regular festival of new music in Dublin was another challenge. 1991 saw the demise of the city's Accents Festival in only its second outing (the first was in 1989). Outside Dublin, festivals of new music cropped up in Waterford and Sligo, and Belfast's Sonorities Festival, established in 1981, went from strength to strength. Meanwhile, other institutions contributed in varying degrees. For example, the Contemporary Music Centre provided an information and archive service for Irish composers, but remained uninvolved in the presentation of performance. The music touring and development agency, Music Network, encouraged the performers it engaged to include works by Irish composers in their programmes.

In this period, when simply getting new music heard could be a major challenge, two composers stood out for their commitment to performance. In 1990 Benjamin Dwyer (b. 1965), in partnership with pianist Neil Cooney (b. 1968), established the Mostly Modern series of lunchtime concerts in Dublin, regularly offering new music from Ireland as well as elsewhere. Dwyer's own output around this time included the earliest of his various *Crow* pieces for solo instrument and tape—a reflection of his fascination with the *Crow* poems of Ted Hughes—and the beginnings of what would become a substantial set of Études for guitar. There were also a String Quartet (1996, rev 1999), a Guitar Concerto (1998, rev 1999), and a wide range of other works for various instruments, ensembles, choirs, voices and orchestra. It was in addition to all this that he sustained the successful Mostly Modern series which, especially in the second half of the decade, became an important provider of new music. At the turn of the decade the series spawned a festival (of the same name), and Dwyer also established a new music ensemble, Vox21.

Vox21 was a mere infant beside Concorde, Ireland's longest standing new music group, directed since its foundation in 1976 by Jane O'Leary (b. 1946). American-born but living in Ireland since 1972, O'Leary, like Dwyer, maintained a fruitful balance between the creation and presentation of new

Opposite: Donnacha Dennehy trained in his native Dublin, Illinois and the Netherlands, and on his return home was the guiding force behind the Crash Ensemble. He became the twenty-first century's first poster boy of new Irish music. His compositions and his ensemble's aesthetic embraced technology and urban culture— a new development in Irish music. He introduced concerts in a disarmingly downbeat way that masked the stringency of his intellectual approach. Crash's performances acquired something of the aura of a cult rock band, and his teaching post in Trinity College Dublin opened up a whole generation to his thought and practices.

music. Through the 1990s Concorde continued to commission and perform pieces from Ireland's established, emerging and young composers, programming them in the context of new music from elsewhere. At the same time O'Leary continued a personal creative journey which was leading her away from the serialism she had previously adopted following her doctoral studies with Milton Babbitt at Princeton University. Her output in the 1990s included the orchestral commissions from RTÉ, *Islands of Discovery* (1992) and *From Sea-Grey Shores* (1999), both drawing inspiration from the landscapes of her home in the west of Ireland, and chamber works like *Into the Wordless* (1998) and her nature-inspired string quartet, *Mystic Play of Shadows* (1995).

• •

Just when it seemed as though the decade of music in Ireland might close out with this version of the status quo, a birth took place that quite radically disrupted it. In 1997 Donnacha Dennehy (b. 1970) was one of three co-founders (with pianist Andrew Synnott and clarinettist Michael Seaver) of the Crash Ensemble. Following the lead of groups such as New York's Bang on a Can All-Stars, in that it was amplified, experimental, and multimedia, Crash not only imported fresh developments in new music, it uncovered an appetite for them. Early concerts sold out, and the change was not just about numbers. Audiences were notably younger and, simply, different, an impression highlighted at Crash's National Concert Hall debut (in the John Field Room, September 1999), where it was easy to imagine a sort of cultural dissonance between audience and venue.

Whether or not that cultural dissonance actually existed, music in Ireland benefited from the shot in the arm that Crash offered. The ensemble's eclectic style included a rock concert element whose energy Dennehy remembers enjoying, 'particularly for the classical establishment in Dublin, which is probably the stuffiest I've ever encountered,' he said in 2003. By then, Crash had already assumed a leading role within Ireland's new music scene, had attracted support from the Arts Council, and had toured abroad, notably to Sweden, Germany and North America. 'I wanted to set up something for the music I was interested in,' said Dennehy, reflecting on the ensemble's first five years. 'Particularly music for mixed media, stuff that was quite rhythmic, and with a little bit of an urban edge to it.'

Such features were also some of the primary characteristics of his own pieces at the time, for example the now-spacey, now-funky *Junk Box Fraud* (1997) for chamber ensemble, speakers, tape and video, or his first commission from the RTÉ National Symphony Orchestra, *The Vandal* (2000), with its Gerald Barry-like embedding of source material, its abrupt changes and reckless energy.

Through his artistic direction of Crash, Dennehy became the composer at the heart of Irish new music. The ensemble was a new prism of expression for Irish composers including many of the established ones discussed in this chapter. However it is perhaps of even greater importance that Dennehy's Crash Ensemble offered an outlet—and for some, a springboard—to the next, much bigger generation of Irish composers.

The popular touch

ANDREW JOHNSTONE

Through thick and thin over nearly seventy years, RTÉ's policy of maintaining two orchestras testifies to a musical duality less self-evident nowadays than in 1948, when the Radio Éireann orchestra bifurcated into the forerunners of today's RTÉ National Symphony Orchestra (RTÉ NSO) and RTÉ Concert Orchestra (RTÉCO). Then, it was axiomatic that one group could concentrate on the classics, typically under the direction of an international conductor, while the other could provide the lighter kind of music without which contemporary public service broadcasting would have been unthinkable, the roles of arranging and conducting being combined by a local musician.

Over time, the onus for providing popular music has shifted from broadcasters in general to what is now termed the music industry, a turning point being reached in 1980 when the BBC axed or redeployed four of its own light orchestras. The remarkable survival of the RTÉCO has gone hand in hand with an increasing versatility, its repertoire overlapping with the RTÉ NSO's particularly during the annual series of summer lunchtime concerts in which both orchestras take their turns. And while current principal conductor John Wilson's notable surveys of Hollywood film musicals have reaffirmed the RTÉCO's association with popular repertory, his forays into classical repertoire have extended to Brahms's Symphony No. 2. Clearly, this orchestra will not live on light music alone.

Inevitably, the RTÉ NSO's superior forces will secure its hold on the post-Brahms symphonic repertory, while its *raison d'être* of promoting art music will continue to give it first call on the orchestral works of contemporary composers. Yet the new music commissioned and performed by this group is not exclusively of avant-garde types, a point forcibly made by the open-air community music-making exercise with which, at Dublin's Collins

Through *Riverdance*, Bill Whelan is the most widely performed of Irish composers and the best remunerated. But he is not regarded as a fully fledged member of the new music community. He doesn't feature in the subscription concerts of the RTÉ National Symphony Orchestra, but instead in special occasion events, in the guise of a celebrity from another musical world. His most conventional mainstream activity was the composition of *The Currach*, one of the test pieces for the Dublin International Piano Competition of 2009.

Shaun Davey is another outsider in the world of new music. He shot to popular prominence through *The Brendan Voyage* in 1980, a marriage of traditional Irish instruments and orchestral sonority that set the tone for the rest of his career. He writes music for theatre, film and television; periodic all-Davey programmes have made him the composer most performed by the RTÉ National Symphony Orchestra, although the orchestra's subscription concerts remain closed to him.

Barracks on 27 March 2016, the orchestra marked the centenary of the Easter Rising.

Back in 1966, RTÉ commemorated the Rising's fiftieth anniversary with a specially commissioned work that was aimed at a high-end classical listenership and broadcast on television, Brian Boydell's cantata *A Terrible Beauty is Born*. Had they chosen to commemorate the centenary with a comparable new work there would have been no shortage of Irish composers equal to the commission.If, fifty years on, there was a sense that this anniversary concert could and should appeal to a wider audience, then that was in no small part due to the influence of the two living composers whose music made up the bulk of the programme.

Dead composers didn't go without token representation. Handel's *Hallelujah* Chorus, famously premiered in Dublin in 1742, was an obvious choice for the specially convened 1,100-voice metachoir that joined with the RTÉ NSO and guest conductor David Brophy. A selection of folksier moments from Seán Ó Riada's landmark score for the 1959 film documentary *Mise Éire* conjured

up the darker aspects of twentieth-century Irish history, albeit without revealing the full extent of the composer's noted technical adventurousness.

Ó Riada's artistry as a traditional musician would almost certainly have remained untouched by cosmopolitan avant-garde techniques were it not that he undertook formal university training under the renowned Cork professor Aloys Fleischmann. It is probably no accident, then, that Bill Whelan (b. 1950) and Shaun Davey (b. 1948), the dominant figures of the centenary concert, both opted to take their degree in subjects other than music. Both have remained staunch autodidacts, each pursuing his career no less as art than as business (whether or not that business was actually profitable). From international and national perspectives, both may be said to have redefined perceptions of Irish music.

Given his catholic musical tastes and varied background in studio work and as keyboard player for the traditional group Planxty, it is logical that Whelan's creative strategies have been primarily those of an arranger. To be sure, he is a fastidious tunesmith, yet his distinctiveness resides not so much in the tunes themselves as in his subsequent treatment of them. The principle is illustrated in 'Caraçena', the finale of his *Seville* Suite (1992), where an original but basically orthodox jig tune is first heard unadorned on traditional instruments and then repeated with increasing masses of orchestral accompaniment. And the accompaniment grabs and holds the attention with appositely Hispanic cross-rhythms—just the kind of rhythms, of course, that have proved simultaneously a red rag to traditional music purists and the lifeblood of Whelan's *chef-d'œuvre*, the *Riverdance* project (1994).

The *Connemara* Suite (2007), however, which in the centenary concert featured the subtly contrasting talents of Zoë Conway on fiddle and Helena Wood on violin, illustrated that in his introspective moments Whelan can be much more than a consummate arranger of his own tunes. At least until the finale (when choreographic instincts take over to the point of admitting a dancer to the stage), the tension between traditional and classical techniques is handled with a sustained yet delicate autonomy that seems indebted to neither side of the stylistic divide, but is unmistakably Whelan's voice.

It is one of the great 'what ifs?' of recent Irish music that Whelan might have built his fame on a large-scale work he started in the late 1970s but abandoned when he heard that Davey was independently completing something on the same subject and with the same title. *The Brendan Voyage* (1980) was thus destined to be Davey's breakthrough, and the first in a series of ambitious compositions creating a quasi-symphonic context for traditional instruments and Celtic topics, and in the notable case of *Granuaile* (1985, a work now well-known partly thanks to its inclusion in the Department of Education Junior Cycle music syllabus), the voice of Irish folk singer Rita Connolly.

Alongside his hefty portfolio of commercial jingles and television themes, Davey's readiness to provide grandly proportioned scores to mark the tercentenary of the Siege of Derry (*The Relief of Derry* Symphony, 1989) and the 250th anniversary of the death of Jonathan Swift (*Gulliver*, 1995) easily singled him out as RTÉ's go-to composer for the Easter Rising centenary. In contrast to his usual practice of compiling his own texts, the words of *One Hundred Years a Nation* were written and for the most part narrated by Pulitzer Prize-winning poet Paul Muldoon. Yet in no way has this departure distracted Davey's attention from the problems of musical macrostructure: on the contrary, in this instance he may have addressed them with more than customary aplomb.

Davey's importance rests not so much on any one of his epic orchestral works as on his success, in the face of the formidable technical challenges they posed for him, at creating and sustaining a ready market for them. Without a Whelan or a Davey to alter the Irish soundscape in the ways they have done, who knows what genre of music might instead have taken a place in the Easter Rising centenary? There can be no telling on what kind of composer the broadcaster's choice will naturally fall next time the nation celebrates a significant anniversary, or by what steps that composer will have arisen.

In search of the Irish Philip Glass or Meredith Monk …

JOHN SCHAEFER

So much of New York was built by the Irish; or to spite the Irish; or on rare occasions for the Irish. (The small 1870 Brooklyn row house where I live was built for the Irish gravediggers working at nearby Green-Wood Cemetery.) We native New Yorkers have never lacked for Irish music, although when I was growing up, it was always the Wolfe Tones and The Clancy Brothers & Tommy Makem and similar acts who sounded suspiciously like 'your parents' music'. Finding a way into the Irish contemporary music scene proved to be much harder.

My long-running radio program, *New Sounds*, began in 1982 at WNYC, America's flagship National Public Radio station, with the idea of offering a wide-angle view of contemporary music that didn't acknowledge the usual boundaries between classical and vernacular music. Irish music was always represented, but fitfully: Planxty and the Bothy Band; the 'world music' (the term was just beginning to take hold) of Mícheál Ó Súilleabháin (b. 1950) and the oddly-medieval-sounding work of his then wife, the singer Nóirín Ní Riain (b. 1951); the choir Anúna, led by composer Michael McGlynn (b. 1964). It was enough to suspect that there must be more.

I wasn't so interested in learning who the Irish Leonard Bernstein was, or the Irish Aaron Copland, or even the Irish Elliott Carter. Who, I wondered, was the Irish equivalent of Philip Glass, or Meredith Monk? The outliers? The ones you have to actually dig around to find? One answer arrived on a winter's afternoon in 1999 while we were doing a soundcheck for one of the *New Sounds Live* concerts I produce at New York's World Financial Center. Robert Fripp was checking the sound of his electric guitar and digital delay system; chairs had been set up for the evening's performance. A lone figure sat in the middle of an empty row. A crew member asked, 'is that David Bowie?' 'Yes,' I replied, 'but leave him alone.'

With the soundcheck done, we began to plan for the evening show and some music began playing through the space's sound system. I noticed it almost immediately—it was a likable yet twisted sort of lo-fi chamber-folk music. The sort of multi-hyphenated music I was always looking for. I walked over to the mixing engineer and asked what it was. 'I don't know,' was the reply. 'This guy came and left this CD and said to give it to you.' I looked at the CD. *Skipper*, by Daniel Figgis (b. 1961). Now this was an outlier. And, it turned out, he was from Dublin.

In 2001, RTÉ lyric fm invited me to do a week-long residency in Limerick and Dublin. This would finally be my chance to really see what the Irish contemporary music scene had to offer. I found a thriving, multi-generational scene. To my complete lack of surprise, it turned out that the two interviews I set up with artists I'd already known—Daniel Figgis and Michael McGlynn—were not part of that scene. 'I don't have much use for most of those people,' Figgis told me. 'Except for Roger Doyle.' Doyle (b. 1949) turned out to be one of the composers I would meet and interview. Like many of his younger colleagues, he seemed to weave a strong technological thread through his music. And over the course of several days, during numerous interviews with these younger composers, the name Donnacha Dennehy (b. 1970) kept coming up. So I went finally to his office at Trinity College one evening—in, tellingly, the Music and Technology Department. The office was a mess, with piles of CDs and papers, a keyboard, and a pile of LPs near the door. David Bowie's *Scary Monsters* sat atop the pile. Here, I thought, is a man I can work with.

That trip essentially served to open the vaults to the Irish new music scene to *New Sounds* listeners. But it also had several unanticipated results. One was the first American commission of a Donnacha Dennehy work. I thought there was a certain energy to Dennehy's music that reminded me of New York's Bang On A Can organisation, so I asked him to write a piece for the Bang On A Can All-Stars. The other was the chance to introduce Dennehy to conductor Alan Pierson here in New York; that meeting would result in Pierson's long-standing position as the conductor of Dublin's Crash Ensemble, the group Dennehy helped found.

So when a return trip to Ireland came up in early 2015, at the invitation of the Contemporary Music Centre in Dublin, I felt far more comfortable with the musical landscape. But the Irish new music scene had another surprise to offer.

I knew John Godfrey (b. 1962) as a former member of the UK group Icebreaker—a group in the mold of Bang On A Can or Crash Ensemble. John played bass guitar. He played it loud, because Icebreaker was loud. He played it in the Crash Ensemble since moving to Ireland. Again, loud. But then he appeared in Dublin with a new CD, credited to the Quiet Music Ensemble. The

John Godfrey is a man of extremes. In 1989 he was one of the founders of the heavily amplified group Icebreaker in the UK. After moving to Ireland, he was a founding member of another amplified group, Crash Ensemble—he plays keyboards and guitars with aplomb. In 2008 he ran a Quiet Music Festival in Cork and founded a Quiet Music Ensemble, whose performances are sometimes as quiet as its name suggests, and at other times anything but.

band, it turned out, was aptly named. Much of the music hovered around the very threshold of audibility. It incorporated found sounds, altered or not, and blurred the distinction not only between music and noise—an area composers have explored for at least a century now—but between sound and silence.

A trip to Cork revealed the extent to which this 'quiet music' was playing with listeners' expectations—not only of how music should sound, but how it should be made, and in what setting. On a picturesque side street in Cork, in a venue called The Guesthouse, I recorded an evening of live music made by Godfrey, the composer/laptop artist Karen Power (b. 1977), and the duo called The Quiet Club, consisting of Danny McCarthy (b. 1950) and Mick O'Shea (b. 1958). On this particular evening, McCarthy played a collection of amplified coils and houseware items, toys and other odd sound-making

Sound artists Mick O'Shea (above) and Danny McCarthy formed the Quiet Club in Cork in 2006. Hi-tech (amplification, processing and mixing) and lo-tech (self-made instruments) are both their stock-in-trade.

Karen Power's artistic statement couldn't be more direct. 'I am a versatile, enthusiastic and well-received Irish composer seeking to stimulate, engage and interact with audiences. I use two primary sources in my creative output; acoustic instruments and everyday sound-objects and soundscapes.' This photograph captures her at work, making a field recording.

devices, while Mick oversaw the food. The Guesthouse is a modest row house with a sitting room and a kitchen on one floor, and upstairs what is essentially a living room, which is where the performances take place. It seems wrong to call them 'concerts'. Three or four musicians play to perhaps a dozen or so listeners in a setting intimate enough that even the tiniest sonic gesture can be heard. After a break for a beer and a plate of food downstairs, the music resumes upstairs.

That music is improvised, quietly and deliberately, with the sounds often processed through Power's laptop. 'Most of what I do revolves around field recordings,' she explained later. She said she was especially drawn to 'environments that are around us all the time but that we cannot hear.' Examples of that would be activity underwater— the highly amplified sounds of the 'popping shrimp' are a favorite—and sounds in the ultrasonic frequencies. But to cross the psychoacoustic divide between these natural sounds and those of Godfrey's guitar and McCarthy's home-made instruments, she brings all three feeds together in her laptop. (This echoes the decision by American composer John Adams to lightly amplify the orchestra in his operas when he began incorporating synthesisers and sampling keyboards; he found that the use of amplification and speakers bridged the sonic divide between the electric and the purely acoustic instruments.)

Listening to this music is not the passive reception of audio that so much music so easily becomes. It is an activity, requiring a level of engagement that can make the listener as much a part of the experience as the musicians. But despite the small scale of each event, the reach of this quiet music is surprisingly extensive. Composers Irene Buckley (b. 1978) and Ian Wilson (b. 1964), both of whom travel in very different musical circles, are part of The Guesthouse community and were there the night I attended.

'Cork City has this extraordinary and unusual improvisation and sound art scene,' Godfrey told me. He couldn't put his finger on why exactly; Danny McCarthy's influence is central, but as he pointed out, that influence doesn't mean anything if there aren't other people willing to be influenced. Somehow, that scene has reached a critical mass in Cork, where it is small enough to be true to the spirit of this quiet music, but large enough to sustain itself over a period of years.

Here in New York, we have a long tradition with Minimal music. Through an accident of musical history, that term has come to denote the often wildly colourful, rhythmically intense and dynamic music of Philip Glass, Steve Reich and others. In Cork, I found a different, more literally 'minimal' music. In both places, the spirit of John Cage hovers; the quiet music scene in Cork, as Godfrey puts it, is built around an almost perfectly Cageian question. 'What happens,' he said, 'when nothing happens?'

26,400 beats per minute

JOANNA MACGREGOR

I first met Donnacha Dennehy (b. 1970) in 1999, after a recital I had given at the fashionable down-town Project Arts Centre in Dublin. I was playing a programme called *Ultramarine,* which—back in those dark days—brought together video, tape and live music with a great deal of effort; these days virtually everything can be run off an iPhone. The concert included Jonathan Harvey's piano and electro-acoustic masterpiece *Tombeau de Messiaen,* and a performance of John Cage's charmingly eccentric *Water Music,* which involved playing whistles, prepared piano, sirens, a pack of cards and water jugs, and moving the dial around on a Roberts radio. Half the fun was not knowing what might turn up live, on local stations; that night an RTÉ lyric fm broadcaster said 'you couldn't call this music, now, could you?', which brought the house down. It was a propitious way to encounter Donnacha.

I'm sure we shared a glass and a laugh afterwards, and he proposed writing me a piece. I formed the impression of someone very bright, permanently fizzing, funny, but at the same time deadly serious. Despite his extreme youth, he taught a heavyweight music technology course at Trinity College Dublin; he also ran his own ensemble, the Crash Ensemble, which took up an inordinate amount of time administering and promoting other composers' work. He believed passionately in tempting young audiences to invest in challenging contemporary music, using smaller and less conventional venues. He worked extraordinarily hard composing; I think the first piece I heard of his was *Junk Box Fraud* (1997), a piece of exuberant, thumping collage that captured the exhilaration of pop culture, disguised as a London Sinfonietta piece. As a composer, Donnacha was (and is) rather hard to pin down; he had joked 'There is a whiff of high-class vandalism about my work,' but his interests were, it seemed to me, highbrow: the spectral music of Gérard Grisey, Samuel Beckett's late works, Ireland caught in the liminal creative space between Britain and America.

Donnacha duly composed *pAt,* an intricate, abstract twelve-minute piece for piano and tape that—rather marvellously—had an older male voice intoning '24,600 b.p.m. [... and] falling ... and rising ... and constant' throughout, in the style of the BBC shipping forecast. (The voice was his grandfather-in-law.) It was simultaneously playful, ironic and didactic. The recited metrics nodded to nineties' dance culture, but also gave clues to the rising and falling tonalities of the piece; the electronics captured early Stockhausen onwards. The piano textures were precise, rather Nancarrow-like, with Jonathan Harvey-inspired arabesques and curlicues.

Both the live player and electro-acoustic part were woven together rhythmically, but not relentlessly; the piece had a driving momentum and argument that only dissolved towards the end. It was a highly scored and virtuosic piano part, with lots of helpful instructions: 'furiously, like a bell ringer', 'gently, as if patting the keys', 'note the independence of the dynamic marks between hands'. Looking at my old score now, festooned with ghostly phone numbers and scribbles (*Fatboy Slim, Hugh Lane*

The title of Donnacha Dennehy's *pAt* is an acronym of piano and tape, and also spells the word 'tap' backwards. Joanna MacGregor took the piece on a Music Network tour and recorded at a crisis-ridden time in 2001.

Gallery/Parnell Square) I notice how much of the tape part I etched in—rhythms, pedal points, 'click', 'pulsing', 'whoosh'—anything to keep me in the right place. (I've often thought the tape part of a piano-and-tape piece needs to be scored in a more detailed way for the pianist; usually it's left blank, and the pianist listens over and over to the electronic part, writing in signposts and landmarks.) *pAt*, though, was satisfyingly substantial to learn, and fun to put together.

Premieres of new works are rarely as smooth as they seem, as recorded by publishers' websites for posterity. There are—more often than not—bumps backstage. New pieces can be delivered late, they may or may not be the length agreed (quite often they're not), and the actual circumstances of performances are difficult to predict or control. (And it matters, because the first performance affects the future life of a piece.) *pAt* was commissioned as part of an Irish Music Network tour in March 2001, with nine concerts around Ireland, and the programme included Bach and Nancarrow, Piazzolla and Somei Satoh, as well as some music written by myself, the visual artist

Kathy Hinde and the sound artist Matthew Fairclough. For the Dublin premiere we were working in a brand-new venue, the Draíocht Centre for the Arts in Blanchardstown. It was so brand new no one knew yet how to turn on the heating, and it was below freezing outside.

I remember rehearsing *pAt* in the afternoon with gloves on, as the sound equipment failed and everyone became frantic. Kathy's visuals projected the waveforms of the music through a vintage camera, via Logic—a pleasingly Cageian concept—but somehow the extreme cold froze everything. The heating remained off that night (sadly the gloves came off), but the computers decided to work for the performance. A success!

Then, a blow: it was the height of the terrible foot-and-mouth crisis in the UK, and the Irish government quite sensibly decided there should be as little travel as possible around the country, for fear of introducing the disease into farming communities. The rest of the tour was cancelled and we were all sent home, but miraculously we reconvened in May, and carried on. (It's hard to imagine, now, quite how this was pulled off, but it was.)

Audiences were both intrigued and entertained by his piece. At the end of the tour, Donnacha and I went into the RTÉ studios in Dublin and recorded *pAt* for commercial release. It took forty-five minutes, and apparently there was a serious contretemps between composer and sound engineer in the recording booth. Like the occasion when the fire brigade arrived at my home while I was practising, I was completely oblivious; I was too busy trying to get the damn piano part right. The recording was first released in 2001 on an album of Irish electro-acoustic music, *By the New Time;* then again on *Elastic Harmonic,* NMC's full-length portrait of Donnacha's music, in 2007.

I was lucky to meet Donnacha Dennehy on the cusp of a big career in America, and it was delightful to work with someone so energetic, wry and committed. His piece showed the best in him: *pAt* was knowledgeably graceful, crafted to his talented fingertips—and all with a sly dig at the establishment.

Chemical change

BARBARA HANNIGAN

I would have been about nineteen years old in Toronto when I found myself sitting in the audience of a programme of chamber music of Gerald Barry, played by a group called Arraymusic.

It was overwhelming. My young heart was beating with excitement and admiration. I wanted to be part of this game. Intense, almost violent, nearly impossible. Frantic, heartbreaking, passionate. And funny. Very funny.

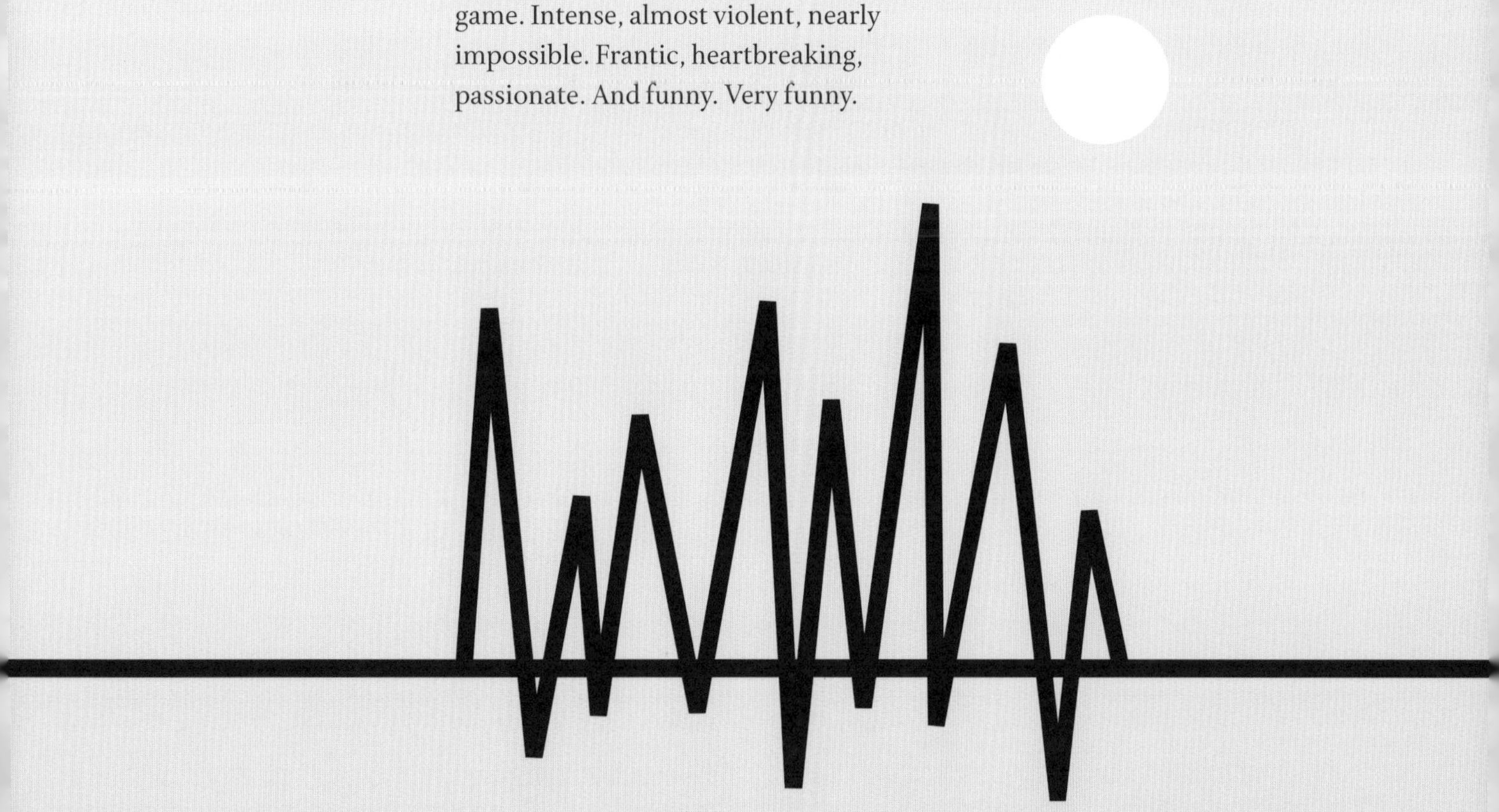

Barbara Hannigan and Gerald Barry in a relaxed moment at the Avanti! Chamber Orchestra's Summer Sounds Festival in Porvoo, Finland, in June 2014.

Over the years our paths began to cross more regularly, and in the early twenty-first century I was asked to audition for his upcoming opera, *The Bitter Tears of Petra von Kant* (2001–04), at English National Opera. I was given the role of Gabi, Petra's adolescent daughter, and we agreed in advance that Gerald would explore the possibility of writing my vocal lines a cappella for much of the time, to have the orchestra cut out completely for long sections as I'd deliver my passages like a virtuoso machine gun. Scary, hysterical, and fun.

As the run of *Petra* was coming to a close, Gerald was already thinking of a new commission for which he had me in mind . . . a setting of Strindberg's monodrama *La Plus Forte*, about an actress who runs into a fellow actress on Christmas Eve, and proceeds to talk at her with breakneck speed until such point as she figures out that this other woman had an affair with her husband.

We gave the premiere in Paris in 2007 (in French) with the City of Birmingham Symphony Orchestra and Tom Adès conducting. Gerald and I prepared my role together . . . he would explain my subtext to me, demonstrate my lines for me in broken and high-octane falsetto, his vocal writing full of dramaturgy and psychological depth. My character (Madame X), was so fully fleshed out by his text setting, at turns comic, poignant, destroyed and proud, that I only had to master the notes and rhythms (which was already a HUGE challenge). I loved his choices and the piece became an incredible dramatic vehicle for me.

Other wickedly fun collaborations ensued . . . Cecily in *The Importance of Being Earnest* (2009–10) (who we think of as a cross between Joni Mitchell and the Undead), and . . . coming up . . . *Alice's Adventures Under Ground*. I haven't seen the score yet but we've had some conversations and I am deliciously shaking in my boots. It's gonna hurt.

I am grateful to him for pushing me as a musician, for seeing something in me and hearing something in my voice that I hadn't yet developed or even recognised, and then challenging me to address it. His music produces a chemical change in me: the whole body shivering in excitement from his combination of notes and rhythm. And warp-speed tempi. And the humour . . . .

When we performed *The Importance of Being Earnest*, concertante, in London and Birmingham, the audience were laughing so loud I couldn't get my next pitch because I couldn't hear the orchestra. We hadn't even staged it but Gerald's musical direction was so clear, and each character's delivery so spot-on, that the audience was wonderfully shocked. And to be onstage during this (!) with Tom Adès simultaneously conducting and chuckling beside me, all of our musical spirits twinkling, dancing, bouncing off the walls of a house that Gerald Barry built. There's nothing like it.

History in the writing

MARTIN ADAMS

A number of issues specific to Irish music and musicology have proved remarkably persistent. And several of these can be seen in the work of the first Irish musicologist to have gained anything approaching an international reputation, the Lismore-born historian, composer and organist, W. H. Grattan Flood (1859–1928). He remains well known for his full-length book *A History of Irish Music* (1905), which is still the only dawn-to-dusk survey of music on this island, and his attempts to prove that some prestigious figures of English music, including John Dowland (1563–1626), Thomas Campion (1567–1620) and Henry Purcell (1659–95), had Irish ancestry and were Roman Catholics, confessed (as with Dowland) or closet.

Musicologists have criticised his methods and his tendency to jump to conclusions. But he cannot be ignored. He is one of the few authors to attempt a synthesis of Ireland's parallel histories of music—on the one hand the aural traditions of folk music such as the harpers, *sean-nós* song and dancing tunes, and on the other music of written transmission.

In an artistic equivalent of the Gaelic Athletic Association's (GAA's) 'foreign games' controversies, the separation between those two musical cultures had become increasingly pronounced during the rise of romantic nationalism across the hundred years or so before Grattan Flood's *History* was published, with traditional music seen as more authentically Irish than the 'imported' repertoires and social functions of classical music. This separation remains a striking aspect of Ireland's musical culture, distinctive in nature and extremity from any other country in Europe. Why this should be and what might be done about it remain topics of lively, sometimes abusive, musicological debate. Grattan Flood's writings reveal a desire for authority, for a prestige whereby Irish music and its history might stand on equal terms with those nations that were internationally recognised as leaders in classical music. His appropriation lends a subtle twist to Declan Kiberd's arguments that an independent Irish cultural identity had been forged partly by making it 'not-England'. At the hands of the Irish musicologist, the so-called English (or sometimes British) Musical Renaissance—which saw Elgar become the first English composer of modern times to achieve international status, which looked to figures such as Purcell and Dowland, and which around 1900 was in full swing—was made to seem not quite as English as the English claimed.

From the late eighteenth century to the 1970s the larger part of the work in Ireland that could be described as musicological had been devoted to ensuring the survival, via publication, of traditional repertoires. Some of the most significant musicological work was written abroad by emigrants. The Dublin-born polymath Frank Llewelyn Harrison (1905–87) forged an outstandingly versatile international career, in several

countries, as an authority on, *inter alia*, English church music, the aesthetics and functions of music in eighteenth-century Ireland, and the sociology of both music and musicology. Jim Samson (b. 1946) was born in Carnlough, Co. Antrim, and has become an internationally recognised authority in various areas of musicology, especially on the lives and music of Chopin (1810–49) and Szymanowski (1882–1937).

Within Ireland a crucial landmark was the 1952 publication, in both Cork and Oxford, of *Music in Ireland: A Symposium,* edited by the indefatigable Aloys Fleishmann (1910–92), who assembled a collection of essays by experts in most areas of music, examining the state of music in the whole island. 'The Composer in Ireland' was written by the internationalist-minded, Dublin-born composer and former director of music at the Abbey

Music historian William Henry Grattan Flood is famous for his extensive body of work, including his *History of Irish Music* and books on the harp, the bagpipe and John Field. He is notorious for claiming Irishness for some celebrated English composers. In his *History* he wrote that 'Ireland can still boast of musical sons and daughters, inheritors of past ages' and listed nearly seventy names, most of them, sadly, now forgotten.

Theatre, Frederick May (1911–85). He praises many musical developments in the Republic over the previous thirty years, including aspects of music education, improvements to the Radio Éireann Symphony Orchestra, and the gradual growth of a public interested in concert music. However, he deplores more than he praises, and most of his complaints are recurrent themes throughout *Music in Ireland*.

This book is far more than a survey: it is also musicology as propaganda and as a tool for campaigning. Both were badly needed to address the Republic's woefully underdeveloped infrastructure for music (Northern Ireland was better developed), the lowly status of the composer in comparison with other countries, the separation between the cultures of traditional and classical music, the poor state of music teaching—the list goes on. *Music in Ireland* does not present a pleasing picture, and nowadays it can only increase one's admiration for those who strove to improve classical music's standing, be they composers, performers, administrators or musicologists.

One of the reasons for the paucity of musicological writing in Ireland before the 1980s was that those who might have been expected to produce it—the holders of the chairs of music at the universities—had to be musical factotums, constantly doing their best to compensate for the lack of infrastructure, of good teaching at primary and secondary schools, and of high-quality public debate about music. This was equally true of Fleischmann, who found the time to complete his main musicological project only after his retirement from University College Cork in 1980 (he had been appointed in 1934), of Brian Boydell (1917–2000) at Trinity College Dublin (appointed 1962), who likewise had his main work published after he had retired, and of Anthony Hughes (1928–2007) at University College Dublin (appointed 1958).

In 1976 the Royal Musical Association published a list of masters and doctoral theses on music produced at universities in the Republic. Just twenty-six completed theses and projects in progress were listed—less than one every two years since the foundation of the state in 1922.

The historically oriented strands in classical and traditional music, represented by the research interests of Grattan Flood, Boydell and Fleischmann, are dominant, via studies of traditional musicians and repertoires, opera in eighteenth-century Dublin by T. J. Walsh (1973), Anglo-Irish music by Ita Hogan (1966), and Irish instruments and iconography. There are also several studies of music in schools. However, there is just one study on Irish classical music from the twentieth century, a master's thesis by Kitty Fadlu-Deen on 'Contemporary Music in Ireland'. And there is nothing on the cultural and ideological tensions that had concerned Grattan Flood and Fleischmann, and that had such a profound impact on composers working in Ireland. It all underlines the fact that up to the 1970s, musicology was an almost invisible art. That was about to change.

In 1988, thirty-year-old Harry White wrote an article, 'Musicology in Ireland'; and high intention is suggested by the fact that it appeared in *Acta Musicologica*, one of the world's oldest and most prestigious musicological journals. White had been a pupil of Anthony Hughes at University College Dublin (UCD), and thereafter studied at the University of Toronto. His survey of musicology since Fleischmann's *Music in Ireland* observed that traditional music had been an exception to the dearth of musicological publication in Ireland, and in support of that point he highlighted the recent work of Breandán Breathnach (1912–85), Tomás Ó Canainn (1930–2013), Hugh Shields (1929–2008), Nicholas Carolan (b. 1946) and the Folk Music Society of Ireland. He rightly found it significant that none of these people was working within a music department, and he observed that, within classical music, the then-recent increase in musicological work had been driven largely by the appointment to university chairs and lectureships of people who were primarily musicologists.

Thanks partly to those appointments made in the 1970s and 1980s the picture changed significantly in the years before and immediately after the publication of White's survey. Numerous monographs, articles and edited collections of essays were published, many of them by major international publishers, and the subjects and branches of musicology ranged as widely as they might in other countries—with one striking exception. In comparison with musicology in countries such as Britain, Germany, France and the USA, there seemed to be little interest in contemporary composition as a subject for research. Any attempt honestly to wonder about that lacuna entails asking discomforting questions. Was it a problem of musicology as then practised in Ireland, or was it a problem with composition? Probably a bit of both. It is hard to escape the conclusion that, justly or unjustly, musicologists did not find any Irish composers interesting enough to devote years of study to them. But one also has to wonder if some of the problems are cultural, rooted perhaps in the intellectual challenges raised by the peculiar position of classical music in Irish society.

For example, at intervals over the last hundred years, even up to the present, people have asked the question, 'Where is the Irish Bartók (or Vaughan Williams or Sibelius)?' All of these composers had found strikingly original ways of incorporating the characteristics of national music into classical composition. Back in the 1930s Aloys Fleischmann had paid special attention to this issue via a number of articles that explored the issue of Irishness in classical music. Moreover, the main figure who sought to write in a self-consciously nationalist idiom, and the only composer to enter into general national consciousness, Seán Ó Riada (1931–71), made his reputation by explicitly moving away from the mainstream European tradition of concert music in which he had started his life as a composer.

Ó Riada's work was covered in *Integrating Tradition: The Achievement of Seán Ó Riada*, edited by Bernard Harris and Grattan Freyer, published in 1981, ten years after the composer's death. Only in the present century have significant studies of living Irish composers appeared, a hundred years after a series of monographs in England, called *Living Masters of Modern Music*, had explored the work of Elgar, Richard Strauss and other composers of that time. The last thirteen years have seen the appearance of monographs, additional to that on Ó Riada, devoted to the life and music of Seóirse Bodley (b. 1933), Raymond Deane (b. 1953), Aloys Fleischmann, John Buckley (b. 1951) and James Wilson (1922–2005). This burst of publication indicates more than increased musicological activity; it suggests a new kind of cultural confidence about Irish classical music in general.

A key event in this change was the appointment of Harry White as Professor of Music at UCD in 1993. He reoriented the college's undergraduate and postgraduate syllabus to emphasise musicology, especially analysis and historical musicology. With the vigorous support of Gerard Gillen (b. 1942), one of his former teachers who had been appointed to the professorship at St Patrick's College Maynooth in 1985, White spearheaded several initiatives that sought to project Irish musicology onto the international stage and to equip it for public debate. These included the foundation of the Society for Musicology in Ireland and of that society's internationally respected *Journal of the Society of Musicology in Ireland,* online at musicologyireland.com; the publication of the ongoing book series *Irish Musical Studies*; conferences in Ireland that attracted international interest and attendance; and the production of the two-volume *Encyclopaedia of Music in Ireland,* which he edited with Barra Boydell, in 2013. Postgraduate students and staff from all Irish universities rode the rising wave of research, and studies emerged from independent scholars, notably Richard Pine (b. 1949), who since the mid 1990s has written or edited a number of historical books on music in Ireland to add to his long list of works on Irish theatre and literature.

When, in 2006, Harry White became the first historical musicologist to be elected to the Royal Irish Academy, it seemed as if it was not just his published output—easily the largest of any musicologist in this country—that was being recognised. So was the distance that musicology, in all its branches, had come in a very few years.

The Society for Musicology in Ireland's register of theses—smimusicthesesregister.com—lists

Opposite: The entry on Ireland in the 1,500 page second edition of the *Encylopedia of Music in Canada* (1992) states that the Irish musicologist Harry White, who studied at the University of Toronto, has used the *Encyclopedia of Music in Canada* as a model for a proposed encylopedia of Irish music. And twenty-one years later, the Irish book was published in two volumes, bringing together more information on Irish music than had ever been assembled in one place before.

nearly 600 projects either submitted or in progress at third-level institutions on this island. Of this surprisingly large number, around twenty are concerned with a twentieth-century or contemporary Irish composer, and most of those are minor theses submitted as a component of a postgraduate degree in performance or composition. However, slimness should not be mistaken for insignificance, for they include critical editions of previously unpublished works, some of which have found their way into a more public domain via the invaluable support offered by the Contemporary Music Centre, in Dublin, and its website, cmc.ie.

Here musicology is performing one of its most valuable functions—promoting the dissemination and performance of music. But critical and analytical studies are crucial too, especially for the possibilities they offer as contributions to public information and debate. In this respect the life-and-works books just mentioned epitomise what musicology can and should do for the contemporary composer. For example, Gareth Cox's account of Bodley's studies in Germany, from the late 1950s to the mid 1960s, and of his later engagement with aspects of Irish traditional music, does far more than observe the ways in which this composer's style developed—it also elucidates the thought, musical and extramusical, that has shaped decisions across a long and varied compositional career.

It is perhaps significant that most of these composer biographies are produced as part of a series edited by two musicologists who are also composers, Séamas de Barra (b. 1955) and Patrick Zuk (b. 1968). That partly explains why these studies prioritise engagement with the music; but it also suggests why both men have been some of the most strident critics of Harry White's views on the history of music in Ireland, which were expounded at length in his 1998 book, *The Keeper's Recital: Music and Cultural History in Ireland 1770–1970*. White maintains that the peculiar position of classical music and its lack of general acceptance within Irish society at large are rooted in the competing claims of nationalist and colonialist cultures, and that such culture of classical music as Ireland had was essentially borrowed from England.

On the whole, White's book has been widely praised in academic journals and elsewhere, and if one of the functions of musicology is to promote public debate, *The Keeper's Recital* has succeeded handsomely. Rightly or wrongly, recurrent themes in responses to the book include the claim that White's thesis reinforces the divide between traditional and classical music, that Irish musical history and its relationship with English music has been richer and more nuanced than he suggests, and that the implications for Irish composition in the twentieth century are unrelievedly and undeservedly dismal. Many of those arguments have been presented in *The Journal of Music*, an award-winning online magazine designed as a forum for information and debate about music of all kinds.

Inevitably, the quality of thought and writing in *The Journal of Music* varies widely, and some of the objections to White's ideas are built on sandy foundations and superficial argument. Perhaps that is why he has not responded publicly to them, though many people have wished he would. Open debate matters. Nevertheless, *The Journal of Music* is remarkable for being a place where the contrasting and sometimes competing strands of Irish music meet on equal terms, a place where discourse between them is actively encouraged. It was founded by a traditional musician, Toner Quinn, in 2000, and was originally a

Opposite: Bob Gilmore was the Irish musicologist who showed the greatest interest in new music, whether Irish or international. His books covered American composers Harry Partch and Ben Johnston and Canadian Claude Vivier, and he wrote insightfully about many Irish composers in *The Journal of Music in Ireland*. He was also director and keyboard player of Trio Scordatura, an ensemble specialising in microtonal music. His untimely death at the age of fifty-three in January 2015 deprived Irish music of one of its most persuasive advocates.

bimonthly printed magazine, *The Journal of Music in Ireland*.

One of its contributors was the Larne-born musicologist Bob Gilmore (1961–2015), whose premature death deprived Ireland of one of its liveliest and most insightful writers on contemporary music. *The Journal of Music* has also offered composers a forum for debate of all kinds, and perhaps the most trenchant writer in that category is Raymond Deane, whose strongly expressed views on numerous topics have provoked responses in subsequent issues of *The Journal*.

Some of the most interesting musicological publications of recent years have been those that, like White's *The Keeper's Recital*, can be regarded as cultural studies. Many of them testify to the endurance of those issues that, some 100 years ago, had so concerned Grattan Flood—identity and authority.

What makes music Irish? When looking at traditional music, nobody seems to have any problem in presenting a convincing answer, as two of the most important books of recent years show—the articles in the award-winning *Companion to Irish Traditional Music,* edited by Fintan Vallely, and Martin Dowling's *Traditional Music and Irish*

Society: Historical Perspectives. Nor does this seem to trouble writers looking at the comparatively recent rise of Ireland as a power in popular music, be it U2, Enya or even that epitome of music as commodity, Westlife. Nevertheless, some attempts to answer that question have been founded on a host of cultural assumptions that at best are intellectually lazy, and at worst musically and culturally ignorant.

One of the challenges for cultural scholars attempting to address the composition of classical music in Ireland is the fact that there never has been a concept of a national school. In this respect too Ireland stands apart from most nations. Yet it seems to me that this is more of a problem for the scholars than it is for the composers, several of whom have, over the last sixty or so years, convincingly refuted arguments that such a school would be possible or artistically desirable. But the issue of Irishness refuses to go away, and it is perhaps telling that several studies addressing this issue are devoted to the area in which Irish musicians have acquired unquestionable international status in recent decades—popular music of various kinds.

However, perhaps the most authoritative studies of Irish musical identity are among the essays to be found in two edited volumes. The first of these, *Irish Music in the Twentieth Century* appeared in 2003 as the seventh volume of *Irish Musical Studies* (*IMS*). Its editors were Gareth Cox and Axel Klein, the latter an important figure in Irish musicology, for he is the author of the first study, in any language (in this case German), of the history of Irish classical music in the twentieth century, and of several other English-language studies of various aspects of Ireland's musical history. The *IMS* volume includes studies of representative works by key composers—Frederick May, Seóirse Bodley, Ian Wilson (b. 1964) and Frank Corcoran (b. 1944), plus chapters on electro-acoustic music, Irish music after Ó Riada, and Klein's own contributions—a twentieth-century Irish music bibliography, and a direct address to the issue of identity, 'Roots and Directions

Opposite: The development of musicology in Ireland brought with it a proliferation of musical conferences. The first conference devoted to women and music in Ireland was held at NUI Maynooth in April 2010.

in Twentieth-Century Irish Art Music'.

The second volume, *Music and Identity in Ireland and Beyond*, edited by Mark Fitzgerald and John O'Flynn, is more wide-ranging than the *IMS* in that its introduction and sixteen essays, spread across some 300 pages, embrace something on many categories of music—traditional, popular, classical, immigrant communities and more. Most essays, including those on classical composition in the twentieth century, address issues of identity with a directness that is both refreshing and, sometimes, brave in its willingness to tackle long-standing, and often unstated, assumptions about Irishness in music.

One of the recurrent aspects of those essays, and of comments made in the *Journal of Music*, is that identity in Irish classical composition, from Thomas Roseingrave in the eighteenth century to composers of today, is seen partly in the heterogeneity, and even the ruggedness, of the works. This is equally true of the individual composers and of any collective view one might take of them. One could say that one of Ireland's most striking national characteristics—the tendency to emphasise individuals rather than institutions or systems, finds, in classical music, a distinctive expression via the differences between and within the outputs of its composers.

Moreover, this analysis seems to fit rather neatly into the picture presented by two recent publications on composition in Ireland. Significantly, a book by the composer, guitarist and musicologist Benjamin Dwyer (b. 1965), which offers an overview of music in Ireland since 1700, and includes interviews with twelve Irish composers ranging in age from twenty-six to eighty, is called *Different Voices*. Secondly, Raymond Deane, in a virtuosic, too-often overlooked essay published in 2005 in *The Republic* (the journal of The Ireland Institute), takes on the thorny topic of Ireland's musical history, especially the presupposition that its discontinuities have stood in the way of developing a healthy musical culture. The title is 'Exploding the Continuum: The Utopia of Unbroken Tradition'. His scepticism is well-founded. Moreover, and as history teaches us, Utopias have a nasty habit of turning into tyrannies.

It is interesting that the rise of musicology in Ireland coincides closely with the rise to prominence of the first Irish composer since Field and Stanford to have attracted widespread international attention, Gerald Barry (b. 1952). Perhaps, in years to come, this parallel rise in compositional and musicological prominence will be seen as a highly specific manifestation of a rise in national confidence. Whatever, no Irish composer before Barry has attracted such critical attention, or has received so many commissions and performances from the most prestigious groups, organisations and venues worldwide. If musicology has been a bit slow in trying to catch up with him, that is perhaps because of the intimidating force of his compositional voice. We await a full-length study, but it is telling that some of the most interesting articles have come from the minds and ears of composers. A striking example is 'Speed and Slowness in the Music of Gerald Barry', by the York-based composer-scholar Daniel March (b. 1972), which addresses, with intellectual clarity and aural acuity, one of the most striking aspects of Barry's distinctive compositional character.

The other composer living and working in Ireland to have attracted significant musicological attention, both because of the strength of his music and because of his distinctive compositional techniques, is South Africa-born Kevin Volans (b. 1949), who made his home here in 1986.

Harry White's *The Progress of Music in Ireland* (2005) has stimulated numerous responses in international peer-reviewed journals, as well as in the online *Journal of Music*. Again, the contentious issues are his views of Irish music's history, but this volume is also significant for including ideas that were to become central to his next monograph. His *Music and the Irish Literary Imagination* (2008) explores the ways in which music has shaped the growth of the Irish literary imagination over the last 200 years, from Thomas Moore to Seamus Heaney and Brian Friel. One of the central tenets of White's historical views is that in Ireland music has been marginalised in favour of literature, to a level perhaps unmatched by any other European country. In this book, music gains ground by becoming attached to the form in which Irish artists have unquestionable prestige, identity and authority. One does not have to agree with everything in it to note, as most reviewers have, that it is a considerable achievement, as much literary criticism as it is musicology.

Although musicology in Ireland still has not found the place in public debate that Harry White and many others would wish for it, it does seem to have come of age. So let's celebrate with a bang. The prize for the best title in all of Irish musicology goes to Mark Fitzgerald, who is one of the most active writers on contemporary Irish composition and an astute analyst. The essential adjective and noun came from the critic Anthony Bye, but even so, Fitzgerald deploys them with flair. His contribution to the eleventh volume of *Irish Musical Studies* is called 'On Constructing a Sonic Gangbang: System and Subversion in Gerald Barry's *Chevaux-de-frise*'. That's stuff for grown-ups.

2001–2016

2001

The Sonic Arts Research Centre (SARC) is founded at Queen's University Belfast.

Axel Klein's *Irish Classical Recordings, A Discography of Irish Art Music* is published by Greenwood Press.

The Orchestra of St Cecilia begins a ten-year series of the complete church cantatas by Bach, in partnership with a wide range of soloists, choirs and conductors.

2002

The first RTÉ Living Music Festival is held at the newly opened Helix, a venue with a 1,250-seat concert hall, 450-seat theatre and 132-seat black box space, on the campus of Dublin City University.

Composer Ian Wilson is appointed director of the Sligo New Music Festival.

2003

Marcus Patton's *The Opera Hat of Sir Hamilton Harty*, a collection of musical illustrations, caricatures and concert posters, is published by Grand Piano Press in Belfast.

The Dundalk Institute of Technology establishes a music department, Ceol Oirghialla.

The Life and Music of Brian Boydell, edited by Gareth Cox, Axel Klein and Michael Taylor, is published by Irish Academic Press.

The ConTempo String Quartet, formed in Bucharest in 1995, becomes Galway's first ensemble in residence.

2004

The new £4.5 million Sonic Arts Research Building at Queen's University Belfast, which includes a suspended performance space with an acoustically transparent floor that allows for sound projection from above and below as well as laterally around the audience, is formally opened by Karlheinz Stockhausen and hosts its first concert during the Sonorities Festival.

Harpsichordist David Adams gives the first concert promoted by the Young Composers' Collective, founded by composer and guitarist David Flynn.

2005

Richard Pine's *Music and Broadcasting in Ireland* is published by Four Courts Press.

The Contemporary Music Centre creates its touring exhibition on Irish composers, *The Art of Sound*, for Cork as European Capital of Culture.

2006

At the Printing House Festival of New Music in Dublin in November, American pianist Matthew McCright gives the premiere of Garrett Sholdice's *Étude*, which at ninety-five minutes is one of the longest piano pieces ever written.

The composers Enda Bates, Brian Bridges, Linda Buckley, Simon Cullen, Liam Grant, Daniel Jacobson, Ian McDonnell and Jonathan Nangle, all graduates of TCD, form the Spatial Music Collective.

2007

Kenneth Montgomery succeeds Thierry Fischer as principal conductor of the Ulster Orchestra, and becomes the first Irish musician to hold the post.

The CIT Cork School of Music moves into its €62 million new home on Union Quay.

Fiona Palmer takes up the post of professor of music at NUI Maynooth, becoming the first female professor of music in Ireland.

2008

Elaine Agnew is appointed the first composer in residence of RTÉ lyric fm.

Brian Irvine is appointed associate composer of the Ulster Orchestra.

2009

At the Project Arts Centre in Dublin, Jennifer Walshe curates the first major retrospective of the avant-garde sound art collective Grúpat, all of whose work is actually by Walshe herself.

2010

The First International Conference on Irish Music and Musicians is held at the University of Durham in July.

The government drops plans to build a new auditorium on the Earlsfort Terrace site of the National Concert Hall in Dublin.

The first *Women and Music in Ireland* conference is held at NUI Maynooth in April.

The 2,111-seat, Daniel Libeskind-designed Grand Canal Theatre opens in Dublin.

2011

Gerald Barry's opera, *The Importance of Being Earnest*, after the play by Oscar Wilde, is premiered in concert by the Los Angeles Philharmonic Orchestra under Thomas Adès.

2012

John Kinsella's Symphony No. 10 is premièred by the Irish Chamber Orchestra, cementing the composer's position as the most prolific of Irish symphonists.

2013

The two-volume *Encyclopaedia of Music in Ireland*, edited by Harry White and Barra Boydell, is published by University College Dublin Press.

2014

Benjamin Dwyer's *Different Voices, Irish Music and Music in Ireland* is published by Wolke Verlag.

Galway's ensemble in residence, the ConTempo String Quartet, become the new resident ensemble at RTÉ, replacing the Vanbrugh Quartet.

Composer Raymond Deane's frank memoir, *In My Own Light*, is published by the Liffey Press.

2015

The Kirkos Ensemble performs three carefully themed programmes, all with specially commissioned works, in the dark, with aromas, wine and food, at the Royal Irish Academy of Music in Dublin.

2016

Composing the Island, the largest ever festival of Irish music, surveying the century 1916–2016, is presented by RTÉ and the National Concert Hall with sponsorship from Bord na Móna in September.

The Invisible Art is published in connection with the festival.

Metamorphoses in a new millennium

LIAM CAGNEY

If, as the saying goes, you can't throw a stone in Ireland without hitting a poet, the 2000s saw composers proliferate as alternative targets for stone throwing. In 2016, 186 active living composers were registered with the Contemporary Music Centre (CMC) and between 2000 and 2015 the Arts Council commissioned 235 new works from Irish composers working in all genres, an average of over fourteen per year. In terms of performing groups, Concorde, which was founded in 1976, was joined in 1997 by the Crash Ensemble and later by numerous smaller bands. New music continued to be heard not just in Dublin, Cork and Belfast, but also in other urban centres and in communities visited by Music Network tours. And the Association of Irish Composers (AIC) was joined by the young composers group the Irish Composers' Collective (ICC).

In scholarship, Irish music history was brought into focus by the publication in 2013 of the two-volume *Encyclopaedia of Music in Ireland*, edited by Harry White and Barra Boydell. In journalism, Irish music's forking pathways had a regular unified organ in the bimonthly magazine *The Journal of Music in Ireland*, edited by Toner Quinn, which sat 'Schnittke opposite Willie Clancy' and 'John Coltrane opposite *sean-nós* singing'. If from the point of view of investment and infrastructure things remained far from ideal—'contemporary music has lagged behind other artforms in securing a valued position in the Irish arts world,' remarks the Arts Council's 2006 *Sounds New* report—the resourcefulness of young musicians was encouraging.

In Gerald Barry (b. 1952) Ireland had an internationally fêted composer. In Jennifer Walshe (b. 1974) Ireland had a composer influencing the current of European music through her teaching at the Darmstadt International Summer Course for New Music. In the Crash Ensemble Ireland had a new music ensemble performing at Carnegie Hall. In RTÉ lyric fm's programme *Nova*, Ireland had a radio show disseminating contemporary music around the country at a regular time each week. The success of Bill Whelan (b. 1950) through *Riverdance* was global.

Certainly the Irish music scene had changed since Denis Donoghue's famous 1955 remark that 'internationally, contemporary Irish music does not exist'. Not only had Irish music matured; it had mutated. These changes were most apparent in the way that long-established music styles were joined by new registers like noise music and, most prominently, amplified post-minimalist music.

Crash and Boom

Up till 2000 the predominant influence on young Irish music was Europe, but with the rise of the Crash Ensemble the scales tipped towards America. Donnacha Dennehy (b. 1970) returned to Ireland in the mid 1990s after Fulbright-sponsored studies at the University of Illinois and a period in the Netherlands. He took with him the idea of a new music ensemble, similar to America's Bang on a Can or the Netherlands' Orkest de Volharding, that would perform his own music as well as the hard-edged sounds coming out of New York City and Amsterdam. In the wake of a sell-out first concert in 1997 attended by the group's spiritual godfather, Louis Andriessen, Crash established a loyal following in boom-time Dublin. Over the subsequent decade, Dennehy's standout compositions and the ensemble's aesthetic, not to mention Dennehy's position as lecturer in music and media technology at

The Crash Ensemble, founded in 1997, and its artistic director, Donnacha Dennehy, brought a cool front that contemporary music in Ireland had never had before. Dennehy cemented the American orientation of his outlook when he brought Alan Pierson onboard as principal conductor in 2006.

Trinity College Dublin, influenced a generation of young Irish composers. 'I wanted the music to feel necessary to the world of today, not some sort of diligent, well-meaning continuation of a museum culture,' Dennehy said. 'The bias in mainstream Irish cultural life is towards commercial pop and rock and a traditional music that should know its place. Many would be surprised by the current vitality of the new "classical" music coming from Ireland.'

This was 'the new Irish classical': contemporary classical for the iPod generation, for music lovers who considered Sonic Youth as valid as Schubert. A key representation of the aesthetic is Dennehy's 2007 portrait CD on NMC Records, *Elastic Harmonic,* which features performances by the Crash Ensemble, the RTÉ National Symphony Orchestra and others. 'Streetwise, soulless,' wrote *Gramophone* magazine, 'hymning the urban jungle and having nothing to do with pastoral escapism, nostalgia or spirituality.' *Streetwalker* (2003) for ensemble trudges along with repeated stabs and octaves in the piano, groans in the winds, syncopated thuds in the double bass and distorted electric guitar; *O* (2002) for orchestra, all insistent pulses and woozy glissandi, is pummelling in a manner directly comparable to the experimental rock bands playing most nights in Dublin basement venues. Dennehy's music, with its rock lustre, had broader appeal than much other contemporary music. A 2005 episode of the television series *The Symphony Sessions* featured Dennehy's RTÉ-commissioned violin concerto *Elastic Harmonic* (2005). This non-traditional concerto, performed by Ioana Petcu-Colan with the RTÉ NSO, is based on hypnotic rhythmic loops with edgy elements including a group of 'prepared violins' with paper clips attached to their strings. The broadcast showed the nation that rarest of things: an Irish composer on prime-time television.

The main Northern Irish composer in the new Irish classical is Ed Bennett (b. 1975). Like Dennehy, Bennett founded an ensemble, Decibel, based in Birmingham, and the group's first album of Bennett's music, *Dzama Stories* (2010), mixes coruscating tenor saxophone improvisation by Paul Dunmall, tight ensemble playing, and electronics by the composer. Bennett's portrait CD for NMC Records, *My Broken Machines* (2011), features performances by Garth Knox (viola), the ConTempo String Quartet, the Fidelio Trio and others, and lounges in cartoonish violence and sharp colour contrasts. *Suspect Device* (2014), at once hard-edged and finely wrought, features electric guitar and bass, amplified violin and crashing percussion in a tortuous tonality; its title is at once a reference to a well-known Troubles-era euphemism and an eponymous song by the punk band Stiff Little Fingers. *Togetherness* (2015), written for Decibel, shows a stylistic development, taking the slowly shifting soundscapes of French spectral composers like Gérard Grisey and bringing them into Bennett's own particular universe of disorientation and funnelled intensity: a slow textural drift of instrumental colour gradually and all but imperceptibly moulds itself into a two-chord riff pumped out by trombone, alto sax, clarinet and strings, with snare-heavy drum kit creating a chugging rhythm reminiscent of No Wave rock before dissolving in violin tremolo and melodica drone.

David Fennessy's (b. 1976) has been a more independent voice. Professionally based at the Royal Conservatoire of Scotland (the former Royal Scottish Academy of Music and Drama), he is published by Universal

Opposite: Like one of his teachers, Brian Irvine, Ed Bennett is a composer whose mixing of musical ingredients and interest in improvisation can make categorisation of his work fluid. As Irvine has pointed out, Bennett's often high-voltage approach produces 'Music that grows from the cracks in the usual categories.'

Edition and his style is multifarious. In *La Rejouissance—La Paix* (2010), commissioned by Ensemble Modern for its thirtieth birthday, material from Handel's *Music for the Royal Fireworks* is used to create a contrast between a glowering ensemble and a beaming chord. *Caruso (Gold is the sweat of the sun)* (2012), scored for four samplers and electric guitar, nods towards Werner Herzog's film *Fitzcarraldo*, using a haunting recording of tenor Enrico Caruso to evoke an exotic fluvial dream. In *BODIES* (2010), commissioned by the RTÉ NSO, ebbing and flowing strings combine with resonant gongs to create a lustrous texture. Fennessy had mainstream success in the UK with the (as he put it) 'sort of' opera *Pass the Spoon* (2014), a collaboration with artist David Shrigley, the action of which takes place on the set of a daytime TV cookery show and whose quirky dramatis personae include June Spoon, Philip Fork, the giant Mr Granules and The Banana (a giant Latino banana).

An exceptional work of the new Irish classical was Andrew Hamilton's (b. 1977) *music for people who like art* for soprano and ensemble, commissioned by the Crash Ensemble; its 2011 premiere, sung by Michelle O'Rourke at Crash's annual Free State concert, caused a stir. Unlike Bennett and Dennehy,

Below: Composer and guitarist David Fennessy is a man for whom unpredictability seems to be the only certainty. *Big Lung* (2008) sets up a Brobdignagian tug of war between two heavily armed percussionists and the monster sonorities of an organ. *Music for the pauses in a conversation between John Cage and Morton Feldman* (2010) offers exactly what the title suggests. There's never any knowing where he will venture next.

Overleaf: Gerald Barry's setting of Oscar Wilde's *The Importance of Being Earnest* has become the runaway Irish operatic success of the twenty-first century. Pictured here from the Wide Open Opera/NI Opera production, directed and designed by Antony McDonald, are: in the photo on the left, Peter Tantsits (Jack), Jessica Walker (Gwendolen); in the photo on the right, Aoife Miskelly (Cecily), Jessica Walker (Gwendolen).

Hamilton has no interest in rock music: 'I was never in a rock band and I was formally trained in the Western classical tradition from the age of seven, studied fugue and counterpoint and auditioned for the Late Late Toy Show.' Hamilton's music uses lots of repetition—'to create a state of unease, ambiguity, and sometimes joy'—presenting a sort of cubist rendering of tonality wherein the fabric of the common practice Western tradition comes at the listener in a flurry of shreds. *music for people who lose people* (2008) is an aural counterpart to Duchamp's *Nude Descending a Staircase No. 2*, all lines and angles and colours. Short motifs are reiterated and expanded incessantly, steel drum and electric bass guitar prominent among an ensemble also featuring piano and brass—'zany' is one over-simplistic adjective, 'deranged' another; at base it is just focused, exuberant and original music.

Traditions

A touchstone for each of the above composers to some degree is Gerald Barry. The 2000s saw Barry's stock rise both at home and in the wider classical world, and internationally he is currently the most successful living Irish composer. When I interviewed him one sunny afternoon in London in spring 2012, he discussed the short-lived new music group he co-founded back in 1981 in Cologne along with Kevin Volans and Chris Newman: the Society for Newer Music. 'We never did anything,' Barry said, 'but we wrote a manifesto. The manifesto said something grand, like that we considered all music to be ours'—shades of Stephen Dedalus; and Barry went on, 'our aim was to write music with a sense of wonder. And it's quite good that, actually. That is something that has stayed with me all my life: the main thing is to write music with a sense of wonder.'

Wonder and risk characterise Barry's most successful work to date, the opera *The Importance of Being Earnest* (2012). Here he successfully negotiated the feat of setting Wilde's famous text in a composition on a grand scale that gives lie to the notion that one can't simultaneously be musically avant-garde and capture popular attention. Barry's idiosyncratic approach saw him cast Lady Bracknell as a bass and write vocal parts careering in spitfire fashion and containing more angles than a Picasso portrait.

A memorable scene is the catty duet of Gwendolen and Cecily, which features the ladies chatting bitchily to each other through megaphones; its

climax sees a percussionist valiantly smashing plates in time to a long sentence of Gwendolen's, each plate-smash punctuating a gap in her speech; as well as this delicacy the percussionist, for good measure, fires a few gunshots from an air gun, slams a carnival-hammer into the ground, and along with another percussionist whacks two pairs of boots into the ground, the boots worn on their arms like long black gloves. Hailed by the *Los Angeles Times* after its world premiere concert performance as 'maybe the most inventive Oscar Wilde opera since Richard Strauss' *Salome* more than a century ago', *Earnest* went on to win Barry the 2013 Royal Philharmonic Society Music Award for Large-Scale Composition, and sold out for every night of its staging at the Royal Opera's Linbury Theatre in London; the NMC CD release was nominated for a Grammy Award.

'The fact that you call a piece a concerto doesn't mean it's in a classical form,' Raymond Deane (b. 1953) has remarked. The 2000s saw Deane compose in a variety of such traditional forms, including a concerto and nocturnes; the most high-profile was the opera *The Alma Fetish*, a collaboration with librettist Gavin Kostick that is one of the major Irish compositions of the past twenty years. The plot, suggested to Deane by RTÉ lyric fm producer Ethna Tinney, is based on the bizarre-but-true story of the painter Oskar Kokoschka's infatuation with Alma Mahler, widow of the composer Gustav Mahler, which led the mentally-ill Kokoschka, once she rejected him, to have an anatomically accurate full-scale model of her made. The painter subsequently stepped out in the dining rooms and streets of Vienna with this life-sized doll. The opera's action also takes us to Dresden and Venice. 'The story is a gift,' as Kostick remarks. Certainly *The Alma Fetish*'s theme of the kaleidoscope of sexual practices chimed with the times, in a period when drag queen Panti Bliss received the popular moniker of Queen of Ireland.

Several other composers created important works in traditional forms. Ian Wilson's (b. 1964) long solo piano work *Stations* (2007) is arranged into fourteen sections corresponding to the Stations of the Cross. It inevitably calls Oliver Messiaen's *Vingt regards sur l'enfant Jésus* to mind, and it is a rare example of recent Irish music engaging with Ireland's Christian Heritage. Kevin Volans's Sixth String Quartet (2000) is one of the major contributions to that genre internationally, a work wholly built on a slow-moving, two-chord vamp in a minor key.

Other important string quartets include John McLachlan's (b. 1964) *Where we are* (2012), in which the quartet's members are spatially distributed around the audience like celestial bodies; Rhona Clarke's (b. 1958) *Pas de Quatre* (2009), a single-movement work based on repeating cellular loops and ostinatos, performed to a specially created video by visual artist Marie Hanlon; Siobhán Cleary's (b. 1970) *Scenes from a Dongba Script* (2012), alternately beautiful and brutal, which sets folk melodies from the Naxi Ancient music tradition within a contemporary idiom; and Elaine Agnew's (b. 1967) *Ready, Steady, Go!* (2004), a brief quartet in a Bartókian style.

Volans also composed the delightfully fragmented Trio Concerto (2005) for violin, cello and piano, featured on his RTÉ lyric fm portrait CD. John Buckley added to his Organ Concerto with Concertos for Bassoon (2001), Flute (2006) and Violin (2008). Gráinne Mulvey's (b. 1966) *Akanos* (2006) for orchestra and the cello concerto *Excursions and Ascents* (2014) evoke natural, sometimes violently tectonic processes. Jane O'Leary's (b. 1946) Piano Quintet (2005) encapsulates the stillness and colour of a lake at sunrise in the dawn air. Among the works composed since 2000 by John Kinsella (b. 1932), one of Ireland's most fecund composers, were Symphonies Nos 9 (2004) and 10 (2012), Cello Concerto No. 2 (2000), String Quartet No. 5 (2013) and the neo-romantic *Cúchulainn and Ferdia—Duel at the Ford* (2008), which latter, premiered at the RTÉ NSO's 60th Anniversary Concert, recalls our mythic past. Of the younger generation, meanwhile, Seán Doherty (b. 1987) was among the most promising, winning several awards for choral works and composing the insistently undulating orchestral work *Hive Mind* (2015).

Music evoking traditional Irish music remained the default choice for some of our cultural programmers. At *A Nation's Voice*, a March 2016 outdoor orchestral concert with large choir that was part of the state's Easter Rising centenary celebrations, Shaun Davey (b. 1948) and Bill Whelan (b. 1950) took the spotlight. Another composer seeking to fuse traditional and classical music, albeit with the emphasis more weighted towards the former than is the case with Davey and Whelan, is Mícheál Ó Súilleabháin (b. 1950). In 2001 Virgin Records released Ó Súilleabháin's album *Templum*, featuring works mostly from the previous decade performed by the Irish Chamber Orchestra and the National Chamber Choir. In *Templum* Ó Súilleabháin appealed to a mainstream audience, for example in *In Search of Ancient Ireland* (2001), originally composed

Composer and pianist Mícheál Ó Súilleabháin built an academic empire as professor of music at the University of Limerick, where he created the Irish World Academy of Music and Dance as 'a space where musicians, dancers, composers, singers, conductors and choreographers explore together.'

to accompany the television documentary of the same name and which, in a manner analogous to Ó Súilleabháin's teacher Seán Ó Riada's *Mise Éire* Suite (1959), orchestrates a group of traditional Irish melodies. 'Streetwalk' (2000) features modal writing and less metrically obvious rhythms, and here, as often, Ó Súilleabháin sets a slow, lyrical instrumental solo (on cello) to a background of more or less static chords. In certain ways this music chimes with so-called Holy Minimalism, and in terms of tonality it is not far from the music composed by some younger Irish composers.

The New Sincerity

The fallout of the 2007–08 financial crisis inevitably saw cuts in arts funding. But less predictably it also witnessed the appearance of a new ethos among young composers. If the boom period was about braggadocio and spikiness, the recession brought a certain sentimentality and introspection. This New Sincerity was most clearly signalled in the change of direction in Dennehy's music with the 2011 Irish premiere at IMMA of his Celtic Twilight song cycle *That the Night Come* (2010). As soprano Dawn Upshaw, watched from the walls of the Great Hall by portraits of nobility past, sang the lines of W. B. Yeats's 'The White Birds' ('I would that we were, my beloved, white birds on the foam of the sea!'), her gentle minor scales delicately backed by piano and flute, it was obvious something had changed. 'There has been a real problem in contemporary classical music of this "ironic detachment" from feelings,' Dennehy commented, 'and [recently] my music has become more unbridled emotionally.' This turn towards sentimentality and direct emotion resonated, too, with currents in the broader arts sphere, such as the work of American author David Foster Wallace. 'Today's risks are different,' Wallace said. 'The new rebels might be artists willing to risk accusations of sentimentality, melodrama. Of overcredulity. Of softness.'

Dennehy's new stylistic direction and engagement with Ireland past was foreshadowed in *Grá agus Bás* (*Love and Death*) (2007) for *sean-nós* singer and ensemble, and continued in *The Hunger* (2014) for soprano, *sean-nós* singer, vintage recordings, electronics, video interviews and ensemble. The new style turned away from dissonance towards a more palatable neo-tonalism and swapped urban grit for pastoral hues. Dennehy distinguished his presentation of traditional Ireland from that of composers who 'exploit it for commercial gain,' people 'usually from the world of light entertainment, who exploited elements of the dance music in what seemed like a definite attempt to appeal to largely conservative native Irish and Irish-American tastes.' Nonetheless, his move to a more sentimental vein undoubtedly broadened his appeal both in his native country and his adopted United States. Dennehy's style of the New Sincerity was displayed on his album *That the Night Come* on Nonesuch Records (home to Steve Reich among others) and heralded a shift among a number of younger composers towards a revised tonality and an avoidance of conceptual complication.

Prominent in all this has been Ergodos, a label and production company founded by two of Dennehy's former pupils, Benedict Schlepper-Connolly (b. 1985) and Garrett Sholdice (b. 1983). Aimed at 'presenting beautiful, transformative performances to diverse audiences,' Ergodos has since the beginning tended to eclecticism. Its concerts and record releases embrace traditional Irish music and settings of J. S. Bach as well as contemporary classical and microtonality. Schlepper-Connolly and Sholdice's compositions invoke the idea of the minimal rather than minimalism per se. In this approach the slow repetition and gradual variation of a minimal number of elements is used to create a maximum effect, with the aim of leading the listener, absorbed in the carefully stripped-down sound-world, to a subtly ecstatic experience. Accordingly, the music is at times presented with a quasi-spiritual undertone.

Ergodos's first album, *Dubh* (2010), features performances by Trio Scordatura of works by Linda Buckley (b. 1979), Judith Ring (b. 1976), Peter Moran (b. 1981) and Scott McLaughlin (b. 1975), as well as Schlepper-Connolly and Sholdice themselves, and was something of an aesthetic mission statement. In terms of later works, Schlepper-Connolly's *Bridge* (2013) for ensemble, named after the artist Nigel Peake's reductions of complex configurations into simple geometric forms, and *Shelter* (2012) for large ensemble, are slow-moving, tonal and meditative, with sustained pitches, repeating gestures and delicately weighted timbres; while Sholdice's *The Root and the Crown* (2016) for ensemble is quiet, slow-moving and graceful, draped in a melancholy arboreal mythos, and the clarinet concerto *Am Obersee* (2013), written for Jonathan Sage, balances still melody with startling microtonal harmonies.

Benedict Schlepper-Connolly (left) and Garrett Sholdice (right) are the composers behind the music production company Ergodos. Ergodos promotes concerts and issues recordings that freely cross boundaries between musical genres and style. Unlike the RTÉ lyric fm label, where the focus is national, the Ergodos label's artistic reach is international.

Linda Buckley's path, broadly speaking, has not been dissimilar to that of her teacher, Dennehy. In *Do You Remember the Planets?* (2004) a solo violin is pitted against a fantastically brutal electronic part, reminiscent of the glitch music of acts such as Autechre. Yet, like Schlepper-Connolly and Sholdice, her music can also veer towards the sedative, and more recent works have embraced a neo-tonal surface. In 2011 she was announced as RTÉ lyric fm's composer in residence for three years. On the announcement, she said she wanted her music to be communicative, and the head of lyric, Aodán Ó Dubhghaill, indicated that the brief in part involved composing music that would lend itself to repeated performance and listening. Buckley's works resulting from this tenure include *Chiyo* (2011) for orchestra, inspired by the haiku poetry of Chiyo-ni (and which was also

performed by the BBC Symphony Orchestra), a work of beautiful intertwining string textures in the vein of Arvo Pärt, with a nod, perhaps, to Barber and Vaughan Williams. This direct emotionality continued with *Ó Íochtar Mara* (*From the Ocean's Floor*) (2015) a song cycle for *sean-nós* singer and string quartet, written for Iarla Ó Lionáird and the Vanbrugh String Quartet, setting Irish poetry going back to the seventh century.

Also part of this movement is Seán Clancy (b. 1984). As well as bypassing irony for emotional directness, Clancy's music meditates on the idea of 'artistic intervention'. The artwork here engages objects and situations from the everyday world to give them a new and personal charge, as in *Findetotenlieder* (2011–12) for soprano and ensemble. This six-verse song sets text from the visual artist Gabriel Orozco's piece *Obit*, a compendium of single lines from obituaries in *The New York Times*. Following two scores commissioned and premiered by the RTÉ NSO, *Changing Rates of Change* (2012) and *Ten Minutes of Music on the Subject of IKEA* (2014), Clancy's first

Linda Buckley is a founding member of the Spatial Music Collective, and her work engages with non-Western musical cultures and cultivates electro-acoustic treatment with finesse. Her sister Irene is also a composer and the two have worked on projects together. The late Bob Gilmore wrote of her, suggesting that certain works engage 'with an area of experience that new music is generally shy of, which, simplified and reduced to a single word, I'd call ecstasy.'

Composer and guitarist Benjamin Dwyer has always had a hands-on approach to musical life. He was co-founder of the Mostly Modern concert series, which spawned its own ensemble, VOX21, and he has written two books, *Different Voices: Irish Music and Music in Ireland*, and *Constellations, The Life and Music of John Buckley*.

album was released in 2015, *Forty-Five Minutes of Music on the Subject of Football*. Scored for four electric guitars, *Forty-Five Minutes* explores pastness and nostalgia, and its musical form is modelled on a key moment in Irish cultural memory, the first half of the football game between the Republic of Ireland and Italy at World Cup 1994 in the USA. The musical material at any given time—the pitch content and the members of the quartet playing—alters according to which team is in possession of the ball at the corresponding moment in the football game. The concept of *Forty-Five Minutes* recalls the pop art of Andy Warhol, an updated equivalent to the luminous, nostalgia-tinged screen prints of Monroe and Elvis; it also reflects the rock scene through which many young Irish composers these days pass.

The Trans-Generation

Rather than seeking solace in landscapes and lyricism, some composers sought to rethink the country entirely. In this regard a few conjured the

Opposite: Jennifer Walshe, here photographed in 2004, is a composer and performer whose work crosses not only musical boundaries but trawls also through the worlds of theatre and visual art. Her intellectual voracity is no barrier to a style of vocal performance that has a rare, let-it-all-hang-out rawness. Her energy has driven her to create a series of alter egos, artistic ancestors she feels she never had in the often placid history of composition in Ireland.

primordial past. Frank Corcoran (b. 1944) explored the mythopoetic imagination in works such as his Cello Concerto (2012). 'What was this little island I came from? Contemporary Ireland didn't interest me at all, nor does it today,' he told fellow composer Benjamin Dwyer (b. 1965). 'But, by God, fifth- and sixth-century Ireland did. This was my big myth.' For Dwyer, 'The renovation of lost cultural and spiritual practices thus forms the basis of Corcoran's project to reinvent Ireland through music rich in mythic significance.' Dwyer's own *Scenes from Crow* (2014) for amplified ensemble, soprano and tape, based on Ted Hughes's poetry collection *Crow: From the Life and Songs of Crow* (1972), is a furious, dissonant work, while *SacrumProfanum* (2015), composed with poet Kimberly Campanello and scored for an ensemble featuring viola, soprano, electronics and uilleann pipes, focuses on sheela-na-gigs, overtly sexual images of women found on stone monuments around Ireland.

No composer probed Irish cultural identity as inventively, however, as Jennifer Walshe (b.1974). In the early 2000s, after studies in in Glasgow and Chicago, Walshe became known internationally as an avant-garde *enfant terrible* with works such as *XXX LIVE NUDE GIRLS!!!* (2003), a music theatre piece for Barbie dolls. Afterwards she branched out into inventing musical personas and in the mid 2000s she created *The Observation of Hibernation Law*, a four-hour installation piece based on myriad text documents outlining the complex administration of an imaginary country based on Ireland. 'The whole idea was to try and create a massive system of procedures that describe how an imaginary country runs—Hibernalia, my alternative Ireland. One of the Milker Corporation's functions is as the monolithic administrator of every aspect of hibernation life.'

The imaginary Milker Corporation begat Grúpat, a collective of fake composers and musicians, each invented and performed by Walshe herself. These include Detleva Verens, an Estonian composer interested in 'the affective power of the spatiality of sound' (parodying the propensity for jargon among composers), the Dowager Marchylove, a human sampler of environmental sounds who performs in grand fashion in full Celtic gown, black tousled hair and moustache, and Turf Boon, who creates 'music' via silent movies. Walshe notes: 'Beckett said that when he was writing he had to be the actor saying the lines, the audience watching the play, and the playwright controlling it, all at the same time. You shift through these different roles; performing, or improvising, is something I do a lot when composing'.

Walshe's work spans different media, and often involves her own virtuosic vocal talent. It inhabits a unique and not often visited crossing point between contemporary composition, folk music, art rock, theatre, performance art and film. The exciting thing is the way she strings these different strands together in a knot, leaving the audience to untie it while she uses the result in her performative skipping rope. Walshe terms this recent movement towards a multimedia avant-gardism the New Discipline; the poet Dave Lordan calls it the Trans-Generation. High points of the Trans-Generation so far include Walshe's *THE TOTAL MOUNTAIN* (2014), a spirit journey through internet chaos performed by a costumed Walshe along with tape and video, and *Aisteach*, a fake history of the Irish avant-garde, conceived and edited by Walshe (who commissioned various composers and writers to contribute to it), that blurs the lines between literature and musical composition.

A precedent for Walshe's play of personas and artistic media is the work of Roger Doyle (b.1949). 'You jump in,' Doyle has said of working with digital technology, 'and you're never quite sure what's going to come out at the other end.' Following his magnum opus to date, *Babel* (1981–99, released on five CDs in 2007), Doyle has worked on a large-scale opera, *The Death by Fire of Giordano Bruno*, based on the titular sixteenth-century heretic, a touchstone for Joyce and Beckett. Other composers also probed such interstitial zones. Bernard Clarke's (b. 1967) radiophonic art alternates fierce satire and hellish audio-visions, as in *Litany* (2015) with poet Karl Parkinson. Donal Sarsfield's (b.1980) *Gallivanting/The Suitcases Piece* (2010), a frenetic melange of sounds evoking travel, airports and suitcases, won first prize in the 2011 Luigi Russolo International Sound Art Competition; 'I preferred to use sounds that were everywhere heard but seldom noticed,' Sarsfield said. Judith Ring (b. 1976) created a hyper-real electro-acoustic female voice in *Mouthpiece* (2006). Jürgen Simpson's (b. 1975) work shifted between media, from straight-ahead computer music, *Sigilum* (2008), to opera, *Air India [Redacted]* (2015). London-based Paul McGuire (b. 1988), in *Marshes* (2013), uses the electric guitar ensemble as generator of a dread-inducing sound-mass. And many

Vicky Langan typifies some of the recent mutations in Irish music. She works in both sound and film, within the underground and in established arts venues, and has built an international reputation for her visceral live performances. She has appeared in music magazine *The Wire*, which also sells a Vicky Langan Limited Edition T-shirt.

composers, among them Scott McLaughlin, Fergal Dowling (b. 1965), Brian Bridges (b. 1977), Rob Canning (b. 1974) and Ailís Ní Ríain (b. 1974), delved into microtonality, noise and digital sound synthesis.

In Cork, a particular scene has become established of composers pursuing noise- and quiet-based music. Of these Ann Cleare (b. 1983) has built an international reputation, works such as *to another of that other* (2009–13), for trumpet, trombone, clarinet and orchestra, establishing her as one of Ireland's most talented composers. Having studied at UCC, IRCAM and Harvard University, Cleare developed an aesthetic which channels technical excellence and intimate knowledge of instruments into a probing of corporeality and darkness. Her series *eyam I–V* (2009–15), named after a seventeenth-century plague village in England that isolated itself rather than allow the plague to spread, harnesses unforeseen contours of instruments.

The chamber opera *rinn* (2014–15), a collaboration with Hans-Peter Jahn based on fragments from the 'Sirens' episode of Joyce's *Ulysses*, which premiered in Salzburg, saw her branch out into dramatic works.

The concerts of Cork's Quiet Music Ensemble—which includes composers John Godfrey (b. 1962) and Karen Power (b. 1977)—often present works balancing field recordings and instruments, such as Power's *flies who dreamt of more than windscreens* (2008) for ensemble and tape, in which musicians play subtly alongside a tape part featuring the sound of crickets and birds and a motorbike occasionally driving by. Vicky Langan (b. 1986) explores noise, samples and analogue electronic equipment in a more underground way, while Danny McCarthy (b. 1950) and Mick O'Shea's (b. 1958) The Quiet Club presents quiet electronic ruminations, as well as collaborating with other artists—including the composer Ian Wilson on the opera *The Last Siren* (2013–14), an experimental chamber monodrama based on Homer and acted by Elaine Mitchener.

Composing a Nation

Towards the end of Joyce's *Ulysses*, Stephen Dedalus and Leopold Bloom, tired and tipsy, are engaged in banter at a cab shelter about the artist's responsibility to his country. Having been told by Bloom that he has as much right to live by his pen as the peasant does by his labour—'You both belong to Ireland,' Bloom notes, 'the brain and the brawn'—Dedalus replies: 'You suspect that I may be important because I belong to the *faubourg Saint-Patrice* called Ireland for short. But I suspect that Ireland must be important because it belongs to me.'

Ireland belongs to me: this artistic credo points to the past as something owned, as something *invented* (thus the Irish nation as a *faubourg*: a faux-borough or made-up place). The power to invent the past is the artist's birthright: it's what the Literary Revival authors did a century ago and what our best composers are doing now. From Jennifer Walshe's catalogue of imaginary Irish composers to Gerald Barry's repurposing of any and all music that comes his way, our best composers continue to refashion the collective conceit we call Ireland, and they do so with a sense of wonder.

Notes on Being an Irish Composer, 2016

JENNIFER WALSHE

Performance artist Marina Abramovic describes reading about Chris Burden crucifying himself on the bonnet of a VW Beetle in 1974. There was no proper documentation, there was no internet. She misunderstood the article and thought that Burden had people drive around L.A. with him fixed to the bonnet. Abramovic thought something along the lines of 'if he's going that far, well, hell, I better raise my game.' Years later, she found out the engine was simply revved for two minutes.

When I was growing up in Dublin it was difficult to access information about, let alone listen to, experimental music. So I tried to imagine it, and in some ways I am still chasing after those imagined sounds, so rich in their total gonzo weirdness and shimmering vibrancy.

Literature was easier to access. Beckett, in particular *Krapp's Last Tape* and *Not I*; Flann O'Brien—these formed models for what I wanted to do with music. I regard them as compositions rather than plays. Not music theatre—compositions. Directed as well as written by the composer.

In 2002 *Cremaster 3*, the final instalment in Matthew Barney's *Cremaster* film series is released. The entire series is shown over the course of a week in Meeting House

Above and opposite: Stills from Jennifer Walshe's *THE TOTAL MOUNTAIN* for voice and film, which has toured Europe, the U.S. and Australia and is available on DVD on Neos as part of a set covering performances from the Donaueschinger Musiktage festival in 2014.

Square in Temple Bar (there's five in total; the numbering system is out of order). Securing this screening is considered a coup—it's the first time all five films have been screened together. *Cremaster 3* is loaded with references to Ireland and Irish figures and performers. Aimee Mullins slicing potatoes using modified prosthetic legs; Paul Brady singing; the Giant's Causeway; Fionn Mac Cumhaill. In my favourite section from the film 'The Order'—Matthew Barney scales the inside of the Guggenheim, ascending through a gauntlet of chorus girls, hardcore punk bands and bagpipes to Richard Serra. There are no stuntmen, no safety ropes, Barney climbs the Guggenheim himself and it is beautiful and touching and profound.

I go to every screening with Donnacha Dennehy. We spend the

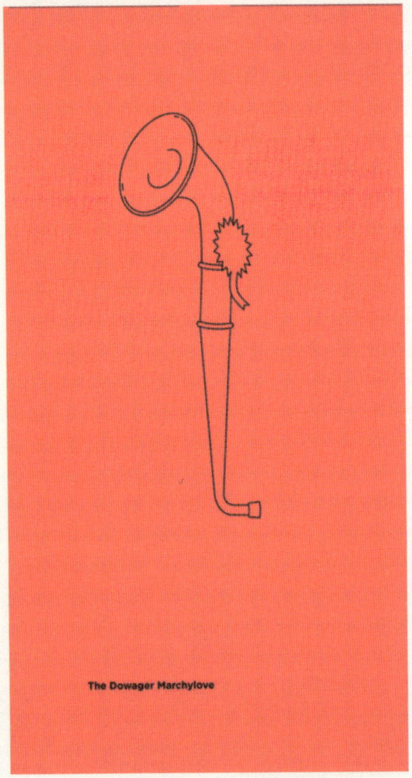

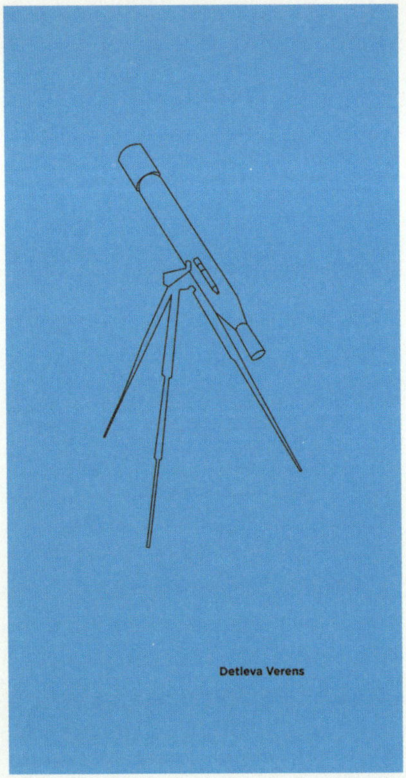

whole week either watching, thinking or talking about *Cremaster*. One afternoon we go out to Kevin Volans's house and lie on the floor listening to Feldman, but I can't concentrate because I'm in the world of *Cremaster*. I'm finally feeling what I was supposed to feel when I saw the *Ring* cycle but didn't. That something huge is at stake. That a language is evolving in front of us. And that this level of commitment is what should be demanded of opera, of the performer, of music. This level of world-building, imagination, symbolism, abstraction. It's challenging. You have to be awake and confused and paying attention. And in all this there is no choice other than that the composer function as auteur.

•• •• •• •• •• •• •• •• •• •• ••

Something shifted during the crash, after the crash. I felt it first and most strongly playing a Kaleidoscope gig at the Odessa Club in 2010. A beautiful beauty was born. Gorgeousness became an option. And who could blame anyone for this? For coming in from the cold? Hadn't we been told to be less difficult for years? I

Jennifer Walshe invented the Grúpat sound art collective for a project commissioned by South Dublin County Council. She wrote the members' histories, created their works, posed for their photographs, recorded their music, and created their fake media coverage. Grúpat's work was exhibited in the Project Arts Centre in Dublin in 2009, and documented in a book and on two CDs. The images above are the pages introducing the sections of the book on The Dowager Marchylove, Detleva Verens and Violetta Mahon.

admire beauty, but it's not for me. I want lipstick on the teeth, drunken confidences and complications. Chris Kraus and Mykki Blanco.

•• •• •• •• •• •• •• •• •• •• ••

James Joyce wrote: 'No one who has any self-respect stays in Ireland, but flees afar as though from a country that has undergone the visitation of an angered Jove.' He also wrote: 'When I die, Dublin will be written in my heart.'

I'm watching Vivienne Dick's work for the first time, at a weekend festival dedicated to her films at the Tate Modern. There is an abrupt cut, between a scene filmed at a party in the Lower East Side to people hiking in the west of Ireland. We see NYC No Wave artists partying in dresses, then we see an ad for Blue Band margarine on an Irish TV. Something makes sense to me in a way no Irish art I've seen has up to this point and I am brought to tears.

•• •• •• •• •• •• •• •• •• •• ••

Bob Gilmore is irreplaceable.

•• •• •• •• •• •• •• •• •• •• ••

In 2015 I launched a project called *Historical Documents of the Irish Avant-Garde*. For this project, I worked in collaboration with a wide number of people to create a fictional history of Irish avant-garde music, stretching from the mid 1830s to the 1980s. All the materials related to this project are housed at aisteach.org, the website of the Aisteach Foundation, a fictional organisation which is positioned as 'the avant-garde archive of Ireland.' The site contains hours of music, numerous articles, scores, documents and historical ephemera. Every detail of this project was composed, written and designed with the utmost care and attention to detail. It's a serious exercise in speculative composition, fiction and world-building. In Aisteach, Irishness becomes a *medium*.

Two of Aisteach's most respected fellow travellers include Afrofuturism and Hauntology. The latter in particular seems like an obvious native choice for Irish-based art, embedded as we are in ghosts, superstition and nostalgia. But Hauntology functions differently in Ireland—Aisteach is haunted by a past which suppressed, marginalised and erased many voices. Aisteach is not interested in fetishising this past. The crackle on the recordings is not there for cosy retro warmth or nostalgia for the rare oul times—it's sand on the lens, grit between the tape heads, violently hacking history to urge us to create a better future. And a better future means being alert and responsible to the present.

• •

In the nineteenth century, the King family built a folly on Castle Island in what is now Lough Key Forest Park in Roscommon. You can admire the ruin from the shore or rent a boat and picnic there. Or you can drive around and look at real ruins—the ghost estates where we witness temporally confused spectres from the future.

All sci-fi is ostensibly about the future, but in reality about the present. I am for a music which is more sci-fi. I am for a music which is dedicated to grappling with the times we live in. As William Gibson points out, in 2016 we live in the most sci-fi of scenarios—we Western Europeans, dressed in athleisure, quantising our steps, mired in debt, wracked by fundamentalism, AIDS and the Zika virus, we content- and data-providers for the Stacks, thrilled, oblivious and terrified in equal measure by the super-fresh tech and changing world of the Anthropocene.

Roscommon, Easter Monday 2016

Clearing the fog of uncertainty

MICHAEL DERVAN

Andrew Hamilton can't remember ever wanting to be anything other than a musician. 'I'm the son of a Methodist minister, so I was brought up with lots of hymns all the time. Ministers' sons are always troublesome, like Nietzsche. My mother says I was always singing. Then my brother got a chance to learn the violin. He was ten and I was six. He was playing one day, and I said, "I want to play that." I just demanded it. From that point on I was never really interested in anything else. I was obsessive.'

Michael Dervan, left, in conversation with composer Andrew Hamilton.

The violin was his initial focus. 'I suppose half of me did have these notions of becoming a concert violinist. And then when I was sixteen, I went to Chetham's School in Manchester as a violinist.' Chetham's is the largest specialist music school in Britain. 'I had studied in Dublin with Maeve Broderick. She was teaching at Chetham's. That's how I ended up there. And then when I was there I realised I was never going to become a concert violinist. The standard was so high. It was a big shock.'

Years before he went to Chetham's he had already started composing. 'I think I was ten. It was very natural. I just wrote down things. I think the problem was that I was nearly more excited at that stage about writing than practising. And I loved listening to music. I think the first tapes I bought were the four last symphonies of Mozart conducted by Karl Böhm. I would save up and listen to music more than practise.'

As a composer he regards himself as having been fortunate in his teachers. 'I had very strong-willed teachers. My main teacher was Kevin Volans. I learnt from him editing, that you had to edit, and I learnt from him not to worry about style. And fearlessness. From Louis Andriessen, I think, attention to detail. He said if you're going to write music that's not so complex, you have to present it the right way, make sure it's clear. I do remember coming out of every lesson in Amsterdam with Andriessen. closing the door behind me, and my first thought was always, "I know nothing." I always thought that I knew nothing.

'When I was eighteen, I showed a lot of my work to Gerald Barry. That was when I first met him. He was quite ruthless. He went through all my scores and said, "That's you! That's not you!" Which was quite interesting.' And, says Hamilton, he was right.

Hamilton comes across as unassuming, almost self-deprecating, though his conversation is peppered with gusty laughter. As a student he didn't like to wrangle. 'I learnt by absorbing like a sponge. I was never someone who talked a lot. I was talking to Kevin recently and he said

I was "very non-communicative" as a young person. I didn't say very much. I never fought with teachers and took it all.'

A word that crops up a lot in his conversation is 'obsessive'. And the quality is to be found in some of his compositions, too, when he latches on to an idea and pursues it with the kind of fixity you can find in Schumann. Think of the relentless ride of Schumann's Toccata, or the gentler recursions of his *Arabeske* or *Blumenstück*—patterns which repeat and repeat. But in Hamilton's work you need to factor in a kind of creeping corruption that wreaks intentional havoc, as if the music is made to stutter or experience glitches.

The harmonic and melodic content of his music often has an aura of familiarity about it. But traditional chords and straightforward-seeming lines can be minced and reconstituted in ways that are not just unpredictable, but that can also linger in the mind with ear-worm-like tenacity. It's hard to say exactly why, but there's something in the intricacy of the procedures that's not unlikely to prompt a fit of the giggles the way a Heath Robinson drawing can when it pursues a flagrantly absurd idea to its logical conclusion.

'There's a sense of playfulness in it,' he says. 'Yeah. I am interested in art that's playful. When I was younger I used to get upset when people said my music was witty or fun. I found that awful, because I thought I was a really serious artist [he laughs]. And people would laugh in concerts. I would be so upset. But now I've sort of accepted it. If you set out to be funny, it would be awful. I would find it easier to write dark, grey pieces. It's not that hard. People whose writing I love, like Flann O'Brien and Beckett, there is that sort of dark laugh in the background.'

His new orchestral work, *C*, was written for the *Composing the Island* festival. The title reflects his current position that 'I don't want any titles to suggest anything. It's like a frame, to make them abstract, to give them more freedom.'

So how does it all begin? How does he actually get started on a piece like *C* ? 'A lot of mess,' he says, laughing. 'Before I was given this orchestral commission for the RTÉ National Symphony Orchestra, I suddenly became obsessed with Paul Klee's *Notebooks*. For the past year I've been going through them in an abstracted way. I don't know if you know them. There are lots of diagrams . . . looking at nature, art that exists in nature, patterns that exist in nature. I think that was maybe the starting point. And also, with this one, because I've been teaching orchestration formally to people, I wasn't as scared of the orchestra as before, probably.'

He professes uncertainty about how he makes the transition from Klee's *Notebooks* to notes on a page. 'Hmmm. That's a good question. I'm not sure. I knew I wanted it to be more organic, or somehow related to patterns in nature. But that didn't really help me with the pitches.'

Did he take visual patterns or word patterns and make musical patterns from them? Or is the connection altogether more oblique? 'Very oblique. I don't try to force things into being too theoretical. At the beginning of the process I always go through my notebooks. I keep notebooks from every year. I try to see if there is any musical material that might be interesting to work with. I did find a group of chords that I'd written a few years ago, and I decided they would be the foundation of the piece.'

I ask about the notebooks. Are they are jottings of ideas that come spontaneously? Or are they the fruit of sessions where he's working things through on an instrument? He shows me the notebook for *C*, explaining, 'It's just notes of pitches, abstract ideas.'

The notebooks, he says, get filled in at random times of the day. 'You could be walking down the street and an idea comes. Sometimes most of what comes is just useless. At the beginning of the process I did do all the stuff that composers are supposed to do, take the chords and analyse them and rotate them, and all that stuff. It was useless. I think I always find that all the tricks of the trade are useless.'

Unless of course the 'useless' work is a part of the process of eliminating possibilities. 'They're eliminating possibilities, yeah. I pretend to be a serious technical composer and then I realise that it doesn't help at all.'

The process of identifying the material is anything but straightforward. 'It's very hard. You have to be very patient, I think, to wait for something that has meaning to appear from all of that. I think a lot of composers stop at the technical stage a lot of the time. They think if they've made a nice harmonic field, or something, that's the composing. But for me it's only the first stage of many, many stages. It gets you going and then you have to throw it away.'

I'm curious about how the Klee connection and the small amount of raw musical material evolve into the final composition. How does the first potentially durable bit come out of it? 'A lot of rewriting and rewriting. For this piece I think it's around ten times I've rewritten most of the piece—so that the pacing is correct. I think the major breakthrough for me in this piece was a quote from Mondrian: "I realised I had to interrupt constantly the line I was producing," if that makes any sense.' In the actual piece, 'it's an interrupted melodic line that's gradually filled in, ultimately as if filled in by a heavy marker.'

Is that a mystery, I ask, the making of that connection, the identification of a principle that's going to have to be applied to the new work? 'I suppose it is a mystery. It's not very formalised. I have loads of his writings—I've taken the bits I like from Mondrian's writings. They're always there, and they sometimes pop up.

'My whole process is very messy, I suppose. It's not a beautiful, sit down and we have a lovely clear outcome. I was thinking so much of this painting by Mondrian, *Pier and Ocean*. The thing about Mondrian is that people think it's all so worked out, don't they? When I actually saw this in real life, I think I was twenty-three, you could see all of his rubbings out, how he was constantly changing the lines. It gave me hope that my process was maybe useful. Because I'm constantly changing. It's very much intuition-based.'

A page from Andrew Hamilton's notebook of 28 August 2015. It relates to the orchestral work C. There is no significance to the use of two colours. The composer just wanted to cheer himself up. The drawing in the bottom right corner refers to the bell-ringing of the Corsa del Ceri at Gubbio in Italy.

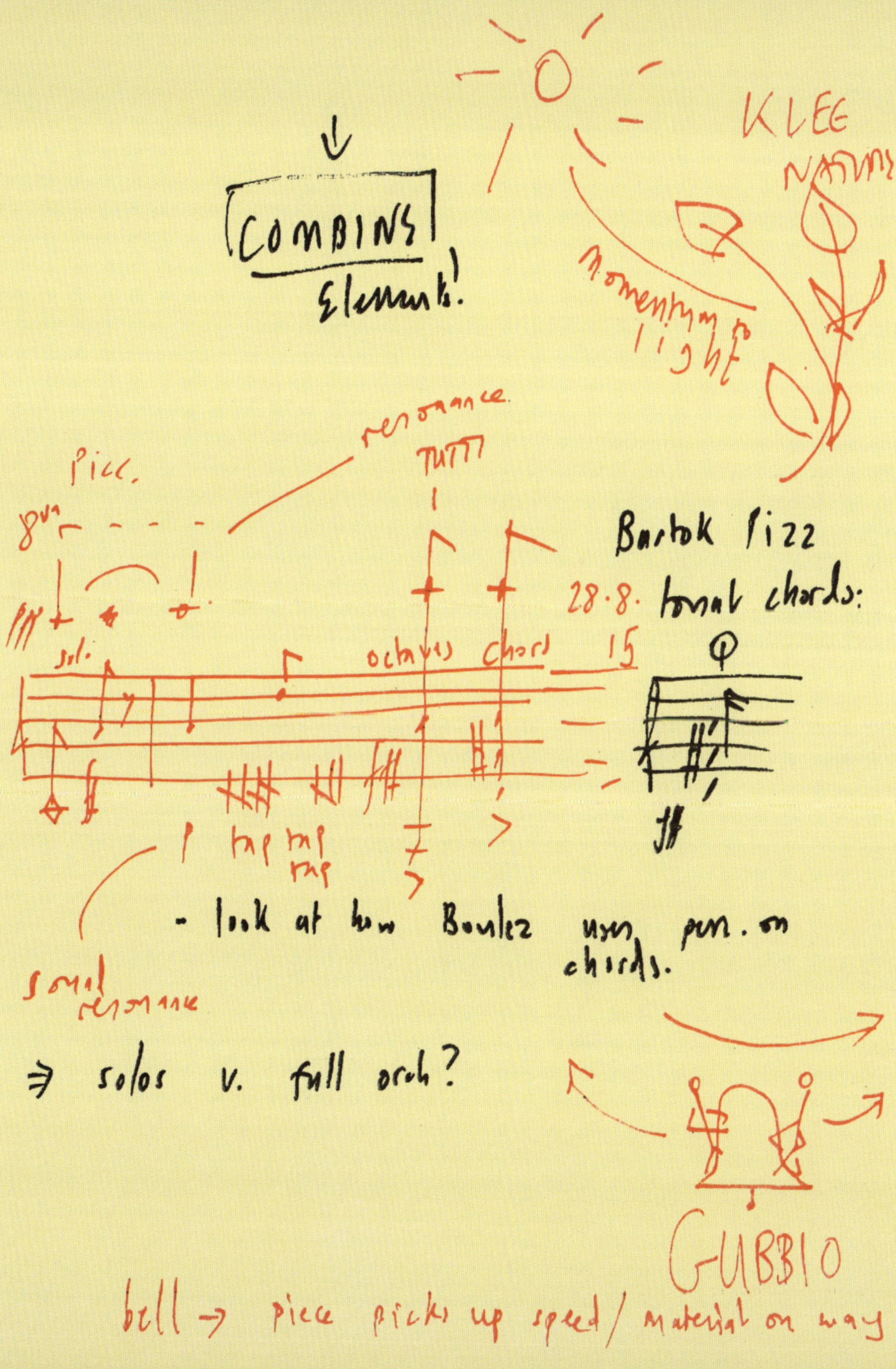
COMBINE
Elements!
KLEE
NATURE
momentum of
light
resonance
Picc.
8va
TUTTI
solo
octaves
chord
15
Bartok pizz
28.8. tonal chords:
p tap tap
tap
- look at how Boulez uses perc. on chords.
sound resonance
⇒ solos v. full orch?
GUBBIO
bell → piece picks up speed / material on way

Intuition is central to Hamilton's way of working. And now that he's teaching, too—he's a visiting tutor in composition at Birmingham Conservatoire—he's trying to help his students develop their intuitive skills as well as their compositional technique.

Is there any constancy or consistency in the creation of a piece? Or can a piece be generated—or generate itself—in ways that are just for that piece, and don't happen in any other piece? 'I really believe that with any piece there's always hundreds of thoughts behind it. For every piece I do the same process. I'll take a bit of material and probably try to disrupt it, break it up, fracture it. The main thing I've been trying to do in the past few years is fracture time more, destroy time, maybe, play with the structure far more. I always do that with every piece I start. Kevin Volans always says, modernism means nothing is given. I don't try to formalise what I'm doing, maybe. I'm reinventing the wheel all the time.'

He contrasts this with his early efforts. 'When I was eighteen, nineteen, twenty, I wrote pieces which were all about using rows and harmonic fields. It's not that hard, really, to be honest. You can get away with . . . you can hide a lot behind techniques. These days I will look for patterns in the harmony and chords. Maybe if you play them a lot a rhythm will come out of it. I'll test it out and see how long I can use that rhythm for. Push it. There is a process of testing out the material. Definitely.'

This takes place at the keyboard, and for C, also on the violin, 'because I knew from the beginning that it would start with a solo violin. I'll try it on the violin as well, to see if and how it works. There's a lot of testing. Trying to get to know the material, I think. Bash things out, test them, and pray that something comes out of it. It's testing an idea to see if you can make it last more than a few minutes. That's also intuition; you have to know what material can be used further.'

What tends to clarify first while working on a new piece? 'That's a hard one as well. What's clear first? I'm often in a fog of uncertainty for most of the time.' The main strategy is writing and rewriting. 'Testing, retesting. Then, suddenly, there's a moment—you know the writer David Foster Wallace, he called it the click—there's a click where you hope this will work.'

Technology comes into the picture. Recording has become part of the business of sifting the material. 'I have started recording, yeah. And I have started using the iPhone and singing into it if I'm walking along and I get an idea in my head.' He generally writes compositions straight into the computer, and has 'no shame' about using the synthesised playback that computers provide. In spite of that, he says, 'I think I was fortunate to do most of my training before computers were a given. I didn't start using music programs until I was thirty. I feel like an old fogey now with the young people. I tell them we used have to transpose everything by hand, all the horns and saxophones. They've no comprehension.'

Hamilton doesn't see himself as a fast worker. 'I started thinking about the orchestral piece a year ago, and I've been constantly working on it for six months. I've learnt now that I have to start thinking about a piece at least a year before I hand it in, because the way I work is very intuitive. I have no system to fall back on.'

He describes himself as very stubborn about getting a work finished to his satisfaction, and admits to missing deadlines. The longest he's ever spent on a work is two years, 'on a piece for Crash, *music for people who like art* (2009). It was a year late.' The main problem was 'I hadn't found the right text. It has a voice. I tried loads of different texts. None of them rang true. And writing for Crash can be very hard, because of the line-up'—the work is for piccolo, clarinet, trombone, percussion, electric guitar, piano, voice, violin, viola, cello and double bass. 'I hadn't found a convincing solution for myself. I'm annoyingly stubborn about handing things in. I don't want something I'm not happy with going out.'

Stravinsky famously described himself as the 'vessel' through which *The Rite of Spring* passed, as if he was the medium rather than the creator. Does Hamilton find himself surprised when he hears his own works for the first time? 'To some extent. I'm surprised often by the energy from them. I don't feel they reflect my personality. I don't try to reflect my inner life, maybe. I don't know if that makes sense. I'm writing away from life, and trying to find a different quality to everyday life.'

So many people think that when someone like Mozart was depressed or short of money he would be unlikely to write music that's exuberant. Surely, I suggest, pieces are more like a character in a novel, with a life of their own. Authors don't always know what's going to happen next, but they're delighted to find out. 'That's exactly it. I find when it's going really well, the music nearly tells you what it's going to do. I love when that happens. It takes on its own complete, independent life.

'You mentioned Mozart's happy music. I also like cheering myself up with my music. I write to cheer myself up. Because if I wrote about my daily paranoias or how I was bored, I wouldn't want anybody to listen to it. For me it's a form of escaping from conventional reality—to get beyond the surface of daily preoccupation. Writing away from life. I think you can divide composers mainly up into composers who write from their lives, and others who write away from their lives.'

The connection of creator to work can even come to seem tenuous. 'The piece that I wrote for Crash, *music for people who like art*, has been played by three groups now. It was done by a group of people in London last December. I have this very strange feeling towards it, that I don't have anything to do with it at all. I can't believe that I made it. A very bizarre feeling. It seems to affect lots of people, and I'm just sitting there going, I can't believe that I wrote it.'

I am not a clockmaker

Interview with Ann Cleare

CAROL McGONNELL

Growing up in Offaly, what kind of contemporary culture were you exposed to, if any?

To my memory, I didn't experience much newly created music, literature or visual art until I was a young adult. But looking back there are some significant influences and experiences from my youth in Offaly that point to a career as an artist … my mother's side of the family are gifted embroiderers, and would make textiles with the most intricate patterns and layering. Although I didn't have much of a talent for it, I had such admiration for their skill, attention to detail and geometric imagination.

And my father was an extraordinary singer. He had an incredibly rich tone and effortless virtuosity in his voice. Most of my early memories are of people huddling around him in the hope that he might sing a song for them. I think both of these experiences planted seeds in my mind of how special it is to create something from your own hands and imagination, and of how stirring live performance can be.

I studied classical music from a young age, and was absolutely fascinated by musical instruments. I loved learning about how they worked and what type of sounds they could make. I don't seem to have ever discriminated between music and noise as very different things. Even though I enjoyed understanding its workings, I remember thinking that tonal music was very limited by its systems—I always felt like there were so many other sonic worlds to be found in between and outside of its practices. There were sounds from the everyday that I thought held far richer systems of colour and motion than the tonal music that I was playing. I suppose this is now representative of the music that I write: it is written for classical instruments but for the experimentally minded performer and listener—I want to guide my listeners' ears and minds to where they haven't been before.

As a young musician, I did attend a handful of concerts in the National Concert Hall in Dublin, but all I ever heard was music by dead white men, and so this is what I assumed a composer was. To be honest, I didn't even know that there were living composers until I went to university at the age of eighteen. Of course there was music being written and programmed by living composers, but unless you proactively went searching for it, I don't think you would have ever encountered it.

I don't hear the influences of other Irish composers in your music, however your music seems so essentially 'Irish' to me. If I recognise the ghosts of any of our cultural forebears in your music they might be Samuel Beckett or James Joyce. Does this make any sense to you?

To my thinking, my music has always been a place of invisible theatre. To many listeners it may seem completely abstract, but for me it is a space that is alive with sonic characters and drama. I think it would be fair to say that theatre and literature are generally more inspiring art forms for me than concert music—they tend to explore the ideas that I want to explore, but I want to explore these ideas with sounds and not with words.

An idea that is quite prominent in my earliest to most recent pieces is the happenings of a piece taking place in some type of scenic situation, whether it be a spatial arrangement of musicians to evoke the idea of different characters or beings on a stage, or thinking of a piece of music as a type of geographical or architectural place with different materials at work. This has involved the invention of instrumental characters or elements that are thought of as part-human/part-nonhuman, that emit shades of a human language and shades of a language from nature, and that are often placed in a type of surreal or unknown situation. Even though it was long before I became a composer, seeing Beckett's *Happy Days* as a teenager was an absolutely earth-shattering experience, and a pivotal moment in the formation of what I think of as the scenic/sonic situation in my music.

I don't think that any of this is completely removed from what other Irish composers are doing or have done. I can hear similar artistic aims in the music of Gerald Barry, Jennifer Walshe, early Donnacha Dennehy, Andrew Hamilton and others. But we are differentiated by our individual tastes and preferences in how we choose to realise these ideas.

You wrote a solo clarinet piece for me called eyam i (it takes an ocean not to) (2009–13) *and you actually began to learn how to play the clarinet in order to compose the piece. This is so impressive on so many levels! Do you try to get to know every instrument you compose for intimately when writing a solo piece, or piece for small forces?*

Yes, I generally do try to get my hands on every instrument that I write for. Both because I think it's important to have a sense of what it is like to play the music that I'm

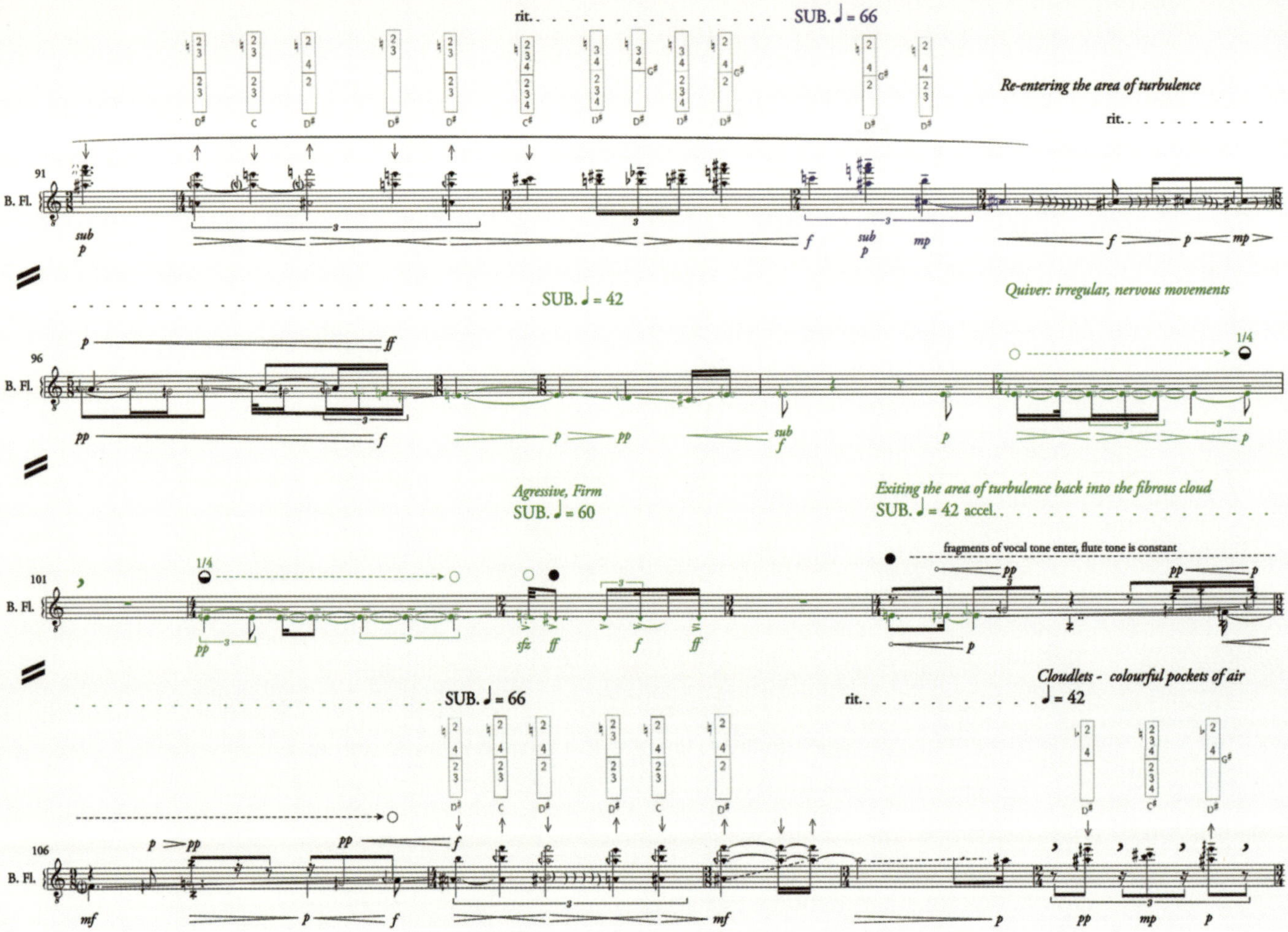

writing, and as a way of researching the sonic material that I will use in a piece. I thrive on combining and juxtaposing sonic materials, almost like a sculptor would combine different materials to make a sculpture. As *eyam i* was the first solo piece (without electronics) that I ever wrote, it was a very difficult task because I only had one instrument, which generally plays in a monophonic fashion, and I am interested in complex spectrums and polyphonic movement. And this is why it was absolutely essential for me to start playing the clarinet and strategise on how I could make it into a multiphonic, polyphonic instrument so that it was capable of representing the idea that I had for the piece. In a sense I was teaching the clarinet and you to be something that I needed you to be for the artistic vision that I had.

A page from the score of *eyam iii (if it's living somewhere outside of you)* for solo bass flute. The fingering charts above the stave are for multiphonic sonorities. The coloured parts are a guide to help the performer characterise musical material which relates to specific other pieces within the *eyam* series. The work also exists in a version in which the flute is shadowed by one low wind instrument and one string instrument.

Back to you learning the clarinet. I have to say that in some ways this made my job way more challenging. You were writing techniques that you, as a beginner clarinettist, could do that I had a really hard job trying to replicate as a 'pro'. I often felt I needed to 'unlearn' the clarinet. It was really frustrating at times because you could get all these amazing sounds that I couldn't figure out how to make as well as you. But ultimately you really expanded my mind as to the possibilities of the instrument, and this was so much fun and enlightening. Do you similarly torture other performers for their own benefit, or just friends?

No, my intention is never to torture anyone, but performers enter at their own risk! Over the years, I have learned how crucial it is for my music that the right type of performer plays it. I know that I ask a lot of performers: the music is very detailed and, on top of grasping the correct pitches/rhythms/dynamics, it requires an interpreter who can convey the highly psychological, risky drama that is at work in a piece.

What does your mammy think of your music?

She often describes it as mind-boggling, which I think is great! I would much rather boggle a listener's mind than bore or falsely appease it. When asked if my music is too challenging or harrowing or unpleasant for a listener, which it is often described as, I suggest that if you want to pretend the world is a lovely, comfortable place, then stay at home and find something mind-numbing to watch on TV. I make work that challenges and reflects the world we live in—I believe that this is what art is for. I work and think hard about how I can make my ideas clear to a listener, to invite them into the experience, but not in a way that compromises or simplifies the complexity of the situation in question.

Since graduating with a doctorate from Harvard, do you feel like a superior human being? How was it to study at this prestigious institution and in what ways did it change you? Or not?

Previous page: Ann Cleare at work. The pages on the floor are from *Claustrophobia* for string orchestra (2005–06), a work which has not yet been performed. Although she produces her final scores using computer music typesetting technology, she still works out the earlier stages with pencil and manuscript paper.

The years that I spent at Harvard were a gift, and a gift that I am immensely grateful for. I've never been in such an engaging, critical, supportive and fun environment. Thanks to my incredibly insightful composition teachers and colleagues, my music developed in ways that I could never have predicted. The resources in the Music Department are things that most composers could only ever dream of having access to, and, outside the department, Harvard offers so much . . . if you take a sudden interest in chemistry or sign language or architecture, it's very easy to enrol in courses across the campus. In fact most departments welcome it. Its a very positive environment, from administration to professors, full of bright people who want to learn and teach and share.

How this has shaped my work? I would say that the music I write now is a lot more detailed than previously. Also, the time and shapes within my pieces have expanded in scope. I have a much more critical relationship with my work now, and sometimes I wish that I didn't. But I think it will be of benefit to me in the long run. I would say that travel of any kind is so beneficial to an artist: rather than living in an environment that you know, spending time in a country that's not your own, and even where you don't speak the language, helps you to understand who you really are, which can only contribute towards forming the most individual and honest voice that you can.

You also spent time at IRCAM in Paris. Physical musical instruments don't really change much over time, but electronics and electro-acoustic possibilities change constantly. How do you feel about using a medium that ages so rapidly, and does this affect how you use it?

Whether acoustic or electronic, good art never ages. Stockhausen's *Kontakte* or *Mikrophonie*, which were written around fifty years ago, sound as new to me as any newly written electronic music of today. It's important to keep the technology up to date so that the music can be performed into the future. But if the music is good, then it won't age regardless of any trends that come and go around it.

This interview was carried out by email.

Bibliography

This photograph was taken in 1962 when the Radio Éireann Symphony Orchestra was en route between Dublin and Cork, whose City Hall was then credited as being the best-sounding venue in which to hear the orchestra.

A Sense of Ireland programme book (Dublin: A Sense of Ireland Ltd, 1980)

Blom, Eric (ed.), *Grove's Dictionary of Music and Musicians*, fifth edition (London: Macmillan Press, 1954)

Boydell, Brian, *A Dublin Musical Calendar, 1700–60* (Dublin: Irish Academic Press, 1988)

Boydell, Brian, *Rotunda Music in Eighteenth-Century Dublin* (Dublin: Irish Academic Press, 1992)

Brown, Terence, *Ireland: A Social and Cultural History, 1922–1985* (London: Fontana Press, 1985)

Butler, Patricia, & O'Kelly, Pat, *The National Concert Hall at Earlsfort Terrace, Dublin, A History* (Dublin: Wolfhound Press, 2000)

Byers, David, *Contemporary Composers: A Troubles Archive Essay* (Belfast: ACNI, 2012) (troublesarchive.com/essays)

Byrne Bodley, Lorraine, *A Hazardous Melody of Being: Seóirse Bodley's Song Cycles on the Poems of Micheal O'Siadhail* (Dublin: Carysfort Press, 2008)

Byrne Bodley, Lorraine, *A Community of the Imagination: Seóirse Bodley's Goethe Settings* (Dublin: Carysfort Press, 2013)

Cox, Gareth, *Seóirse Bodley* (Dublin: Field Day Publications, 2010)

Cox, Gareth, 'Serialism in Ireland' in Cox, Gareth & Horton, Julian (eds.), *Irish Musical Studies 11: Irish Musical Analysis* (Dublin: Four Courts Press, 2014)

Cox, Gareth & Klein, Axel (eds.), *Irish Music in the Twentieth Century*, Irish Musical Studies 7 (Dublin: Four Courts Press, 2003)

Cox, Gareth, Klein, Axel & Taylor, Michael (eds.), *The Life and Music of Brian Boydell* (Dublin: Irish Academic Press, 2004)

Dawney, Michael, 'A Register of Theses on Music at Universities in the Republic of Ireland' *R.M.A. Research Chronicle* 13, 1976

Deane, Raymond, *In my own Light* (Dublin: The Liffey Press, 2014)

Deane, Raymond, *Exploding the Continuum: The Utopia Of Unbroken Tradition* http://www.raymonddeane.com/articles_results.php?id=11

Deane, Raymond, 'Must Music be Accessible?', *The Journal of Music* 1 July 2004 (journalofmusic.com/focus/must-music-be-accessible-0), and subsequent exchanges with Desmond Fennell, *The Journal of Music* 1 September 2004 (journalofmusic.com/focus/must-music-be-accessible)

de Barra, Séamas, 'Aloys Fleischmann and the idea of an Irish Composer', *The Journal of Music*, 1 September 2005 (journalofmusic.com/focus/aloys-fleischmann-and-idea-irish-composer)

de Barra, Séamas, 'The Symphonies of John Kinsella' PhD. Diss., (Durham: 2012)

de Barra, Séamas, *Aloys Fleischmann* (Dublin: Field Day Publications, 2006)

Devane, James, 'Is an Irish Culture Possible?' *Ireland To-day* 1:5, 1936

Dibble, Jeremy, *Michele Esposito* (Dublin: Field Day Publications, 2010)

Dowling, Martin, *Traditional Music and Irish Society: Historical Perspectives* (Farnham: Ashgate Publishing Ltd, 2014; Abingdon: Routledge, 2016)

Dwyer, Benjamin, *Constellations: The Life and Music of John Buckley* (Dublin: Carysfort Press, 2013)

Dwyer, Benjamin, *Different Voices* (Hofheim: Wolke Verlag, 2014)

The Encyclopaedia of Music in Ireland, 2 Vols, general editors Harry White and Barra Boydell (Dublin: UCD Press, 2013)

Fitzgerald, Mark, 'On Constructing a Sonic Gangbang: System and Subversion in Gerald Barry's Chevaux-de-frise', *Irish Musical Analysis*, Cox, Gareth and Horton, Julian (eds.), Irish Musical Studies 11 (Dublin: Four Courts Press, 2014),

Fitzgerald, Mark & Flynn, John (eds.), *Music and Identity in Ireland and Beyond* (Farnham: Ashgate Publishing Ltd, 2014

Fitzgerald, Mark, *The Life and Music of James Wilson* (Cork: Cork University Press, 2015)

Fleischmann, Aloys, 'The Outlook of Music in Ireland', *Studies* 24:93, 1935

Fleischmann, Aloys, 'Composition and the Folk Idiom', *Ireland To-day* 1:6 1936

Fleischmann, Aloys, 'Ars Nova—Irish Music in the Shaping', *Ireland To-day* 1:2, 1936

Fleischmann, Aloys (ed.), *Music in Ireland A Symposium* (Cork: Cork University Press, 1952) ucc.ie/celt/AloysFleischmannMusicIreland2013.pdf

Fleischmann, Aloys, *Sources of Irish Traditional Music c. 1600–1855: An Annotated Catalogue of Prints and Manuscripts, 1583–1855*, 2 Vols, eds. Ó Súilleabháin, Mícheál and McGettrick, Paul (New York & London: Garland, 1998)

Flood, W. H. Grattan, *History of Irish Music* (Dublin: Browne & Nolan, 1905) http://www.libraryireland.com/IrishMusic/Preface.php

Gannon, Charles, *John S. Beckett The Man and the Music* (Dublin: The Lilliput Press, 2016)

Gillen, Gerard, & White, Harry (eds.), Irish Musical Studies 1 *Musicology in Ireland* (Dublin: Irish Academic Press, 1990)

Grünefeld, Hans-Dieter, Corcoran, Frank (eds.), *Frank Corcoran: Festschrift At Seventy* (No publisher identified, ISBN 9783000501531, 2015)

Harris, Bernard & Freyer, Grattan (eds.), *The Achievement of Seán Ó Riada: Integrating Tradition* (Dublin: Irish Humanities Centre, 1981)

Hast, Dorothea E. & Scott, Stanley, *Music in Ireland—Experiencing Music, Expressing Culture* (New York & Oxford: Oxford University Press, 2004). See also Axel Klein's review in *Music and Letters* k86/2 (2005), 274–275

Hogan, Ita, *Anglo-Irish Music, 1780–1830* (Cork: Cork University Press, 1966)

Hunt, Una & Pierse, Mary (eds.), *France and Ireland Notes and Narratives* (Oxford: Peter Lang, 2016)

Kennedy, Brian P., *Dreams and Responsibilities. The State and the Arts in Independent Ireland*, The Arts Council/Chomairle Eala on (Dublin: Criterion Press,1990)

Kiberd, Declan, *Inventing Ireland: The Literature of a Modern Nation* (London: Jonathan Cape, 1995)

Klein, Axel, *Die Musik Irlands im 20 Jahrhundert* (Hildesheim: Georg Olms Verlag, 1996)

Klein, Axel, 'Irish Composers and Foreign Education: A Study of Influences', Devine, Patrick & White, Harry (eds.), Irish Musical Studies 4: *The Maynooth International Musicological Conference 1995: Selected Proceedings* Part One (Dublin: 1996)

Klein, Axel, 'Celtic Legends in Irish Opera, 1900–1930', *Proceedings of the Harvard Celtic Colloquium* Vol. xxiv (2004), (Cambridge and London: Harvard University Press, 2009)

Larchet, John F., 'A plea for music: an analysis of the present condition of music in Ireland and the needs of the future', *The Voice of Ireland*, W. Fitzgerald (ed.) (Dublin: 1924)

McAllister Hart, Nuala, *From Farquhar to Field Day: Three centuries of music and theatre in Derry—Londonderry* (Dublin: The History Press Ireland, 2012)

Ó Canainn, Tomás & Mac an Bhua, Gearóid, *Seán Ó Riada: A shaol agus a shaothar* (Dublin: Gartan, 1993)

Ó Canainn, Tomás, *Seán Ó Riada: His Life and Work* (Cork: The Collins Press, 2003)

O'Connell, Kevin, *On Seán Ó Riada* (kevinnoconnell.com/blog/blog18.html).

Ó Gallchobhair, Éamonn, 'Music—Atavism', *Ireland To-day* 1:4 1936

O'Kelly, Pat, *The National Symphony Orchestra of Ireland, 1948–1998, a selected history* (Dublin: RTÉ, 1998)

O'Neill, Joseph, 'Music in Dublin', *Music in Ireland A Symposium* Aloys Fleischmann (ed.) (Cork: Cork University Press, 1952)

Patton, Marcus, *The Opera Hat of Sir Hamilton Harty* (Belfast: Grand Piano Press, 2003)

Pine, Richard, (ed.), *Music in Ireland 1848–1998* (Cork: Mercier Press, 1998)

Quinn, Toner, '"Are You Talking to Me?": Traditional and Classical Music in Ireland', *The Journal of Music*, 1 May 2005 (journalofmusic.com/focus/are-you-talking-me-traditional-and-classical-music-ireland)

Rosen, Charles, 'Music à la Mode', *New York Review of Books* 23 June 1994. See letters in response from Lawrence Kramer (September 22, 1994) and Rita Steblin (20 October 1994), and Rosen's replies.

Ryan, Philip B., The Lost Theatres of Dublin (Westbury: The Badger Press, 1998)

Slonimsky, Nicolas, *Music Since 1900*, fifth edition (New York: Schirmer Books, 1994)

Smyth, Gerry, *Music in Irish Cultural History* (Dublin: Irish Academic Press, 2009)

Tóibín, Colm, *A Guest at the Feast: A Memoir* (Penguin, 2011)

Vallely, Fintan (ed.), *Companion to Irish Traditional Music*, 2nd, revised edn (Cork: Cork University Press, 2011)

Walshe, Jennifer (ed.), *Grúpat* (Dublin: Project Press, 2009)

Walshe, Jennifer (ed.), *Historical Documents of the Irish Avant-Garde* (Milker Corp and the Aisteach Foundation, 2015) www.aisteach.org

Walsh, T. J., *Opera in Dublin 1705–1797: The Social Scene* (Dublin: Allen Figgis, 1973)

White, Harry, 'Musicology in Ireland', *Acta Musicologica,* 60/3 1988

White, Harry, *The Keeper's Recital: Music and Cultural History in Ireland 1770–1970* (Cork: Cork University Press, 1998)

See review by Gearóid Ó hAllmhuráin in the *Journal of Interdisciplinary History* 31/2 (2000), 265–267

White, Harry, *The Progress of Music in Ireland* (Dublin: Four Courts Press, 2005)

White, Harry, *Music and the Irish Literary Imagination* (Oxford & New York: Oxford University Press, 2008)

White, Harry & Murphy, Michael (eds.), *Musical Constructions of Nationalism: Essays on the History and Ideology of European Musical Culture 1800–1945* (Cork: Cork University Press, 2001).

Zuk, Patrick, 'Music and Nationalism', *The Journal of Music,* 1 January 2002, 1 March 2002 (journalofmusic.com/focus/music-and-nationalism part 1), (journalofmusic.com/focus/music-and-nationalism-part-2)

Zuk, Patrick, *Raymond Deane* (Dublin: Field Day Publications, 2006)

Appendix

Festival Programme
Composing The Island: A century of music in Ireland 1916–2016

Sponsored by Bord na Móna and presented by RTÉ and the National Concert Hall as part of RTÉ 1916 and Ireland 2016.

7–25 September 2016

National Concert Hall, Dublin

Concert listings as supplied on 20 July 2016

: :

Irish Rhapsodies

Wednesday 7 September, 8.00 p.m.

RTÉ Concert Orchestra

Kenneth Montgomery conductor

. . . .

Charles Villiers Stanford Irish Rhapsody No. 4 *The Fisherman of Lough Neagh and What He Saw* (1914)

Norman Hay *Dunluce* (1921)

Ina Boyle Symphony No. 1 *Glencree* (1927)

: : : : : : : : : :

In Ireland

Thursday 8 September, 8.00 p.m.

Vanbrugh Quartet

Robin Tritschler tenor

Peter Tuite piano

Clíona Doris harp

William Dowdall flute

Cormac Ó hAodáin horn

. . . .

Hamilton Harty *In Ireland* (arr.) harp, flute, quartet (1918)

Frederick May Four Romantic Songs (1933)

Ernest John Moeran String Quartet No. 2

Ina Boyle Two Poems by John Donne (1939, 1946)

Charles Villiers Stanford Horn Fantasy (1922)

Arnold Bax Harp Quintet (1919)

: : : : : : : : : : :

Songs of Erin: An Irish Song-Book (Volume 1)

Friday 9 September, 1.05 p.m.

Robin Tritschler tenor

Peter Tuite piano

. . . .

Hamilton Harty *My Lagan Love* · *The Stranger's Grave* · *Cradle Song* · *The Two Houses*
Charles Villiers Stanford *The Fairy Lough* · *Trottin' to the fair* · *A broken song* · *Drake's Drum* · *Cutting Rushes* · *Witches' Charms*
Arnold Bax *Youth* · *In the morning* · *When I was one-and-twenty* · *Carrey Clavel* · *The Market Girl*
Herbert Hughes *She moved through the fair* · *Oh! Breathe not his name* · *A good roaring fire* · *The Forlorn Queen* · *The Palatine's Daughter*

: : : : : : : : : : :

Organ Music

Friday 9 September, 6.30 p.m.

David Leigh organ

. . . .

Percy Buck Sonata No. 1 in E flat major, Op. 3 (*Fantasie—Variations—Introduction and Fugue*)
Charles Kitson *Introduction and Passacaglia in A minor* (1919)
Charles Villiers Stanford Sonata Eroica (*Rheims—Adagio molto. Temo di Marcia Solenne—Verdun*) (1917)

: : : : : : : : : : :

Four Masters: Orchestral Music from the 1930s

Friday 9 September, 8.00 p.m.

RTÉ Concert Orchestra
Gavin Maloney conductor
Máire Flavin soprano

. . . .

Howard Ferguson *Partita for Orchestra* (1936)
Frederick May *Symphonic Ballad* (1937)
Hamilton Harty *The Children of Lir* (1938)
Aloys Fleischmann *The Four Masters* (1944)

: : : : : : : : : : :

Dispensing Musical Understanding to the People

Saturday 10 September, 1.05 p.m.

Band of the Defence Forces School of Music

. . . .

A. J. Potter *The Blackthorn Wattle*
A. J. Potter *Finnegan's Wake* (1969)
Thomas C. Kelly *A Wexford Rhapsody* (1954)
Col. Wilhelm Fritz Brase *The Frost is All Over* (1940)
Col. Wilhelm Fritz Brase *General Mulcahy March* (1924)
James Bolger *Rollicking Rakes*
Col. Fred O'Callaghan *Air from Co. Derry* (Rev. 2014)
John F. Larchet *Lament for Youth* (1939)
Sammy Nestico *The Boys of Wexford* (1963)
Hamilton Harty *The Fair Day* (from *An Irish Symphony* 1904) (arr. Eric Richards)

: : : : : : : : : : :

Gaelic Revival and Foreign Influences: Chamber Music of the Early Twentieth Century

Saturday 10 September, 7.30 p.m.

Fidelio Trio

. . . .

E. J. Moeran Piano Trio in D major (1920–25)
Joan Trimble Phantasy Trio (1940)

Michele Esposito Sonata for Violin and Piano No. 3 in A, Op. 67 (1913)
Charles Villiers Stanford Piano Trio No. 3 in A, Op. 158 *Per aspera ad astra* (1918)

: : : : : : : : : : :

Chamber Music between the Wars

Sunday 11 September, 3.00 p.m.

Vanbrugh Quartet
Chiral Quartet
Matthew Manning oboe

. . . .

Ina Boyle Quartet in E minor (1934)
Brian Boydell Oboe Quintet, Op. 11 (1940)
Frederick May Quartet in C minor (1936)
Aloys Fleischmann Movement for String Quartet (1927–32)

: : : : : : : : : : :

New Beginnings

Wednesday 14 September, 8.00 p.m.

RTÉ Concert Orchestra
David Brophy conductor

. . . .

Brian Boydell *In Memoriam Mahatma Gandhi*, Op. 30 (1948)
Seán Ó Riada *Hercules Dux Ferrariae* (1957)
John Larchet *By the Waters of Moyle* (1957)
Éamonn Ó Gallchobhair Waltz from *Nocturne sa Chearnóig* (1959)
Thomas C. Kelly Fantasia for Harp & Orchestra, on two Irish Airs · (*O'Carolan's Lament* and *The Heather Glen*) (1960)
Noel Kelehan *Cuchulainn's Lament* (1967)
Gerard Victory *In Memoriam James Connolly* (1966)
A. J. Potter *Sinfonia de Profundis* (1969)

: : : : : : : : : : :

Choirland: 100 Years of Irish Choral Music

Thursday 15 September, 8.00 p.m.

Chamber Choir Ireland
Paul Hillier conductor

. . . .

David Fennessy *chOirland* (2002)
Charles Villiers Stanford Three Motets (1905)
Arnold Bax *This worldes joie* (1922)
Brian Boydell *O my thoughts surcease* from *Three Madrigals* (1967)
Aloys Fleischmann *Na Trí Captaení Loinge* —a choral dance suite (1956)
Stephen McNeff *A Half Darkness* (2016)
(With a commissioned text by Aoife Mannix)
Gerald Barry *Long Time* (2012)
David Fennessy *Letter to Michael* (2014)
Eoghan Desmond *More Mother Goose Melodies* (2015) *world premiere

: : : : : : : : : : :

A Celebration of 21st Century Piano Music

Friday 16 September, 1.05 p.m.

Michael McHale piano

. . . .

Philip Hammond *Miniatures and Modulations* (2009–13)
David Byers *A Full Moon* (2009)

Ian Wilson *Sonnenwende* (2009)
Benedict Schlepper-Connolly New work (2016) *world premiere
Ronan Guilfoyle *Bystanders* (2016) *world premiere

Old and New: Organ Music 1945–1990

Friday 16 September, 6.30 p.m.

Fergal Caulfield organ

. . . .

Joseph Groocock Choral Prelude on *Hanover* (1945)
Daniel McNulty *Reverie* (circa 1955)
James Wilson *Jeu des Tierces* (1966)
Raymond Deane *Idols* (1971)
Paul Hayes *Coda* (1975)
Gerald Barry *Sur les Points* (1981)
Walter Beckett Organ Voluntary (1985)

: : : : : : : : : : :

Visions of Irish Modernism: Exploring New Horizons

Friday 16 September, 8.00 p.m.

RTÉ National Symphony Orchestra
Gerhard Markson conductor

. . . .

Seóirse Bodley *Configurations* (1967)
Roger Doyle Four Sketches for Orchestra (1969)
Gerard Victory *Miroirs* (1969)
Raymond Deane *Sphinxes* (1972 rev. 2015)
Seóirse Bodley *A Small White Cloud Drifts over Ireland* (1975)
Raymond Deane *Embers* (1973/1978 rev. 2015)
Gerald Barry From *The Intelligence Park* (1986)

: : : : : : : : : : :

Closing the 20th Century

Saturday 17 September, 7.30 p.m.

Concorde

. . . .

Gerard Victory *Runic Variations* (1988)
Philip Martin *Garments of the Night* (1981)
James Wilson *Three Play Things* (1983)
Deirdre McKay *through still pollen* (1998)
Eric Sweeney *Strings in the Earth and Air* (1988)
Jane O'Leary *Poem from a Three Year Old* (1976)
Rhona Clarke *Purple Dust* (1987)
Frank Corcoran *The Quare Hawk* (1974)
Stephen Gardner *Trane* (1996)

: : : : : : : : : : :

Twentieth Century Irish String Quartets

Sunday 18 September, 3.00 p.m.

RTÉ Contempo Quartet

. . . .

Seóirse Bodley Quartet No. 1 (1968)
John Kinsella Quartet No. 3 (1977)
Raymond Deane Quartet No. 1 *Silhouettes* (1981)

: : : : : : : : : : :

Love and Death— Grá agus Bás

Tuesday 20 September, 8.00 p.m.

Crash Ensemble
Iarla Ó Lionáird singer
Michelle O'Rourke singer
Alan Pierson conductor

. . . .

Ann Cleare *Dorchadas* (2007)
Andrew Hamilton *music for people who like art* (2009)
Gerald Barry *First Sorrow* (2006–07)
Donnacha Dennehy *Grá agus Bás* (2007)

: : : : : : : : : : :

Alchemy

Wednesday 21 September, 8.00 p.m.

RTÉ National Symphony Orchestra
Gavin Maloney conductor

. . . .

John Buckley *Taller than Roman Spears* (1977 rev. 1986)
John Kinsella Symphony No. 3 *Joie de Vivre* (1990)
Kevin O'Connell *North* (1998)
Siobhán Cleary *Alchemy* (2001)

: : : : : : : : : : :

The Irish Piano

Thursday 22 September, 7.30 p.m.

Hugh Tinney piano

. . . .

Aloys Fleischmann Three movements from *Sreath do Phiano* (Piano Suite) (1933)
Le líonrith (Agitato) • *Mall calma, diaidh ar ndiaidh ag sírneartú (Largo risoluto)* • *Gasta gealadhramach (Presto scherzando)*
Brian Boydell *Dance for an Ancient Ritual* (1959) • Capriccio (1958)
Seóirse Bodley Aislingí Nos. 1 & 5 (1977)
Ian Wilson *Lim* (1998)
Siobhán Cleary *Suantraí* (2003)
E. J. Moeran *Irish Love Song* (1926)
Howard Ferguson Five Bagatelles (1944)
Gerard Victory Prelude and Toccata (1962)

Philip Martin *The Rainbow Comes and Goes* (1987)
Jane O'Leary *Forgotten Worlds* (1987)
Raymond Deane Three pieces from *Noctuary* (2011) • *Minerva's Owl ...* • *Duskiss* • *Couchant*

: : : : : : : : : : :

Songs of Erin: An Irish Song-Book (Volume 2)

Friday 23 September, 1.05 p.m.

Rachel Kelly mezzo-soprano
Una Hunt piano

. . . .

Philip Martin *He Wished for the Cloths of Heaven* • *I am of Ireland* • *The Lake Isle of Innisfree* • *The Fiddler of Dooney* (from *Five W.B. Yeats Songs* 1973–1989)
Hamilton Harty *My Lagan Love* • *Sea Wrack*
Bernadette Marmion *When you are old* (1974) • *Bright Cap* (1968–69)
Philip Hammond Three songs to texts taken from Thomas Moore's *Irish Melodies*
Thomas C. Kelly *Huisabá a Bháibín Óig* • *The Mother*
Herbert Hughes *I know where I'm goin'* • *Down by the Salley Gardens* • *The Star of the County Down*

: : : : : : : : : : :

Organ Music: 1990–2016

Friday 23 September, 6.30 p.m.

David Adams organ

. . . .

Donnacha Dennehy Work for Organ (1992/8) • *Mad, Avid, Sad* (2000)
Kevin O'Connell Chorale, Toccata and Fugue for Organ (2001)

Jonathan Nangle Toccata *L'homme armé* (2014)
Sebastian Adams Work for Organ (2013)

: : : : : : : : : : :

New Century

Friday 23 September, 8.00 p.m.

RTÉ National Symphony Orchestra
Gavin Maloney conductor
Elaine Clark violin

. . . .

Deirdre Gribbin *Venus Blazing* (2001)
Donnacha Dennehy *Crane* (2009)
Stephen Gardner *NEVER...NEVER...NEVER...* (2003)
Brian Irvine *Big Daddy, Motorhead* (2009)
Andrew Hamilton C (2016) *world premiere/RTÉ commission

: : : : : : : : : : :

New Century Quartets

Saturday 24 September, 1.05 p.m.

RTÉ Contempo Quartet

. . . .

David Fennessy *bow your head* (2008)
Enda Bates Quartet No. 1 (2008)
Gráinne Mulvey *Entropy* (2009)
Seán Clancy *Neue Kraft Fühlend* (2013)

Here and Now:

Saturday 24 September, 3.00 p.m.

Crash Ensemble
Roger Doyle
Raymond Deane
Andrew Hamilton

. . . .

Deirdre Gribbin *Invitation to a journey* (extract) (2014)
Judith Ring *Swelt belly at dawn* (2013)
Barry O'Halpin *Lipids* (2014)
Roger Doyle Performance by composer
Linda Buckley *Fiol* (2008)
Deirdre McKay *Ice Etchings* (2002)
Raymond Deane Performance by composer
Donnacha Dennehy *Bulb* (2006)
Andrew Hamilton Performance by composer
Garrett Sholdice *Tanka for Aki Takahashi* (prelude #5) (2012)
Ed Bennett *Magnetic* (2010)
Jonathan Nangle *Pause* (2014)
Kevin Volans *White Man Sleeps* (1997)

: : : : : : : : : : :

Five Decades of Music for Guitar

Saturday 24 September, 7.30 p.m.

John Feeley guitar

. . . .

Andrew Shiels *The Voyage of Maeldún: The Island of the Black Mourners—The Island of the Little Cat*
Mary Kelly *Adagio—Moderato* from *Shard* (1982 rev. 1998)
Frank Corcoran *Prologo* from *Three Pieces* (1990)
Brian Boydell *Fantasia* from *Three Pieces* (1974)
John Kinsella Guitar Fantasy (1974)
Jerome de Bromhead *Gemini* (1969)
Greg Caffrey *Takemitsu's Dream* (2008)
Philip Martin *Chorale* from *Due Angeli* (1992)
Jane O'Leary Four pieces (1993)
Eric Sweeney *An Chailín Álainn: The Beautiful Girl* from *Three Irish Folktunes for Guitar* (2003)
John Buckley Guitar Sonata No. 2 (1998)

: : : : : : : : : : :

Wayfarers

Sunday 25 September, 3.00 p.m.

Vanbrugh Quartet

Chamber Choir Ireland

Ian Wilson conductor

Abbi Temple soprano

Jeffrey Ledwidge baritone

. . . .

Deirdre Gribbin *hearing your genes evolve* (2013)

John Kinsella Quartet No. 5 (2013)

Ian Wilson *Wayfarers* (2016) *world premiere

: : : : : : : : : : :

Voices of the Future

Sunday 25 September, 6.30 p.m.

RTÉ Cór na nÓg

RTÉ Contempo Quartet

Mary Amond O'Brien choral director

Dan Bodwell double bass

. . . .

Sue Furlong *Fáilte* and *Don't Let the Flame* from *Peace Songs from County Wexford* (1995)

John Gibson *Codladh Sámh* (2004)

Michael McGlynn *Cúnnla* (2004)

Michael Gallen *The Most Beautiful Flowers of All* (2016)

Havelock Nelson *The Girl with the Buckles* (1967)

Elaine Agnew *Wait and See* (with string quintet) (2000)

Michael Holohan *Riverbed* (1997)

: : : : : : : : : : :

Out of the Cradle: A Choral Finale

Sunday 25 September, 8.00 p.m.

RTÉ National Symphony Orchestra

RTÉ Philharmonic Choir

Mark Hindley conductor/chorus master

. . . .

Norman Hay *The Wind Among the Reeds* (1921)

Rhoda Coghill *Out of the Cradle Endlessly Rocking* (1923)

Picture credits

Page	
ix	© Lee Miller Archives, England 2016. All rights reserved. www.leemiller.co.uk
x	This image is reproduced courtesy of the National Library of Ireland [L NS 05380].
xv	© NIRC 1971. Digital images courtesy of Michael Dervan.
xix	Reproduced by kind permission of Michael Dervan. Digital image courtesy of Michael Dervan.
xxi	Digital image © Max Fleischmann. Aloys Fleischmann Collection, University Archives, University College Cork. www.aloysfleischmann.ie.
6–7	Digital image courtesy of Michael Dervan.
9	Image courtesy of the Irish Traditional Music Archive.
11	RTÉ Archives.
12	© The Master and Fellows of Trinity College Cambridge.
15	Portrait of Michaele Esposito, Pianist and Composer, 1926 by Sarah Cecilia Harrison (1863–1941). Photograph courtesy of the National Gallery of Ireland ©.
18	Digital images © Max Fleischmann. Aloys Fleischmann Collection, University Archives, University College Cork. www.aloysfleischmann.ie.
20	© Marcus Patton.
21	Special Collections, Queen's University Belfast.
26	© The Board of Trinity College Dublin.
28	© The Board of Trinity College Dublin.
29	© The Board of Trinity College Dublin.
31	© The Board of Trinity College Dublin.
34	Digital image © David Byers.
36	Digital image © Max Fleischmann. Aloys Fleischmann Collection, University Archives, University College Cork. www.aloysfleischmann.ie.
39	© Immediate Media Company London Limited. Digital image © David Byers.
46	Digital image © Max Fleischmann. Aloys Fleischmann Collection, University Archives, University College Cork. www.aloysfleischmann.ie.
49	Illustration from *Dublin Opinion* © Frank and Bairbre Kelly.
51	© BBC. Reproduced by kind permission of the BBC Community Archive.
52	Digital image © Max Fleischmann. Aloys Fleischmann Collection, University Archives, University College Cork. www.aloysfleischmann.ie.
53	© The Board of Trinity College Dublin.
54	Image courtesy of Cork City Libraries ©. Reproduced by kind permission of An Gúm/Foras na Gaeilge ©.
56	This image is reproduced courtesy of the National Library of Ireland [Ir 9141 s 1].
58	Image courtesy of Axel Klein. Digital image © Axel Klein.
63	Reproduced by kind permission of Aoife Taylor. Digital image © Clement Mac Mánuis.
64	Digital image © Max Fleischmann. Aloys Fleischmann Collection, University Archives, University College Cork. www.aloysfleischmann.ie. Image reproduced by kind permission of Independent Newspapers.
65	Digital image © Max Fleischmann. Aloys Fleischmann Collection, University Archives, University College Cork. www.aloysfleischmann.ie. Reproduced by kind permission of the Gaiety Theatre.

66 © The Board of Trinity College Dublin.
70 © RTÉ Lyric FM.
71 RTÉ Archives.
76 Image courtesy of the West Cork Chamber Music Festival ©.
77 Photo by Eugene Langan. © Contemporary Music Centre.
78 Image courtesy of the West Cork Chamber Music Festival ©.
87 © Cork International Choral Festival. Images courtesy of Cork City Libraries ©.
89 Image © Media & PR, Bus Éireann.
91 RTÉ Archives.
92 RTÉ Archives.
93 RTÉ Archives.
95 RTÉ Archives.
97 RTÉ Archives.
99 © Marcus Patton.
101 RTÉ Archives.
102 RTÉ Archives.
103 © The Board of Trinity College Dublin.
104 © The Board of Trinity College Dublin.
107 © Marcus Patton.
108 © BBC.
110 Photo reproduced courtesy of Frank Gavin Photography. Digital image courtesy of Michael Dervan.
117 © Marcus Patton.
124 *Soundpost* image reproduced by kind permission of Michael Dervan.
Gramophone image © NIRC 1972. Reproduced by kind permission of Gramophone.
Digital images courtesy of Michael Dervan.
126 © RTÉ Document Archives.
127 RTÉ Archives.
128-9 Artist and Architect: Raymond McGrath. Digital image © Norman McGrath.
130 © Gerald Barry. © The Estate of Samuel Beckett. Samuel Beckett's letter to Gerald Barry dated 2 May 1973 reproduced by kind permission of the Estate of Samuel Beckett c/o Rosica Colin Limited, London. Digital image © The Board of Trinity College Dublin.
133 Photo © Edmund Ross used by permission of John Buckley.
134-5 RTÉ Archives.
138 © The Board of Trinity College Dublin.
141 RTÉ Archives.
142 RTÉ Archives.
144 © Gerald Barry. © The Board of Trinity College Dublin.
146 RTÉ Archives.
148 © Seóirse Bodley. Digital image: Contemporary Music Centre.
153 Image © Keith Gemerek.
158 Photo by Betty Freeman. © Gerald Barry.
161 Libretto © 2010 Meredith Oakes. Annotations © Gerald Barry. Digital image © The Board of Trinity College Dublin.
163 Flyer for *The Intelligence Park* © Almeida Theatre. Digital image courtesy of Michael Dervan.

Music Ireland cover reproduced by kind permission of Michael Dervan. Digital images courtesy of Michael Dervan.

165 © Gerald Mangan.

166 Image reproduced by kind permission of Raymond Deane, Derek Ball and Brian Beckett. Digital image courtesy of Michael Dervan.

171 Photo by Eugene Langan. © Contemporary Music Centre.

172 Photo by Eugene Langan. © Contemporary Music Centre.

173 Image © Steve Rogers Photography.

174 RTÉ Archives.

177 Photo by Britt Olsen-Ecker. © Donnacha Dennehy.

180 RTÉ Archives.

181 Image © Shane McCarthy: www.shanemccarthy.ie.

187 Image © Agata Ożarowska-Nowicka.

188 Image © Patricia Klich.

189 Image © John Godfrey.

193 Image courtesy of Music Network ©. Digital image courtesy of Michael Dervan.

196 Image © Heikki Tuuli.

200 Image courtesy of Margaret Franklin and the family of W. H. Grattan Flood. Digital image © Margaret Franklin.

205 Cover reproduced by kind permission of UCD Press ©. Image permission courtesy of The Central Bank of Ireland.

207 Image © Paolo Giudici and Orpheus Institute.

209 Concept © Dr Jennifer O'Connor-Madsen. Design © Declan Madsen.

219 Image © Ros Kavanagh.

221 Image © Giorgia Fanelli Photography for Civitella Ranieri Foundation.

222 Image © Tanya Kiang.

224 Image courtesy of Wide Open Opera ©.

225 Image courtesy of Wide Open Opera ©.

228 Image © Maurice Gunning.

231 Benedict Schlepper-Connolly image © Benedict Schlepper-Connolly. Garrett Sholdice image © Andrew Kohn Photographer: www.andrewkohnphotographer.com.

232 Image © Shane Scollard.

233 Image © Brian Kavanagh.

234 Photo by Eugene Langan. © Contemporary Music Centre.

237 Image © Joseph Carr Photography.

240 © Jennifer Walshe.

241 © Jennifer Walshe.

242 © Jennifer Walshe.

246 Image © Eugene Langan.

251 © Andrew Hamilton.

258 © Ann Cleare.

259 Image © Brian Redmond AIPPA, Roscrea.

262 RTÉ Archives.

286 © Lee Miller Archives, England 2016. All rights reserved. www.leemiller.co.uk

Biographies

Musicologist and critic MARTIN ADAMS was born in Littlehampton, Sussex, and began his musical education in Pembrokeshire with William Whitehall. He studied at Southampton University, and worked at the University of Leeds before being appointed lecturer in music at Trinity College Dublin, where he later became a college fellow. His research centres on English music of the seventeenth, late nineteenth and early twentieth centuries. His monograph, *Henry Purcell: The Origins and Development of His Musical Style* was published in 1995. He also contributes reviews to *The Irish Times*.

• •

ITA BEAUSANG (née Hogan) was born in Cork, where she studied under Aloys Fleischmann at University College Cork. She wrote the first Irish PhD to be submitted in musicology, which in 1966 was published as a book, *Anglo-Irish music, 1700–1830*. She has taught at the Cork School of Music, the DIT Conservatory of Music and Drama (where she was involved in the establishment of Ireland's first full-time third-level performance course), on the executive committee of the Feis Ceoil and on the advisory group for Music Network's feasibility study, A National System of Local Music Education Services. Her next book is a study of Ina Boyle.

• •

Educator, musicologist and writer HILARY BRACEFIELD was born in Dunedin, New Zealand and studied at Otago University. She worked in England, in Birmingham and Worcester, before moving to Northern Ireland as a lecturer in music at the Ulster Polytechnic, now the University of Ulster, where she later served as head of music. She has served on the committee of the Sonorities Festival and the board of the Contemporary Music Centre, and founded the Irish chapter of the Royal Musical Association in 1987. She has written widely on new music from around the world.

• •

Composer, musicologist, music producer and orchestra executive DAVID BYERS was born in Belfast. He studied with Raymond Warren in Belfast, James Iliff in London and, with the assistance of a Macaulay Fellowship from the Arts Council/An Chomhairle Ealaíon, with Henri Pousseur in Liège. He was northern editor of *SoundPost* and *Music Ireland* magazines, has served on the Arts Council, and on the boards of the Tyrone Guthrie Centre, the National Concert Hall and Wexford Festival Opera. His website byersmusic.com is a cornucopian source of information on music and musicians associated with Northern Ireland and byersfamilies.com includes a genealogy of Byers families in Ireland.

••

LIAM CAGNEY was born in Donegal. After graduating from University College Dublin with a double first-class honours BA degree, he gained a PhD in Musicology from City University London. He is Occasional Lecturer at the School of Music, University College Dublin. His forthcoming publications include chapters for *The Oxford Handbook of Spectral Music* and *The Routledge Research Companion to Musical Modernism*. As a music journalist he is a regular contributor to *Gramophone*, *Opera*, *The Journal of Music* and other publications. His fiction has been published in *Gorse* and *The Moth* and read out on RTÉ Radio 1.

••

Originally from Montreal, MICHAEL DUNGAN is a secondary-school teacher of English, music and RE in Hartstown in Dublin. He is a former full-time music critic, columnist and broadcaster, writing variously for *The Irish Times*, *The Sunday Times*, the *Irish Examiner* and the *Evening Herald*, and presenting music programmes on RTÉ radio. His work includes interviews with a great many Irish composers. He studied in Trinity College Dublin, in Hungary at the International Kodály Institute of the Liszt Academy, and at the University of London and NUI Maynooth. He is married to the conductor Bernie Sherlock.

••

MARK FITZGERALD was born in Dublin and studied at Trinity College Dublin. He is a lecturer at the DIT Conservatory of Music and Drama and has written articles for *The Encyclopedia of Music in Ireland* (2013) and *The New Grove Online Dictionary*. His study *The Life and Music of James Wilson* was published in 2015. Other recent publications include *Music and Identity in Ireland and Beyond* (co-edited with John O'Flynn, 2014) and an essay on

Gerald Barry's *Chevaux-de-frise* in *Irish Musical Studies 11* (2014). His edition of Frederick May's songs, with recordings, will be published shortly.

••

Multi-award-winning Canadian soprano and conductor BARBARA HANNIGAN grew up in Waverley, Nova Scotia, and studied in Toronto and The Hague. She works with leading conductors, orchestras and opera houses, and was a singer for choice for composers György Ligeti and Henri Dutilleux. Other composers she has worked extensively with include Pierre Boulez, George Benjamin, Gerald Barry, Salvatore Sciarrino, Pascal Dusapin and Hans Abrahamsen, whose symphonic song cycle, *let me tell you*, was commissioned for her by the Berlin Philharmonic Orchestra. Her signature operatic roles include Lulu and Marie in *Die Soldaten*. As a conductor she has worked with the Munich Philharmonic, Göteborgs Symfoniker, Mahler Chamber Orchestra and l'Accademia Nazionale di Santa Cecilia in Rome.

••

Violinist DAVID HARRINGTON was born in Portland, grew up in Seattle and is the founder and artistic director of the Kronos Quartet. For more than forty years, San Francisco's Grammy-winning Kronos Quartet and its non-profit Kronos Performing Arts Association have reimagined and redefined the string quartet experience through thousands of concerts, more than fifty recordings, collaborations with composers and performers from around the globe, more than 850 commissioned works, and education programs for emerging musicians.

••

Organist, university lecturer, musicoloigst, arranger and critic ANDREW JOHNSTONE was born in Preston, Lancashire and has been based in Dublin since 1989. As assistant organist of the city's two Church of Ireland cathedrals he broadcast on RTÉ and BBC and recorded four CDs. In 2015 he was appointed assistant director of music at St Bartholomew's, Clyde Road. He has served since 1992 on the staff of the music department at Trinity College, where he teaches historical musicology and composition techniques, and has contributed reviews of more than 300 music performances to the columns of *The Irish Times*.

••

Independent German musicologist AXEL KLEIN was born in Münster in 1962, and studied at the University of Hildesheim and Trinity College Dublin. Since the publication of his groundbreaking study, *Die Musik Irlands im 20. Jahrhundert*, in 1996, he has become the most widely published writer on Irish music of the nineteenth and twentieth centuries, including three monographs and two co-edited volumes. He was the advisor on Ireland for the German encyclopedia *Die Musik in Geschichte und Gegenwart* (MGG, 1999–2008), and an advisory editor for the *Encyclopaedia of Music in Ireland* (2013).

••

Dublin-born, New York-based clarinettist CAROL MCGONNELL studied with Brian O'Rourke in Dublin, and in Belfast, Frankfurt and New York. She has been hailed by *The New York Times* ('an extraordinary clarinettist') and the *LA Times* ('elastic, exacting, stupendous'). She is a founding member of the Argento Chamber Ensemble, and has premiered over 100 new works. She has just completed a two-year residency with Trio Ariadne at Weill Hall at the Green Music Center in Sonoma and currently teaches at the Aaron Copland School of CUNY and Juilliard. Her next CD is of works by Philippe Hurel. Carol is a member of the Carnegie affiliate ensemble, Decoda.

••

Multi-faceted pianist JOANNA MACGREGOR was born in London and read music at Cambridge University. Her deep interest in new music has led to many landmark premieres, innovative multimedia projects and collaborations, as well as performances worldwide of classical repertoire. She was artistic director of the Bath International Music Festival (2006–12), the multi-arts festival Deloitte Ignite 2010 at the Royal Opera House, London, and curated *Aventures*, an orchestral series for the Luxembourg Philharmonie (2012–13). She is Head of Piano at the Royal Academy of Music in London, Professor of the Univeristy of London, and artistic director of the Dartington International Summer School and Festival.

••

Musicologist MICHAEL MURPHY was born in Dublin and studied music at University College Cork, where he has also lectured. He co-edited *Musical Constructions of Nationalism* with Harry White (2001) and *Music in Nineteenth-Century Ireland* with Jan Smaczny (2007) and was a subject editor for the *Encyclopaedia of Music in Ireland* (2013). He broadcasts on RTÉ lyric fm and is an active member of the council of the Society for Musicology in Ireland, and a Research Associate with the Research Foundation for Music in Ireland. Since 2001 he has lectured in the Department of Music, Mary Immaculate College, Limerick.

••

Composer KEVIN O'CONNELL was born in Derry, where he studied with Redmond Friel. At Trinity College Dublin he studied composition with Joseph Groocock and Brian Boydell. He is currently lecturer in composition at the Royal Irish Academy of Music. His orchestral works *North, Four Pieces for Orchestra* and Symphony have appeared on an RTÉ lyric fm CD played by the RTÉ National Symphony Orchestra. His three chamber operas and extensive list of chamber works have been widely performed. He was artistic director of the 2005 RTÉ Living Music Festival and is a member of Aosdána.

••

Conductor and composer PROINNSÍAS Ó DUINN was born in Dublin, where he studied piano and cello at the Royal Irish Academy of Music and served as music director of the Gaiety Theatre. He held principal conductorships with the Iceland Symphony Orchestra and the Orquesta Sinfónica Nacional del Ecuador and has been conductor of the RTÉ Singers and the RTÉ Concert Orchestra, of which he is now conductor laureate. He was the founding music director of Opera Theatre Company, and is music director and conductor of Our Lady's Choral Society. His compositions include a symphony and two string quartets.

••

Composer and pianist JANE O'LEARY was born in Hartford, Connecticut. She studied at Vassar College and Princeton University, including composition with Milton Babbitt. She settled in Ireland in 1972 and is director of Ireland's first contemporary music group, Concorde, which she formed in 1976. Her works have been widely performed and recorded, and she has held posts at the Royal Irish Academy of Music and the DIT Conservatory of Music and Drama. A member of Aosdána, she has served on the Arts Council and the board of the National Concert Hall, and has chaired the

Contemporary Music Centre. Through Music for Galway she was involved in the establishment of The Galway Music Residency.

••

Musicologist and conductor JOSEPH RYAN studied at University College Dublin and Maynooth University, where he completed his PhD on *Nationalism and Music in Ireland* in 1991. Following a period as a second-level teacher in Dublin, he entered the Defence Forces in 1980 where he served as executive officer and principal conductor of the Army No. 1 Band. He has also contributed to *A New History of Ireland VII, Ireland 1921–1984* (2003), broadcast on RTÉ lyric fm and directed the Gaudete Singers and the Palestrina Choir. He is currently vice president academic and registrar at Athlone Institute of Technology.

••

JOHN SCHAEFER was born in New York and studied Creative Writing at Fordham University. He has hosted and produced WNYC's radio series *New Sounds*—'The No. 1 radio show for the Global Village' (*Billboard*)—since 1982. His extensive writings about music include the books *New Sounds: A Listener's Guide to New Music* (1987) and *The Cambridge Companion to Singing: World Music* (2000), and sleeve notes for more than 100 recordings. He is a regular contributor to the World Science Festival and the White Light Festival at Lincoln Center; he has also written about horse racing and was a regular panelist on the BBC's soccer-based program *Sports World*.

••

'The most original compositional voice to emerge from Ireland in the past 20 years' (*The Irish Times*) and 'Wild girl of Darmstadt' (*Frankfurter Rundschau*), composer and performer JENNIFER WALSHE was born in Dublin. Her music has been commissioned, broadcast and performed all over the world. She has been the recipient of fellowships and prizes from the Foundation for Contemporary Arts, New York; the DAAD Berliner Künstlerprogramm, the Internationales Musikinstitut, Darmstadt and Akademie Schloss Solitude among others. Recent projects include a fictional history of Irish avant-garde music, www.aisteach.org, and *THE TOTAL MOUNTAIN* for voice and film, which has toured Europe, the U.S. and Australia and is available on Neos.

OYAL BANK

Acknowledgements

Lee Miller's 1946 *Vogue* assignment for illustrations to accompany Constantine Curran's article, 'When James Joyce Lived in Dublin,' took her to 'quiet Foster Place', where Stephen Dedalus left his mother and his brother and one of his cousins to wait while he went with his father and 'drew forth his orders on the governor of the bank of Ireland for thirty and three pounds'. The pipers' band is unidentified.

It has to be somewhat of a surprising fact that this survey of the work of Irish composers in the twentieth century and beyond is the first of its kind in the English language. But, as the book makes clear, it is rather less surprising that the idea for the book originated outside the official structure of Irish musical life. The vision that gave birth to *The Invisible Art* came from John Horgan, a passionate music lover, a musical amateur in the best possible sense. Without him, this book simply wouldn't exist.

Nor would it have come into being without the imaginative spur provided by the Composing the Island festival initiated by the executive director of RTÉ's performing groups, John O'Kane, with the chief executive of the National Concert Hall, Simon Taylor. And it would not be the book that it is without the all-out commitment of its executive editor Clíodhna Ní Anluain of RTÉ, the labours of its indefatigable illustrations researcher Caitríona Ní Dhunáin and the visual flair of its designer Fidelma Slattery.

My thanks go to all the contributors, who showed patience and thoroughness with the briefs I gave them. Ita Beausang and David Byers in particular shouldered a lot that was above and beyond the call of duty.

Many composers, especially Seóirse Bodley, Ann Cleare, John Kinsella, Jane O'Leary, Andrew Hamilton and Jennifer Walshe, gave generously of their time and energy, and the co-operation of composers' families, friends and descendants was also invaluable. I would also like to thank those individuals other than contributors who read all or parts of the book and gave valuable feedback: Linda Buckley, Siobhán Cleary, Seán Creed, Joe Denny, Niall Doyle, Anna Lardi Fogarty, Jürgen Gahre, Paul Griffiths, Niall Ó Ciosáin, Barra Ó Seaghdha, Eamonn Quinn, Fergus Sheil, Jacqueline Weij and my partner, Margaret O'Reilly, without whose unwavering support and patience this book would not have been possible.

For their particular generosity and assistance, thanks are due to RTÉ Libraries and Archives, including Bríd Dooley, Pearl Quinn, Tina Byrne, Lindsay Dowling and Michael Talty.

The Invisible Art covers a century and more and touches on the lives and careers of hundreds of men and women. Many contributed to various elements required in the book's completion. They include Aisling Lockhart, Claire Allen, Ellen O'Flaherty, Caoimhe Ní Ghormáin, Estelle Gittins, Sharon Sutton, Gillian Whelan, Jane Maxwell, Bernard Meehan and Roy Stanley at Trinity College Dublin; Caitríona Honohan, Jonathan Grimes and Evonne Ferguson at the Contemporary Music Centre; Joan Pepper; Rodney Senior; Ruth Fleischmann; Kitty Buckley; John Mullins, Liam Ronayne and Paul Devane at Cork City Libraries; Aifric Gray and John O'Loughlin Kennedy; Aoife Taylor; Fr Clement Mac Mánuis; Margaret Franklin and Tom Shaw; Catherine Lee, Bernadette Johnston, Caoimhe Buckley, Conor Sweeney, Deirdre McMahon, Assumpta Lawless, Angela Rohan, Niamh Ryan, Odessa Stafford, Tracey Diamond, Joseph Hoban, Kieran Dempsey, Sheila Gallagher, Eoin Brady, Lorelei Harris, Tom McGuire and Jim Jennings at RTÉ; Jenny Costello, Rosita Wolfe and Sinead Doyle at the National Concert Hall; Orla Kane at Bord na Móna; Christine Monk; Ian Woodfield, Jan Smaczny, Aidan Thomson and all the staff at Special Collections and Archives at Queen's University Belfast; Joanna McVey; Berni Metcalfe, Máire Ní Chonnalláin, Caroline Sheehan and Christopher Swift at the National Library of Ireland; Alastair and Graham Nelson; Gerald Barry; Kevin Volans; Nicholas Wilson; Russell Greenberg at Yarn/Wire; Ross Karre; Cay Bubendorfer and Thierry Bruehl at Klang21; Louise Morgan and Barry McLoughlin at the National Gallery of Ireland; Pat Redmond; Brian Fay; Ronan McCrea, Dr Manfred Karallus; Gisela Gronemeyer; Barra Boydell; Brian Beckett; John Buckley; Máire Harris at Gael Linn; Alex Keys at Fáilte Ireland; Eric and Manus Sweeney; Meredith Oakes; Imogen Sarre at Casarotto Ramsay and Associates; Adrienne Meagher, Sean Ó Broin and Friends of Classical Music in Ireland; Seamus O'Neill; Ian Wilson; Wide Open Opera; Mary Jane Walsh and Donald Taylor Black at Poolbeg Productions; Frank and Bairbre Kelly; Lisa Gilbey at Rosica Colin Limited; Ed Bennett; Marc Mewshaw at Civitella Ranieri Foundation; Becki and Joe Gavin at Frank Gavin Photography; Donnacha Dennehy; Mícheál Ó Súilleabháin; Jürgen Krebber at Internationales Musikinstitut Darmstadt; John Fitzpatrick at the Cork International Choral Festival; Benedict Schlepper-Connolly; Garrett

Sholdice; Andrew Kohn; Benjamin Dwyer; Peter Moran; Paul McGuire; John Godfrey; Vicky Langan; Mick O'Shea; Donal Sarsfield and Peter Campbell; Dr Jennifer O'Connor-Madsen; Norman McGrath; Grainne MacNeill, Alan McQuillan, Caroline Downey and Denis Desmond at the Gaiety Theatre; Marcus Patton; Sandy Paul at Trinity College Cambridge; Treasa Harkin at the Irish Traditional Music Archive; Raymond Deane and Renate Debrun; Derek Ball; Éamon de Valera at Irish Press Plc; Éamon De Búrca; Harry White; Josh Hilliard and Pat Nolan at the Irish Independent; Shaun Davey; Elisabeth Smalt; Christopher Fox; Sam South and Susie Newbery at the Almeida Theatre; Niamh Baker and Mark Adair at BBC; Catriona Mulcahy at University Archives, UCC; Emmanuel Wiafe at Immediate Media Company London Limited; Gwen O'Gorman at Lafayette; Eoghan Davis at Claddagh; Bettina Tiefenbrunner-Horak at Universal Edition; Philip Hamilton; Elaine Hill; Joanne Downey at Bus Éireann; David Greer; Jenny Costello at the National Concert Hall; Colum O'Riordan at the Irish Architectural Archive; Nick Maxwell at History Ireland; Anne O'Neill at An Post; Sarah Domican at the OPW; Barra Mac Aodha Bhuí at An Gúm; Jamie Ryan at the Irish Photo Archive; Toner Quinn; Olesya Zdorovetska; Giulia Biasibetti; Cian Brennan; Joanne de Castro at Naxos; Marie Hanlon; Aideen Ireland; Niamh Boyle; Noelle Moran at UCD Press; Katie Philpott at the Central Bank of Ireland; Sandra O'Connell and Clare Finglas at the RIAI; Simon O'Connor at the Little Museum of Dublin; Neva Elliott at the Crash Ensemble; Francis Humphrys at West Cork Music; Stephen Gardner; Irene Stevenson; Tugce Tez at Harrison Parrott; Nikolás McConnie-Saad at the Kronos Performing Arts Association; Louise Walshe at Music Network; Susan Schreibman; Joe Ó Dubhghaill; Celia Donoghue; Denis Donoghue; Caitríona Crowe; Elaine Sisson; Diarmaid Ferriter; Paddy Brennan; John Allen; Gerry Moriarty; David Carmody; Ellen Cranitch; and Catherine Reijans at Insight Creative Digital

Finally, Dan Bolger, Aisling Glynn, Justin Corfield, Edwin Higel and everyone at New Island deserve particular mention and thanks for the book's publication.

Michael Dervan, Editor

Index

T

U

V

W